THE REVELATION OF
BAHA'U'LLAH AND THE BAB

THE REVELATION OF BAHA'U'LLAH AND THE BAB

Book I—Descartes' Theory of Knowledge

by

RUHI MUHSEN AFNAN

PHILOSOPHICAL LIBRARY
New York

Manufactured in the United States of America

To the memory of The Master,

Abdu'l-Baha

Contents

FOREWORD

This book is an exposition of the manner in which Baha'u'llah and the Bab confronted modern thinkers, and of their system of thought. They were both originally from Iran. Baha'u'llah was born in Teheran, in the year 1817, to a family that traced itself back to Nur, a district of Mazendaran. The Bab, who was his junior by two lunar years, was born in Shiraz. This second claimed to usher in the advent of "Him whom God would manifest". Baha'u'llah, in time, declared himself to be that manifestation, bearing a mission from God for suffering humanity. The ready acceptance of their teachings, and the rapidity with which they spread among young intellectuals, made the authorities, both secular and religious, apprehensive. They, therefore, joined forces in its suppression, by executing the Bab in the public square of Tabriz, and permitting Baha'u'llah, who had not yet announced his mission, to depart to Bagdad.

Fearing that the remains of the Bab would be desecrated, his followers hid it, until it was smuggled into Haifa, in the early years of this century; and laid to rest in a sanctuary built for that purpose, on the Eastern slope of Mt. Carmel. As to Baha'u'llah, the Turkish government laid hands on him, and sent him as a prisoner to Acca (August 3, 1868) located on the Eastern shore of the bay facing Carmel. After his death in May 28, 1892, he was buried in Bahji, in the outskirts of that town.

These two sanctuaries, thus represent the twin centers from which modern thinkers can be considered as having been confronted. They provide the guiding light, modern culture demands, and is anxiously groping in the dark to find. Together they afford human thought with the primary premises it needs to

ix

attain truth. They locate the formal cause of man's spiritual and cultural evolution; and thereby designate the source of moral and spiritual values; and the purpose that dominates the universe, and leads man to his destiny. They state what the object of art should be, to help man attain perfection, and realize his supreme objective.

Descartes had previously denied the existence of a formal cause. Spinoza had already sought to support monism and accept its moral consequences. British Empiricists had spread skepticism as to the existence of a dominating primal Purpose, when it eluded human perception and understanding. And Kant's Critique of Pure Reason had made the existence of God, a mere working hypothesis, for practical moral ends. Those twin sources of illumination, confronted these disruptive principles, which constituted the primary premises of thought; and tried to dissipate the darkness that thereby enveloped mankind.

To Descartes, Baha'u'llah and the Bab would have said, that the prophets of perennial religion, constitute throughout the ages, the formal Cause of human evolution. To Spinoza they would have retorted that, being creators of man's spiritual and cultural life, they reveal a different substance from the human spirit; the one is necessary, the other contingent; the one imparts forms, the other acquires them through constant practice. These two substances, therefore, are essentially different and cannot be confused, by including them under one conception, such as "the All". To the Empiricists, Baha'u'llah and the Bab would have answered, that the unity of the universe is not substantial but the result of a dominating Purpose which is creative. And that Purpose is the criterion of the nature and existence of things; not the sense perception of an observer. The primal Purpose of the creator, revealed through the prophets, states what the nature of man is, and what his destiny is to become. Such being the case, and the function they fulfil, the prophets constitute the "appearance" of God; to which the proofs, mentioned by Kant, adequately apply. And the existence of these prophets is not a hypothesis of Pure Reason; but a verifiable fact of history, that could be empirically ascertained.

Such is the nature and scope of the illumination this book tries to elucidate. It is the guiding light, shed from the region of Carmel, upon the rest of the world: the light that can extricate human thought from its impasses, overcome its predicaments, give it the necessary primary premises, and lead it to truth. It is the Glory of the Lord.

In short, just as under the ancient Hebrews, Jerusalem became the place where divine "Presence" was deemed to rest, and from which illumination spread; just as during the spiritual hegemony that Zoroaster achieved the center was located in Media, and thence radiated to east and west, which included Greece; and later under Christian domination reverted to Palestine and Jerusalem; just as in Islam it was located in Hejaz; so in this age, the focal point is in the region of Carmel, and the plain of Acca across the bay. The truth regarding the nature and destiny of man; goodness, as what imparts perfection to the human soul; social justice among nations, races, and classes of society, which alone can insure peace and security; beauty as what uplifts the spirit to achieve its destiny; all these values seem to flow out of that source of illumination: the light pouring out from the twin centers located in the region of Carmel.

In "The Great Prophets," we attempted to show that the revealed religions constitute successive manifestations of the same divine Purpose, pursued down the ages, to stimulate and guide the spiritual and cultural evolution of mankind, individually and socially. For they all were animated by the same purpose, and taught the same conception of God, and of the reality and destiny of man, from which cultural values are derived. In such a case, we held, Hebrew, Zoroastrian, Christian, and Mohammedan cultures should be considered one and the same, periodically reborn and reformed, to satisfy the needs of an evolving humanity.

But if these, which are the main cultural movements recorded by history, are so viewed; what was the role of the ancient culture of Greece, with its rich literary remains? What was its significance, and the part it played, in the intellectual history of mankind? What virtue did it possess? For undoubtedly it filled a recurring gap, and fulfilled a specific task, to make its appearance so periodically, and as a striking contrast to the culture sponsored by revealed religion. In "Zoroaster's Influence on Greek Thought", we confronted that problem, and maintained that pagan thought—for so was ancient Greek philosophy—was a reaction of independent human intellect, to ultimate issues, at a time when revealed religion was itself undergoing a recession in Greece, and therefore, lamentably lacked the necessary power to galvanize human consciousness, guide reason, and proffer adequate primary premises and cultural values. But the result of such self-assertion on the part of human reason, and its venture to formulate ultimate premises as hypothetical conceptions, to operate as ground of its reasoning, was to confront it with impasses and entangling predicaments. These, we tried to show, could have been easily avoided, if Greek thought had sought its primary premises, and source of its basic values, not in hypothetical notions of its own making, especially as regards the nature of God, and of the reality and destiny of man; but in the simple revealed words of Zoroaster, who at that time dominated the spiritual and cultural life of the Persians; on the ground that he was its actual creator. In other words, we maintained that human thought can become certain, and morally, socially, and aesthetically wholesome; not when divorced from revealed religion; but rather, when firmly and squarely built upon it, as the only adequate source of its primary premises.

This book, which was mainly to contrast Zoroaster's teachings with Greek thought, was followed up by "Zoroaster's Influence on Anaxagoras, the Greek Tragedians and Socrates"; which was written to show that historically such influence prevailed, and it can be clearly detected in the system of thought, outstanding figures of that age advocated; individuals who created the golden Periclean age, and maintained it as long as it lasted. For that intellectual productivity continued as long as those individuals were free to express their views. And when these were subjected to persecution and their writings burned, that golden age gradually petered out; and led men, such as Plato, to write disparagingly of Athenian institutions and cultural values.

Humanity is at present confronted with similar spiritual and cultural predicaments. And our contention here is that they are due to the same causes, and similar hypothetical premises adopted. It is the same phenomenon, making its appearance again, in the history of the race. Finding religion an inadequate source for its primary premises, modern thought has stressed the need for separating the field of reason from that of revelation. And having stressed their independence; it has formulated hypothetical notions regarding the nature of God, and of the reality and destiny of man, as sources of cultural values, along the same lines as the ancient Greeks.

Jesus had rebuked the Pharisees for "teaching for doctrine the commandments of men. For laying aside the commandments of God, ye hold the tradition of men" (Mark 7:7,8). Confusing the revelation of the Word of God, with traditions accumulated gradually by man, the Church had ceased to inspire certainty, and ensure the cultural values to European thought. Therefore, it was only natural for it, as it previously was to the ancient Greeks, to fall back on independent human intellect for its primary premises.

Just as Greek philosophy—as we attempted to show—could have avoided its predicaments, and led to adequate unfoldment of the spiritual and cultural life; if it had derived its primary premises, regarding the nature of God, and of the reality and destiny of man, from the simple teachings of Zoroaster; so we try here to establish, that modern thought can serve human weal spiritually and culturally, if it reverts to the teachings of Baha'u'-llah and the Bab, and receives from them the revelation of the Word of God, as yet undefiled by human tradition. For the spiritual and cultural life can be truly served, not when human thought is based upon hypothetical notions, regarding those ultimate truths; but when derived from the creative purpose of Him Who made man, sustains him, and furthers his growth and perfection. It is served when these primary premises, which constitute the sources of the higher values, are derived from the authentic Word of God, as revealed through the prophet of the age. This is the intellectual aspect of the light shining from the region of Carmel.

THE REVELATION OF

BAHA'U'LLAH AND THE BAB

INTRODUCTION

1. THE NEED OF HUMAN THOUGHT FOR PRIMARY PREMISES OF UNDERSTANDING: Human thought is either inductive or deductive. It is either empirical, and constituted of generalizations made of individual collected facts of experience; or idealistic, and derived from a priori premises or ideas already entertained by the mind. In either case, ultimate principles, such as the nature and destiny of man, are indispensable for thought to formulate cultural values. For inductive reasoning, these principles constitute the hypotheses which give at least a provisional meaning, and guidance, to facts of cultural life; and thereby lead to their classification, understanding, generalizations, and also verification through experience. For deductive reasoning, these principles constitute the primary cultural premises, from which these values are logically derived.

2. THE OBJECTIVE VALIDITY OF THESE PRIMARY PREMISES PROVIDE THE TRUTH REGARDING THE SUBSTANCE OF THOUGHT: If we distinguish the formal from the substantial element of thought; that is, differentiate between the logical coherence of a certain trend of reasoning, and its objective reference; we shall observe that the validity of the second, rests wholly upon these primary premises. For deductive reasoning discloses what these primary premises entail and imply; while the inductive method depends upon them to interpret the significance of the facts collected. But the two are essentially formal, and cannot disclose the substantial reality regarding which the major premise makes its assertion. For the empirical method is primarily negative in its operation. Its specific function is mainly to verify principles already assumed, by making the necessary inferences and deductions, and then trying to prove or disprove

1

them in fact. It cannot establish ab initio a premise that is absolutely valid, and hence, assert the absolute validity of thought, and eliminate all elements of uncertainty. Some day, through more advanced methods of verification the initial hypothesis, taken as a premise, and assumed to be true, may be disproved and invalidated, and thereby, the whole system based upon it, rendered untenable. In other words, whatever hypothesis inductive reasoning may take up, to interpret its facts, classify them accordingly, and in its light, draw the necessary conclusions; that premise is provisional and tentative, not certain and final. Left to itself, inductive reasoning cannot establish these ultimate truths, upon which culture rests, and its values are established. It can disprove the primary premises, eliminate false deductions, invalidate wrong hypotheses. It can verify a truth tentatively accepted; but it cannot produce one of its own.

Furthermore, neither can deductive reasoning fare any better. Its province is to make logical deductions and formulate a harmonious system of thought; not to establish truths as primary premises of understanding. Still further, deductive reason cannot dispense with the empirical method; for the latter fulfils a function the former cannot dispense with. That function is to subject the conclusions derived deductively, to close scrutiny and verification, and thus, indirectly ascertaining the validity of the initial premises. Thus, the two systems are complementary. Together they provide man the necessary assurance he requires for tracing his spiritual and cultural life, once the primary premises regarding his nature and destiny are given. Once these ultimate truths are provided, human thought can make the necessary inferences and inductively verify their truth.

3. WHAT CONSTITUTES THE SOURCE OF THESE PRIMARY PREMISES?: What is the fountainhead of those ultimate truths, regarding the nature and destiny of man, from which cultural values are derived? Previous to the appearance of Jesus, the two outstanding systems of thought, that dominated the Hellenic, Hellenistic, and Roman cultures, were the Platonic and the Aristotelian. They were both based upon clear definitions

and possessed inner logical and formal coherence. But had their primary premises objective validity? Were their initial hypotheses true? Being essentially rationalistic, both systems of thought considered the clearly defined mathematical formula, and the coherence of such formula among themselves, the supreme examples of validity. But mathematics is essentially formal in nature. It does not attribute importance to the nature and substantial reality made subject to calculation. A mere hypothesis in that respect fully satisfies its requirements. Ultimate reality, however, must be, at the same time, objectively true and valid to be pragmatic, and lead to a creative cultural process, that is salutary in its effects. The clear coherent system of thought, besides being formally correct, must also be based upon initial premises that are objectively true and valid. How can thought ascertain the objective validity of those primary premises?

4. THE IDEALISTIC THEORY: In his Republic, Plato questions a slave-boy to show that these primary premises of understanding, and hence, the basic cultural values they entail, are inherent in the mind of the generality of mankind, even of a slave-boy, who is admittedly of the lowest strata of society, and presumed to be utterly uneducated. He tries to show that what we term knowledge of these basic values, is mere reminiscence of truths already found in the mind, as ground of the soul. But if we read carefully his dialogue on that subject, we shall observe, that the questions he directs to the slave-boy pertain to the formal aspect of thought: to the relations existing between different mathematical notions, he uses as examples, and their logical entailment; rather than to the substantial reality, which constitutes the theme of the primary premises, such as the nature of God and the reality and destiny of man.

That it is an inherent tendency, and property, of human intellect to be consistent in its logical deductions and inferences, and to formulate a logically coherent and harmonious system of thought, no one can deny. But beneath that formal structure of logical entailment and deduction, there is a positive objective assertion regarding the substantial reality, which acts as the primary premise, and upon which the truth, or falsehood, of the whole reasoning depends, together with their pragmatical values. Now, how can the truth about that individual, objective reality be considered as inherent in the mind of the generality of mankind, or of a mere observer of objective phenomena? What metaphysical ground is there for such a belief, if we do not venture to consider the mind of the slave-boy, in substance and essence, one with the mind of God?

5. THE EMPIRICAL THEORY: Empiricists such as Aristotle would say that ultimate reality is formal and immanent in nature. Man, through his senses, apprehends those forms, and by classifying them and appreciating their significance, discovers them as universal and abiding realities. But it is only to the observer, standing before an already made world, that forms seem immanent in things. To the observer, nature and its many phenomena: that is, the shapes objects possess, the colors they manifest, the qualities they reveal, the functions they fulfil, the properties they habitually display, all these forms seem inherent in nature itself, and immanent in its varied objects. But is there a necessary relation between the observer, and the substance and nature of the object observed, or between him and the forms it reveals as phenomena, to render the knowledge certain and true? The relation of the observer to the object observed is accidental, the connection between the former and the latter is a casual incidence, and hence, not necessary, that the knowledge it imparts should be necessary. Furthermore, neither is the world ready-made, nor man bound to be for ever a mere observer. The world of nature is one of constant becoming, the realm of culture, and the spiritual life, is always in the making or unmaking. God is their maker, and man may partake in that creative process. This is the reason why empiricism, which rests on the outlook of an observer, before a constantly changing nature, and spiritual and cultural life, can never lead to certainty. For neither is the world ready-made, nor does an observer possess the necessary relation to its constant substantial change: a change that is planned, purposed and creative.

4

6. THE PRIMARY PREMISES ARE DERIVED FROM THE PURPOSE OF THE CREATOR: The constant changes we observe in nature, and in the cultural life of man, constitute the stages of a creative process. They are the outward appearances of a physical nature, or a cultural life, in the process of making. The Forms we observe are not inherent in the objects, existent there initially. The constantly changing Forms, that the objects reveal, and the relations they manifest, both in physical nature, and in the spiritual and cultural life of man, are derived from the purpose of the creator. They are imposed upon existing realities, as matter, to generate that constant newness, and rebirth, in the process of evolution the observer beholds. In other words, there is the dominating will and purpose of a Creator creating; and man, to a certain extent, participates in that creative process. The Forms, therefore, originate in the mind of God and man, not as observers; but as creators, and to the extent of their respective part, and function, in that respect. Hence, the Ideas, of which Plato was speaking, and which he located in the mind of the slave-boy, can be considered as logically residing there, only if we consider the latter as factually a participant in the creative process; not if we regard him as a mere observer of the physical nature, and the spiritual and cultural life of man. In short, the Ideas are not initially in the mind of the generality of mankind, as Idealists are wont to maintain; nor are they inherent in nature itself, but originate in the will and purpose of the creator. Ideas and Forms are generated by the will and purpose of God. In other words, the ultimate objective truths, regarding the supreme premises of thought, are not inherent in the mind of man, recalled as reminiscence; nor can they be discovered empirically from the processes of nature; they can be only revealed by the Creator, expressing His will and purpose in His creation. Ultimate truths regarding the nature and destiny of man, can be revealed or disclosed only by the Creator, who made that nature, set that destiny, and pursues its final attainment. "Does He not know! He who has created, the Subtile, the All-knowing?"(1) says the Koran.

(1) The Koran 67:14.

5

7. WHAT CONSTITUTES THE ULTIMATE MEASURE OF REALITY AND BEING?: If the mind of the slave-boy, or generality of mankind, were, according to Plato, the repository of truth, then that mind would also be the measure of reality and being of all things. For, according to such a theory, certain formulas, values, and universal Ideas, would possess substance and reality; because the mind or intellect of the generality of mankind, would be able to judge and decide on their truth; because, as a result of such a reminiscence, the slave-boy would be in a position to decide as to their objective validity, that is, their conformity and correspondence with the inherent Ideas inborn in his own mind, of the harmony and unity that prevails between the two sets of consciousness. It would then recognize their likeness, and be able to judge as to the validity of their correspondence. In short, it would be able to assume the role of the judge to decide on the principle of harmony, correspondence, and likeness that should prevail between the objective reality presented to the mind, and the Ideas already inborn in it.

If, on the other hand, ultimate reality were considered to be a Form immanent, not in human intellect, but in nature; then, the empiricist would say, the measure of reality and being, would be the habitual sensual experience man can have of their operation. That is, not the subjective mind of the generality of mankind, but the accumulated sensual experiences of man, constitutes the measure of the reality and being of all things. For the function of the senses is to detect those Forms, and decide whether they are habitual and universal in their operation.

Thus, in both the Idealistic and Empirical systems of thought, whose peculiar approach to reality is that of an "observer", it is the universal Idea of Form, which is considered real and existent. And the faculty to decide on their validity is either the mind, or the senses, of the generality of man. But does reality and being reside, for example, in humanity, in that universal abstract conception we term mankind, or rather in the individual man? Is not rather the term "humanity" a universal feature, the mind of the observer formulates, to establish certain abstract ideas, necessary for his system of reasoning? Thought seeks the universal, but human thought is an accident of being, and interested in its universal aspects. Human thought has to become creative to determine reality and being; and then its interest is directed, not to the universal aspects of things, but to their individuality. When human thought becomes creative, and its interest is to generate the individual, then it becomes the measure of things it has so created. In other words, reality resides in the individual, and the determinant of the reality and existence of the individual, is its maker or creator, not its observer. Absolute causality functions, not between the mind, or senses, of the observer, and the object perceived; but between the creator and his handiwork.

Furthermore, if the individual, as such, is beyond the field of interest of the observer; if his knowledge is directed to the realm of universal relations, attributes, properties and phenomena that individuals reveal; if the idealistic and empirical approaches are directed only to these incidents of being, then how can we consider the mind, or the senses, of an observer, the measure of individual objective reality, both as to its substance and also its being? The criterion of being, should rather be considered to reside in him whose province of activity is the very production, sustenance, existence, nature and reality of the individual thing, in him who is necessarily bound to the very being of the individual object, or rather in him whose will and purpose the very being of the individual object originated. In other words, the measure of the reality and being of an object, is its creator and maker, who moulded the idea or form he initially conceived, into the matter at hand, and thus brought it as a new individual into being and existence. And if the individual reveals certain general properties, qualities and attributes, and fulfills certain specific functions, in the physical universe or in society, these are grounded in the will and purpose of him who planned their realization. In short, it is not man as an observer that is the measure of all things, but rather God as creator, and man only to the extent that he is creative, or participates in God's creative process.

7

8. THE TWO STRATA OF BEING: THE NATURAL AND THE SPIRITUAL: Man has two levels of existence upon this earth. He is subject to two forms of birth, two grades of creation: namely, a natural and a spiritual. He is first born on one level, and then acquires the other. He is born as a physical animal in the laps of nature, then he is nurtured, or rather, is asked to submit himself to a further process of development in the school of the spirit, to acquire spiritual and cultural perfections, which would lift him above and beyond his original state of animality. That nurture, that cultivation of the spirit of man to acquire spiritual perfections, is the cultural process. This is a creative process because, like any other creative one, it entails the imposition of an idea or form, first conceived by the creator, and then superimposed upon that individual natural man, used as matter or clay, to generate a new reality, a higher grade of being. This creative purpose gives rise to basic needs and values that, if employed, would entail the end desired. That purpose establishes the ultimate nature and destiny of man, traces the path he has to tread, sets his ethical standards, helps to establish the social institutions adequate for his growth, and stimulates in him an urge, or a love and longing for the goal he has to attain.

9. THE TWO TYPES OF CULTURE: THE NATURAL AND THE SPIRITUAL: These two levels of human existence, we said, give rise to two forms of creation: a natural and a spiritual one. We might also apply this distinction between forms of culture, and distinguish between the natural and the spiritual, depending upon the purpose and the end that culture pursues. If the object of that culture is to develop the physical and the mental powers of man, it remains on the level of nature; for these are essentially natural faculties. In this sense Idealism, with its emphasis on the rational powers of man, is as much naturalistic as the materialism and sensualism, it vehemently denounces and tries to combat. If on the other hand, the dominating purpose and end, that culture entertains, is to use these physical and rational powers of man, as mere instruments to stimulate the growth of his higher and fuller personality,

of that higher reality in him which transcends both his senses, and his mind, then that culture becomes spiritual; and instead of keeping man on the level of nature, employs natural means to raise him to the spiritual.

Should we bear in mind this basic distinction between the natural and the spiritual forms of culture; we would find the different ones recorded in history, range themselves into two camps. We will find the trend of the one to have been towards nature; that of the other towards the spiritual life. The one has considered man as essentially a physical being, or a rational animal; the other has regarded him as primarily spiritual, with his rational and physical powers serving as instruments for the attainment of spiritual ends. The one has been sponsored by man in his state of paganism; the other has been advocated and established by prophets, who claimed to have been sent by God to effect the spiritual regeneration and rebirth of mankind. The one is considered pagan because it is essentially naturalistic, stressing the physical and mental powers of man; the other we term revelational, for it asserts divine revelation as the source of its higher values, which delineate the purpose and end, it attempts to serve. The one considers man as the measure of all things; the other regards the prophets, or messengers of God, the mouthpieces of divine revelation, and hence, the source of truth, goodness, justice and beauty. The one seeks the development of the physical and metal powers and potentialities of man; the other employs these for the growth of his whole personality, which is essentially spiritual, as willed and purposed by God. The one considers the social environment, the field wherein physical and mental powers should dominate; the other regards it as the realm where spiritual qualities and perfections should be nurtured and cultivated by the individual. The one goes to nature for its source of aesthetic inspiration; the other to the prophets, as revelations of God's attributes of perfection.

10. THE DIFFERENT REVEALED RELIGIONS CONSTITUTE ONE CULTURAL GROUP: With all the seeming differences, and antagonisms, that at present prevail between the

9

different revealed religions, we can rank them all into one cultural group, advocating one conception of God, and of the reality and destiny of man; entertaining one dominating purpose; seeking one ultimate end; combating the same antithetic form of culture, namely, naturalistic paganism. Every one of these prophets came, not to destroy but to fulfil, and regenerate, that one ancient, perennial, spiritual culture, willed and purposed by God, and to hasten the realization of its promises for mankind.

These prophets, taken as commanding officers of the same cultural camp, constitute the immediate creators of that spiritual culture which made its appearance with the dawn of history. They all entertained the same idea of the reality and destiny of man, sponsored the same cultural purpose, and furthered the establishment of the same Kingdom of God on earth, as the ideal social environment, wherein human development can be ensured. These were creators, because they moulded supreme Forms, they held in common, into the clay presented by man, individually and socially, to produce an ever more faithful image of what they jointly visualized. These are not wishful thoughts, or convictions dogmatically asserted. They are facts of history, and verifiable by a dispassionate student of human culture. And being creators of man's spiritual culture, and the prime movers of his highest destiny, these prophets of God knew with full certainty, the Ideas and Forms they jointly entertained, the purpose they have been pursuing, and the goal they visualize. In other words, they constitute the supreme judge and measure of man's spiritual and cultural values.

11. THE PERSIAN BAYAN OF THE BAB: In religious literature, or, to be more specific, in the Sacred Scriptures of the different revealed religions, there is nothing as outstanding as the Persian Bayan of the Bab, on ultimate conceptions of thought, such as the absolute transcendence of God; the supreme dominion of the divine nature of the prophets, upon the spiritual and cultural life of man; the basic unity of their creative purpose; and the fundamental unity of their progressive revelation. We can easily consider it as constituting part of the classics on

these ultimate subjects of religious interest.

The Bab was born in 1819, and in 1850 was martyred, together with one of his followers, in the public square of the city of Tabriz, in North Western Persia. During the last period of his very short life, and while held in prison in the fortress of Maku, he wrote the Persian Bayan. To the unfamiliar explorer of his writings, the language of the Bayan is as baffling, and forbidding, as the rugged mountains on which they were revealed. But with a little patience, and diligent endeavor, the quest becomes fully rewarding. Its rugged style gradually begins to reveal forcefulness, and ends by becoming winsome and positively captivating; especially when the novelty and directness of its style, is seen to reveal the logic of its thought and deductions, in exposing the vital issues he chooses for elucidation.

Religion, if it is truly divine in origin, knows no national or regional boundaries and interests. It is addressed to humanity as a whole, and its saving grace is proffered to mankind at large. The fact that the message delivered by the Bab spread so fast among the Persians, especially its students and teachers of theology, proves that it conveyed what they earnestly longed for as religious enlightenment. But this search for illumination was not confined and restricted to the Persians. Eighteenth century thought, especially in the West, was deeply religious in its implications. The fundamental premises of thought were being questioned, assailed, and at times exploded; not with any evil intent of destroying cherished prevailing ideas and institutions; but with the earnest hope of attaining "enlightenment," of imparting to religious thought the rationality it sought and required, to pursue its spiritual and cultural mission in the world. And that earnest search for truth, had logically entailed the destruction of cherished ideas, and institutions, that were heretofore dogmatically asserted, and unquestioningly accepted.

It is just as rewarding to study the Bayan of the Bab, in such an intellectual context, as it is to read the New Testament, in the light of contemporary Roman thought. To the same extent that the Sermon on the Mount, delivered on the shores of the lake of Galilee, answered the deep spiritual cravings of humanity,

11

irking under the materialism and naturalism of Paganism in that age; the Bayan, revealed in the fortress of Maku, resolved the basic religious problems that confronted human thought generally, during the eighteenth and nineteenth centuries of our era. And it is in this light that we seek to present the Persian Bayan of the Bab.

Fortunately, what seems at first reading—because of its enigmatic style—involved, and unclear, in the Persian Bayan; was soon after explained and expounded by Baha'u'llah, mainly in his book, "The Iqan", in a language that is lucid, classical, and intelligible, even to the least learned, and least familiar to such ultimate premises of thought, and their discussion. We shall try and avail ourselves of the guidance of both in pursuing our task.

12. THE ABSOLUTE TRANSCENDENCE OF GOD: The Gospel says: "No man hath seen God at any time; the only begotten Son, which is in the bosom of the Father, he hath declared him."(1) Similarly the Koran says: "No faculty of perception can reach Him, but He reaches perceptive faculties; and He is the Subtile, the All-informed"(2). The vision of which Jesus Christ and Mohammed spoke, includes all perceptive faculties, including what mystics term intuition. These verses, and many of the like in the Sacred Scriptures of Judaism, Christianity and Islam, establish the absolute transcendence of God, the Divine Essence, to human thought, on the one hand, and the principle of self-revelation, on the other, and constitute the basis of religious belief. These basic conceptions of all thought, are more fully presented by Baha'u'llah and the Bab.

The heading of the Persian Bayan is: "In the name of God the Inaccessible, the Supremely Sanctified". Then the Bab starts with a full exposition of this basic principle of all revealed religions, the fundamental premise of all their thought. He starts in praise of God the Supreme Sovereign, Who in His Essence is eternally inaccessible to human understanding. And because

(1) John 1:18.
(2) The Koran 6:103.

12

of this essential inaccessibility, He has shed the rays of His light to impart illumination to all created things. In His day of judgment, by which the Bab means, the day of the appearance of the prophets on earth, all things bear witness that God is Unique, Matchless, and absolutely Sovereign over all things. Through that revelation the divine and inaccessible Essence establishes that He is the First and the Last, the Manifest and the Hidden, the Creator and Sustainer of all things, the Sovereign and the Wise. In other words, through the divine nature, revealed in the prophets, these supreme attributes of perfection, which constitute the source of man's spiritual and cultural life, become accessible to human understanding, and object of his knowledge. And this divine nature, revealed in the prophets, constitutes what the Bab terms "The Primal Purpose".

On the same theme Baha'u'llah states in The Kitab-i-Iqan: "To every discerning and illumined heart it is evident that God, the unknowable Essence, the divine Being, is immensely exalted beyond every human attribute, such as corporeal existence, ascent and descent, egress and regress. Far be it from His glory that human tongue should adequately recount His praise, or that human heart comprehend His fathomless mystery. He is and hath ever been veiled in the ancient eternity of His Essence, and will remain in His Reality everlastingly hidden from the sight of men. No faculty of perception can reach Him, but He reaches perceptive faculties; He is the Subtile, the All-Knowing. No tie of direct intercourse can possibly bind Him to His creatures. He standeth exalted beyond and above all proximity and remoteness. No sign can indicate His presence or His absence; inasmuch as by a word of His command all that are in heaven and on earth have come to exist, and by His wish, which is the Primal Will itself, all have stepped out of utter nothingness into the realm of being, the world of the visible"(1).

The term "Mashyyat", translated here into "Will", would be better expressed as "Purpose". Because "Purpose" implies, besides the conative element, the principle of rationalism, and foreknowledge of the goal sought. All these are, as we shall observe,

(1) The Kitab-i-Iqan by: Baha'u'llah tr. by: Shoghi Effendi p. 98.

implied by Baha'u'llah and the Bab, in the expression, the primal "Mashyyat". For the divine nature revealed in the prophets, is a creative spirit the source of all knowledge and understanding, entertaining and pursuing a goal, both social and individual, for further human perfection.

13. GOD'S CREATIVE PRIMAL PURPOSE: Jesus Christ said; "All things are delivered unto me of my Father"; (1) similarly, "I am the way, the truth, and the life: no man cometh unto the Father, but by me."(2) After establishing the primary premise of all thought, namely, the absolute transcendence and inaccessibility of God's Essence, the Persian Bayan proceeds to stress the principle, that all creative activity, hence all names and attributes we refer to God, proceed from the primal creative "Mashyyat", or Purpose, that spirit of Christ, that divine nature, revealed in all the prophets. In other words, that God created the primal "Mashyyat", or Purpose, and then through It, created all things. And that creative Purpose, the Bab adds, has been an eternal and everlasting process, with no beginning and no end.

"The door of the knowledge of the Ancient of Days", Baha'u'llah says, "being thus closed in the face of all beings, the Source of infinite grace, according to His saying: 'His grace hath transcended all things; My grace hath encompassed them all, hath caused those luminous Gems of Holiness to appear out of the realm of the spirit, in the noble form of the human temple, and be made manifest unto all men, that they may impart unto the world the mysteries of the unchangeable Being, and tell of the subtleties of His imperishable Essence. These sanctified Mirrors, these Day-springs of ancient glory are one and all the Exponents on earth of Him Who is the central Orb of the universe, its Essence and ultimate Purpose. From Him proceed their knowledge and power; from Him is derived their sovereignty. The beauty of their countenance is but a reflection of His image, and their revelation a sign of His deathless glory. They are the Treasuries of divine knowledge, and the Repositories of celestial

(1) Matthew 11:27.
(2) John 14:6.

14

wisdom. Through them is transmitted a grace that is infinite, and by them is revealed the light that can never fade. Even as He hath said: 'There is no distinction whatsoever between Thee and Them; except that they are Thy servants, and are created of Thee'. This is the significance of the tradition: 'I am He, Himself, and He is I, myself.' " (1)

These words of Jesus, Mohammed, the Bab and Baha'u'llah mean that human thought can attain an understanding of God's Purpose, to obtain from It, as ultimate source of the spiritual and cultural life, the fundamental conceptions and premises, namely, the truth regarding man's nature and destiny, the forms of virtue he has to acquire to become in the image of God, the type of social environment and institutions: the rights and duties, he has to uphold to stimulate that growth, the form of beauty he has to visualize, and the aesthetic impulses he has to cultivate; that man can attain an understanding of these basic cultural values, only through the intermediary of God's primal Purpose revealed through the prophets. For if man be a creation of God, and the object of His loving and spiritual nurture, he has to be guided and informed as to what constitutes his own true nature and destiny—whether his reality is purely physical and rational, or whether it is essentially spiritual, and transcendent to his bodily senses, and intellectual faculties. He has to be instructed how that reality should be nurtured and perfected, what goal it should seek, what purpose it should pursue, what values it should follow, and what norms of conduct it should conform with. For these define the course of man's intellectual, moral, social and aesthetic life, and hence, the path of his spiritual and cultural evolution. These values and norms should constitute the intellectual atmosphere in which he has to live, move and have his being, if he is to attain his destiny. Any religion, or system of thought, which sheds light on these ultimate issues, carries conviction and inspires confidence; can hope to survive. Otherwise, it will gradually recede from human consciousness, lose its significance, and fall into oblivion.

(1) The Kitab-i-Iqan by: Baha'u'llah, tr. by Shoghi Effendi p. 99.

15

14. THE PRIMAL PURPOSE IS THE PRIMAL POINT:

Besides the expression: "Primal Purpose", the Bab employs that of "Primal Point", to designate the divine nature revealed in the prophets. He attributes two stages to this Point: first that of absolute purity and nudity. In this stage it is absolutely transcendent and identical with the divine Essence, for it is utterly imperceptible. Its second stage, is when it becomes a defining and creative reality, that reveals itself to human thought and understanding. In this stage it is identical with the "Primal Purpose", or the divine nature revealed in the prophets (1). The Point is a defining reality. God, the divine Essence, being absolutely transcendent, and inaccessible to human understanding, cannot be considered as a defining reality, thus making all things object of knowledge, definite and defined. A reality that defines should be the supreme object of understanding; otherwise it cannot impart intelligibility to all other things. Therefore, God, the divine Essence, cannot be by analogy compared to the "Point", which is the primal defining reality. A point is definable and defining. When it is projected in a certain direction, it forms or defines a line. If it then moves in a second direction, perpendicular to the line, it traces the basic elements of a plane. It thus acts as the source of physical definitions. It is also the most primal and elementary reality in the sense that it reveals its possible functions and properties as circumstances develop, and new forms and definitions are required. Furthermore, being a defining principle, and having the power of imparting form to formlessness, it constitutes a creative reality, imparting newness to primordial matter. This constitutes the ground for the identity, the Bab asserts, between the Primal Purpose and the Primal Point, and attributes them both to the divine nature revealed in the prophets. This is the reason Jesus said, "the Spirit of truth . . . will guide you into all truth"(1); it is because that

(1) The Persian Bayan by: The Bab, 1:15. (I have used a mimeograph copy of the original text; but it has been translated by A. L. M. Nicolas into French, under the title "Le Béyan Persan," and published in Paris by Geuthner in 1911-14 in two volumes.)
(1) John 16:13.

16

Spirit will be the creative defining point, which will impart significance and meaning to human thought and activity. That Primal Point, or Primal Purpose, the Bab says, is the reality that differentiates between the good and the evil, that is, between what is conducive to man's spiritual and cultural progress, and what retards or obstructs it.

Referring to this function of the prophets as the Primal Point, which defines all things, and distinguishes the good from the evil, Baha'u'llah says: "I testify that no sooner had the First Word, proceeded through the potency of Thy will and purpose, out of His mouth, and the First Call gone forth from His lips, than the whole creation was revolutionized, and all that are in the heavens and all that are on earth were stirred to the depths. Through that word the realities of all created things were shaken, were divided, separated, scattered, combined and reunited, disclosing, in both the contingent world and the heavenly kingdom, entities of a new creation, and revealing, in the unseen realms, the signs and tokens of Thy unity and oneness. Through that call Thou didst announce unto all Thy servants the advent of Thy most great Revelation and the appearance of Thy most perfect Cause. No sooner had that Revelation been unveiled to men's eyes than the signs of universal discord appeared among the peoples of the world, and commotion seized the dwellers of earth and heaven, and the foundations of all things were shaken. The forces of dissension were released, the meaning of the Word was unfolded, and every several atom in all created things acquired its own distinct and separate character". (1)

15. THE HUMAN PERSONALITY OF THE PROPHETS IS A PRIMARY MIRROR REFLECTING THE LIGHT OF GOD; AND THE HUMAN SOUL IS A SECONDARY MIRROR REFLECTING THE LIGHT SHED BY THE PROPHETS: If the divine nature revealed in the prophets, is the Primal Purpose, or Primal Point, that differentiates the absolutely simple, and hence, undifferentiated and unknowable Essence of God, into its infinite names and attributes, or functions and qualities, and thus

(1) Prayers and Meditations by Baha'u'llah, tr. by: Shoghi Effendi clxxviii.

makes It the source of the spiritual and cultural life of man; then the human nature of the prophet constitutes the primary mirror, in which the light of God is first reflected, and through which, it radiates to mankind. The analogy of a mirror, or glass, was not unfamiliar to religious literature previous to the Bab. We find Paul says: "But we all, with open face beholding as in a glass the glory of the Lord, are changed into the same image from glory to glory, even as by the Spirit of the Lord"(1). "Glass" here refers to Jesus, in whom "the glory of the Lord" was revealed, and through whom it became accessible to human understanding. Paul further speaks of "Christ who is the image of God"(2); and says that that light "hath shined in our hearts, to give the light of knowledge of the glory of God in the face of Jesus Christ"(3). In other words, if the human nature, or personality, of Jesus operates as the primary mirror, in which the light of the divine Essence shines; then man's countenance constitutes a secondary mirror which receives its light from the prophets, and gradually makes it its own, in his process of spiritual and cultural development and regeneration.

In the Persian Bayan we find a full exposition of this principle: namely, that the divine Essence, is the ultimate source of light, that the prophets are primary mirrors; and mankind secondary ones, receiving the light of God through the intermediary of His prophets. We find this principle together with all its logical implications clearly stated. The human personality of the prophet is likened to a mirror in which the image of God, or the Primal Purpose, or Point, is reflected. In this mirror, the Bab says, only the image, not the Essence of God is contained. For the Essence of God, we have already observed, is an absolutely transcendent reality, far beyond physical considerations and categories, which the principle of reflection necessarily entails. Furthermore, this "image" is in the reality, of which it is an "image", not in the mirror itself (4). For if the "image" were initially in the mirror,

(1) 2 Cor. 3:18.
(2) 2 Cor. 4:4.
(3) 2 Cor. 4:6.
(4) The Persian Bayan by the Bab IV:1.

the Bab says, it would be ingrained in it, and not dependent on a transcendent source for its being, knowledge and gradual acquirement, on the part of man. In other words, if the "image", or the Primal Purpose and Point, and the divine perfections attributed to them, are immanent and ingrained in the human nature of the prophets, that nature would cease to be human, but would be divine. Similarly, if that "image" were immanent in the nature of the generality of mankind, they would be already divine, with no further perfections to acquire, no higher state of being to attain.

16. THE ESSENTIAL UNITY BETWEEN GOD AND THE DIVINE NATURE REVEALED IN THE PROPHETS: Philosophic skepticism springs into being, and starts to disturb human thought, when separation, or distinction of essence and substance, is made, between the reality of an object, and the appearance of its qualities and attributes; that is, between it as a thing in itself, and the phenomena that human senses perceive. This is the reason why the view-point of the observer is bound to lead to skepticism; while that of the creator inspires certainty. The observer possesses no means to verify and hence, no ground, for asserting, the existence and substantial nature of the object; much less to stress its organic unity with the properties and attributes he perceives. While to the creator, the substantial nature of the object, and the attributes he perceives, were initially conceived, willed and purposed, and made to be organically united. The Primal Purpose wills, and pursues the process, which entails the realization of the object; and the Primal Point defines its nature and being; as creator, they fashion a concrete substantial reality, to possess certain specific properties and attributes.

This principle is universally applicable to all creative activity, but it is primarily true of the relation which prevails between God, the divine Essence, and the prophets, who are selfless individuals, totally dedicated to the fulfilment of His supreme creative Purpose. In fact, the Primal Purpose, and Primal Point, which are identical with the divine nature revealed in the prophets, constitute the rays of light projected by the divine

Essence, and merely reflected by the human nature of the prophets. The latter is a creation of God's Purpose, defined by Him, acting as the Point, to reveal such properties, and fulfil such functions, in human society. This is why, while in agony, Jesus said: "Father, if thou be willing, remove this cup from me: neverthess not my will, but thine, be done"(1). His supreme desire was to maintain the unity of purpose between himself, acting as a prophet, and the Father who sent him. It is on this ground that Mohammed says: "Of a truth they who believe not on God and his Apostles, and seek to separate God from his Apostles, and say, 'Some we believe, and some we believe not', and desire to take a middle way; these! thy are veritable infidels! and for the infidels have we prepared a shameful punishment. And they who believe on God and his Apostles, and make no difference between them——these! we will bestow on them their reward at last. God is Gracious, Merciful!"(2). Thus, Mohammed maintains, that separation between God and His messengers, who reveal His purpose and attributes of perfection; or differentiation between the divine nature revealed in the different prophets, are the supreme form of skepticism which leads to perdition.

The Bab says, that the revelation of God may be likened to the sun; though it may rise an infinite number of times; or, as it proceeds above the horizon, shed an ever fuller measure of light, yet it is always the same sun, possessing the same infinite power, bestowing the same regenerating influence. Referring to this essential unity between God and His prophets, as well as between the prophets themselves, Baha'u'llah says: "These Tabernacles of holiness, these primal Mirrors which reflect the light of unfading glory, are but expressions of Him Who is the Invisible of the Invisibles. By the revelation of these gems of divine virtue all the names and attributes of God, such as knowledge and power, sovereignty and dominion, mercy and wisdom, glory, bounty and grace, are manifest. These attributes of God are not, and have never been, vouchsafed specially unto certain Prophets, and

(1) Luke 22:42.
(2) Koran 4:150.

20

withheld from others. Nay, all the Prophets of God, His well-favoured, His holy, and chosen Messengers, are, without exception, the bearers of His names, and the embodiments of His attributes. They only differ in the intensity of their revelation, and the comparative potency of their light"(1).

17. UNITY OF SUBSTANCE AND ESSENCE PREVAILS BETWEEN GOD AND THE DIVINE NATURE REVEALED IN THE PROPHETS: Unity of substance, which mystics, as pantheists, maintain to be universal, and which constitutes the basis of their thought, cannot apply to the relation between the creator and the created: between the artisan and his artifact: between the inventor and his invention. By no flight of imagination can an object of art be considered essentially and substantially one with the artisan himself. It may reflect his personality, represent his genius, and reveal his thought, talents and sentiments; but these cannot be considered to be in substance one with him. Such unity of substance, and essence, prevails only between God and, the divine nature revealed in the prophets, which is His Primal Purpose and constitutes the Primal Point that defines all things. The Bab says that, in the Bayan, he has revealed what constitutes the gist of all truth in the following utterance, proclaimed by God as creator, namely: "I am God, and there is no other God but Me. All other than Me is My creation, O My creation, worship thee Me." Then, the Bab adds: "Hence, all things, which can be considered as things, are other than God, constitute His creation, and are subject to formation, generation and contingency."(1) This primary premise of all thought, stated as a dictum by the Bab, contrasts revealed religion, from all other systems of thought, which repudiate the principle of creation; and specifically from the monism and pantheism of mysticism.

In a special chapter dedicated to this theme, Abdu'l-Baha states in his "Some Answered Questions," that we should distinguish two forms of proceeding from God: first proceeding through "manifestation," and second, proceeding through "creation,"

(1) The Kitab-i-Iqan by: Baha'u'llah tr. by: Shoghi Effendi p. 103.
(1) The Persian Bayan by: The Bab 3:6.

though the term "creation" has been loosely applied to include both. In proceeding through "creation," a new substance, and individual reality, is brought from non-existence into being. The object of artistic production, is a new individual substance and reality, which the artist desires and generates. In proceeding through "manifestation," or "revelation," on the other hand, the same substance assumes a new form. Thus the divine nature revealed in the prophets, is in substance and essence, one with God. The Primal Purpose, and Point, are His functions as a creative reality. His attributes of perfection, or rays of His light, are in substance and essence one with Him, as source of all illumination. These are outpourings of His nature, over-flows of His substance, not things, "other than Him," and "made" by Him.

Thus, in contrast to the attitude of the Idealist, the Empiricist, and the mystics, who assume the role of an observer before nature, and the spiritual and cultural life of man; we have that of the prophets, who, as revelations of God's Primal Purpose, pursue a constant, and eternal, process of creation and regeneration, and as Primal Point, define the existence, nature and substance of all things. And being the creators, and knowing the truth regarding their creation, they impart it as illumination, which guides human thought, and understanding, by providing it with its primary premises. The result is, that whereas these other systems of thought, are bound to lead to skepticism, the one advocated by the prophets inspires certainty.

18. THE DIVINE NATURE REVEALED IN THE PROPHETS IS A CREATIVE REALITY: But the Primal Purpose, or Point, is not a semi-passive reality, an object of mere contemplation, as is a natural phenomenon, which awaits the observation of man to reveal itself, which when it does become the object of perception, it is tinted with characteristics that are essentially subjective to man, and cast in categories that are specifically his. The Primal Point is like an active projecting source of light, that sheds illumination, that enters a magnetic field to polarize every single atom of its being, that imparts new values to human thought and activity, by giving them all a new definition. The environment in

which the Primal Purpose, or Point, appears, and the circumstances under which it operates, act as merely the occasion for the simple, undifferentiated divine Essence to reveal its infinite attributes. By revealing these attributes of perfection, it dominates the environment, and reshapes it. It does not become subject to it. The circumstances of the revelation: the functions the prophet fulfils in society, his life and teachings, the way he acts and reacts towards his environment, the various aspects of the spiritual and the cultural life in which he takes an active interest, all these help the revelation of attributes inherent in his divine nature. These become aspects of divinity which the nature of that specific cultural field demands to be regenerated. For qualities, or characteristics, we term divine and exemplary, are habitual forms of activity the prophets reveal, while pursuing their spiritual and cultural purpose. As Baha'u'llah remarks, adjectives spring from verbs. Conceptions are habitual forms of activity. Qualities we term divine, are derived from acts these prophets perform as emissaries of God in human society. And because the Primal Purpose, or Point, that is, the divine nature revealed in the prophets, expresses these attributes of perfection to man, sets for him the exemplary life, generates in his heart love and longing to act similarly, and gradually acquire them; because of this positive activity on the cultural and spiritual life of man, that reality is considered creative. It imparts a new form to the reality of man, acting as clay. It raises him to a higher level of being.

19. THIS CREATION IS PRIMARILY SPIRITUAL AND CULTURAL, EFFECTED THROUGH ILLUMINATION: In his first epistle to the Corinthians, Paul says: "For who hath known the mind of the Lord, that he may instruct him? But we have the mind of Christ."(1) "If the mind of the Lord," or the divine Essence, is absolutely inaccessible to man, then the sole source of illumination is the mind of Christ, or the divine nature revealed in the prophets. "In him was life; and the life was the light of men. And the light shineth in darkness; and the darkness com-

(1) 1 Cor. 2:16.

prehended it not. . . . That was the true Light, which lighteth every man that cometh into the world." (1)

In the same strain Mohammed said: "God is the light of the heavens and the earth. His light is like a niche in which is a lamp—the lamp encased in glass—the glass, as it were a glistening star. From a blessed tree is it lighted, the olive neither of the East nor of the West, whose oil would well nigh shine out, even though fire touched it not! It is light upon light. God guideth whom He will to His light, and God setteth forth parables to men, for God knoweth all things." (2) "Now hath a light and a clear book come to you from God, by which God will guide him who shall follow after his good pleasure, to paths of peace, and will bring them out of the darkness to the light, by his will: and to the straight path will he guide them." (3)

When the oil, which might be taken to correspond with the Primal Purpose, is produced by the outstretched and universal tree of the divine being, and poured into a lamp that is encased in the physical body and personality of the prophet, it sheds its light, as the source of illumination, to all mankind. The light potential in the oil, through the personality of the prophet, or lamp, reveals its different hues, or qualities and attributes. The words and sayings of the prophet, within that social environment, and as part of it; and his actions on its dominating forces, provide the occasion for those divine characteristics to be revealed, and expressed, in a manner comprehensible to man. Attributes that were inherent, but hidden in the divine Purpose, become distinct and evident; truths inaccessible to human thought, become direct objects of human experience and understanding; pious beliefs, that were inferential in nature, become factual and historical. This process of illumination, though on the plane of the spiritual and cultural life, is essentially creative. As the Bab says, (4) the objective reality of things is generated, when, through the inter- mediary of the prophet, God utters His fiat. When that word is uttered, all things are reborn. "For the thingness, or objectivity

(1) John, 1:4, 5, 9.
(2) The Koran 24:35.
(3) Ibid. 5:16.
(4) The Persian Bayan 2:1.

24

of things, become revealed through the operation of the Primal Purpose, in the world." (1) Baha'u'llah explains the operation of this phenomenon, by giving the example of a dark room which contains many objects. Being in utter darkness, these objects are indistinguishable, and undefined; and hence, non-existent to an observer. They cannot, as such, constitute the objects of his sense experience, and thought. When light is introduced into the room, or, to put it in the words of John, when "the light shineth in darkness," then those objects begin to act on the senses, and stimulate thought; then will the observer distinguish their form, color and characteristics. The creator, or the one who made those objects, knows of their being, and is certain of their nature and existence; but the human observer cannot distinguish, define and understand those things, unless light is introduced and the objects are illuminated. The intellectual, moral, social and aesthetic values that the prophets reveal, through their teachings and exemplary life, operate as such a light. And in consequence of that illumination, the human observer can appreciate the reality of things. Remove that light, that is, renounce those values, and the objects of human experience will cease to have spiritual and cultural significance, and lose their objectivity. Even within the field of purely physical experience, objects of perception are grasped, and become significant, only in the light of the values, and interests, man already possesses. Remove those values and interests, and those impressions made on his senses, will not be recorded by his mind. It is only in the light of those values, that the observer can acquire an objective understanding of things.

When the prophets reveal the truth regarding the nature and destiny of man, state the attributes of perfection he has to acquire, tell of the ideal social order, or Kingdom of God on earth, he has to establish as the optimum environment, which the human soul requires to achieve that perfection; then and only then, will the incidents of life, and facts of nature, reveal their true significance, arouse cultural interest, and enlighten spiritual understanding. On the other hand, if that light is tinted then all objects will appear under that shade of color. If the primary

(1) The Persian Bayan, 7:19.

premises of understanding are not objectively true, but incorrect or hypothetical, then the basic values, and with them, all facts of experience will be distorted, and become invalid.

20. "THE WORD," DENOTES THE CULTURAL SIGNIFI-CANCE OF THE DIVINE NATURE REVEALED IN THE PROPHETS: "In the beginning was the Word, and the Word was with God, and the Word was God. The same was in the beginning with God. All things were made by him; and without him was not any thing made that was made."(1) Just as the conception of "Primal Purpose" conveys the creative aspect of the divine nature revealed in the prophets; and the "Point" expresses its defining function; so does the term, "The Word," denote its significance as the source of cultural life, and specifically its intellectual and moral one. It is in this sense that Paul said of Christ: "In whom are hid all the treasures of wisdom and knowledge."(2)

In the Koran,(3) Mohammed likens the "Word" to the "good tree," which with firm roots, and outstretched branches, bears its fruits regularly in every season of the year. It thus corresponds fully with the divine nature revealed in the prophets, which produces its spiritual and cultural regeneration of mankind, according to a cyclic process.

We have observed the Bab state that, "the word, which sums up all knowledge is this: 'I am God, there is no other God but Me. All other than Me is My creation. O My creation worship Me.'"(4) This dictum contains the Primal Purpose or "Word" of God,(5) regarding the nature of all "other than Him," as well as their supreme destiny, namely, His worship. The instrument of that creative Purpose is His Word. Inasmuch as the divine Essence is eternally the same, He creates the Word to reveal Him. For the latter can be of the past or future, that is, subject to

(1) John 1:1-3.
(2) Col. 2:3.
(3) Koran 14:24.
(4) The Persian Bayan, by The Bab, 3:6.
(5) Ibid. 2:14.

26

temporal considerations.(1) This Word revealed by the prophets down the ages, constitutes the "Tree of Truth," or the source of all thought and understanding.(2) Being essentially creative, this Word of God is totally unlike the utterances of man. It imparts form to the latter, and gives unity to its elements. As an example of the creativeness of the Word, the Bab mentions the establishment of the "Vilayat" of Ali; which in Christian history, corresponds to the apostleship of Peter, and the founding of the Church. In either case the institution was the product of the creative Word of the prophet.

Being the source of all truth, the Word also acts as the supreme standard of the moral life of man, it defines the nature of the good, and judges man accordingly. This is the reason why the supreme attainment of man is to acknowledge its revelation.(3) Being creative, it generates the spiritual and cultural life, sustains it, lets it perish and then revives it again.

Another consideration that can bring out the cultural significance of the term "word," is its function as an element in human thought. The letters of the alphabet are mere sounds and scripts, with purely physical and material being, and devoid of any spiritual and cultural significance. It is with the word that thought starts. As the Bab says, every word possesses a spirit,(4) that is, conveys a thought, and bears a significance. In fact, if the letters bear any virtue, it is because of the word which they construct. Similarly, individual human beings, acquire their value, and their thought and behaviour become virtuous, only in so far as they reflect characteristics the prophets reveal. If, like him, they reflect attributes that are divine, they can be considered "letters of illiyin" that is, exalted and heavenly in nature; if, on the other hand, they express, in their thought and behaviour, attributes that are "other than illiyin," they are evil. In any case the moral and ethical nature of the individuals, or "letters," is derived from their conformity, or non-conformity, with the "Word" of God, as uttered by the prophets.

(1) Ibid. 2:14.
(2) Ibid. 3:2.
(3) Ibid. 3:2.
(4) Ibid. 2:4.

Thus, in the Word which is the Spirit of Christ that animates all the prophets, "are hid all the treasures of wisdom and knowledge." (1) And if that Word is the repository of truth, man has to turn to it for knowledge and understanding. He should, as a secondary mirror, turn to that source for his rational life. Hence, he should follow the counsel of Paul and develop "humility of mind"; (2) and not arrogantly, in the manner of pagans, consider himself—his mind and sense perception—the measure of all things: of things that are that they are, and of things that are not that they are not. Human knowledge and understanding should not, in that case, seek to assert its independence, but in all humility, turn to divine revelation, to the Word, for its primary premises, upon which man's cultural life is to be raised. And having acquired a true knowledge of what constitutes man's real nature and destiny, thought can make its logical deductions, render them fully coherent, and also true and in conformity with the objective nature of things.

In short, Platonic Idealism considered the ultimate premises of thought, and the supreme principles of the cultural life, to be as abstract notions, inherent in the mind, or soul, of the generality of mankind, even of the ordinary slave-boy who is utterly untutored. Aristotelian Empiricism, on the other hand, regarded Ideas, or Forms, immanent in the nature of things, and ingrained in their physical being, as the soul is in the body of man. Thus, his logic led him to believe, that human reason is a mere potentiality, which depends upon a superior, active, reason, to provide it with the ultimate premises it requires. He termed that reality, "the active reason," to contrast it to "passive reason" and seems to identify the former with God as the Form of all forms. For these primary premises of "active reason" act as forms for "passive reason." To revert to the example of the mirror, and the distinction we observed the Bab make, Aristotle seems to favor the idea, that the "image" is immanent in the mirror, and not transcendent to, and detached from, it; as the Bab maintained.

In contrast to these two points of view: the Idealistic and the

(1) Col. 2:3.
(2) Acts, 20:19.

28

Empirical, the Bab presents that of revealed religion, namely, that the ultimate premises of thought are vouchsafed by the prophets, acting as the Word of God. Thus, even if the divine Essence is absolutely inaccessible to human understanding, the revelation of His Word is; and that can afford man the guidance he requires for his spiritual and cultural life. This process is creative, because it moulds these basic premises of thought, into the rational life of man, and gives it unity, coherence, and purpose: a form. In other words, the Word, is the "active reason," the dynamic element Aristotle's logic required. It is the reality human reason requires, to trace the path of man's spiritual and cultural evolution.

21. CREATION OF THE CULTURAL LIFE NECESSITATES A TRINITY OF BEING: Creation, as such, implies only the creator and the created, for according to the Bab's basic premise of all thought: "other than Me is my creation." What the creator seeks is the existence of the substance and nature of the reality created. There is no need for an intermediate reality. The object of spiritual regeneration, or cultural creation and rebirth, on the other hand, is for man to become in the "image" of God; it is to reflect His light by acquiring His attributes of perfection; it is to reflect through his thought, words, and deeds characteristics that are divine. The emphasis here is not on the substantial existence of God, but on the revelation of His attributes and perfections; which should become the object of human understanding, to stimulate man's spiritual and cultural growth. Hence, the prerequisite of cultural life, is knowledge of the attributes we term divine; and such knowledge implies a trinity of being. For it requires, besides the substantial being of the creator, the revelation of His attributes; in other words, His appearance within the field of human understanding, as the highest object of knowledge. For, according to the Bab,(1) we can observe in an object only the qualities of that object, that is, its "appearance," and not its substantial reality. And it is primarily these attributes and perfections that knowledge tries to unravel. In other words, man's spiritual and cultural evolution rests primarily upon an under-

(1) The Persian Bayan, by The Bab 2:8.

29

standing of the attributes of God, upon His revelation, or appearance; which is vouchsafed through the divine nature revealed in the prophets. The Primal Purpose, the defining Point, the Word that this divine nature reveals, are like rays proceeding from the sun, which though, in their original form, are simple and undifferentiated, they become differentiated through the thought, words and deeds of the prophets, and becoming differentiated, and defined, act as supreme objects of human understanding. In short, any process of understanding is based upon the presupposition that there is a trinity of being: of the substance revealing itself; of the functions and attributes revealed, as appearances of that substance; and of the observer himself.

22. THE PRIMAL PURPOSE, OR POINT, OR WORD, THAT IS, THE DIVINE NATURE REVEALED IN THE PROPHETS, IS AN ETERNAL REALITY: But the Primal Purpose, or Point, or Word, or Wisdom, which are identified with the divine nature revealed in the prophets, are eternal and everlasting. Like any appearance, they are co-eternal with the substance they reveal. They cannot be identified with the historical individuality of any single prophet. It is on this ground that Wisdom says: "The Lord possessed me in the beginning of his way, before his work of old. I was set up from everlasting, from the beginning, or ever the earth was." (1) When Jesus was asked whether he was John the Baptist, Elias, or Jeremias, that is, the reappearance of any single one of the previous prophets, he passed the question to Simon Peter. And the latter answered saying: "Thou art Christ," (2) that is, the revelation of the divine nature, which is universal, eternal and everlasting.

Eternally in the past, and eternally in the future, the Bab says, (3) the divine Essence has been, and will remain, inaccessible to human thought. What constitutes the object of understanding are His attributes of perfection, revealed through the thought, words and deeds of the prophets. Their divine nature reveals

(1) Proverbs 8:22, 23.
(2) Matthew 16:16.
(3) The Persian Bayan, by The Bab, 1:15.

God's creative Purpose. They act as the defining Point of the spiritual and cultural life of man. They utter the Word of God. These are everlasting characteristics, true of all the prophets, and manifested periodically to mankind, when a new spiritual cycle sets in. If the Christians failed to accept Mohammed, and repudiated his cause, the Bab says, it is because they failed to appreciate this basic truth,(1) namely, that the divine nature revealed in Mohammed was the same as the one revealed in Jesus Christ, and that the Koran was the same Evangel recording the Word of God. They failed to appreciate that the same Primal Purpose animated them both; and that they equally acted as the Point, defining the values of the spiritual and cultural life of man.

The Bab says(2) that, in fact, there can be no manifestation of God's Primal Purpose, except to usher in a subsequent one; as a further step in its realization, and a fuller revelation of the Word. It is on this basic principle, of progressive revelation of the Word of God that Jesus said: "How be it when he, the Spirit of truth, is come, he will guide you into all truth, for he shall not speak of himself; but whatsoever he shall hear, that shall he speak: and he will shew you things to come."(3) In short, the divine nature revealed in the prophets, as well as the Primal Purpose, the Point and the Word, which are its characteristics, are eternal and everlasting, operating as a source of recurring grace to mankind. They are revealed periodically through the instrumentality of the prophets who succeed one another throughout history, both in past and in the future.

23. THE PRINCIPLE OF PROGRESSIVE REVELATION: "The Day of the Lord," such as referred to by Isaiah,(4) was the main theme of the prophets of Israel before the exile, at the time when the kingdom of Judah in the South, and that of Israel in the North, were fast declining. These prophets had lost hope in regenerating the spiritual, and universalistic, culture of the ancient Hebrews, which had gradually become syncretized with pagan

(1) Ibid. 2:15.
(2) Ibid. 3:4.
(3) John 16:13.
(4) Isaiah ch. 11.

31

beliefs and practices; and looked expectantly to that day of days, to the "Day of the Lord," when he would come, and the spiritual life of all humanity will be reborn. That was a supreme event in the spiritual and cultural development of mankind, which these prophets foresaw, anxiously awaited, and earnestly tried to serve.

Similarly, Zoroaster foresaw the coming of two prophets, or "saviours," at intervals of one thousand years, to further the cause of Ahura Mazda against the evil forces of Ahriman, and thereby prepare for the advent of the supreme turning point in civilization, when "At that Final Consummation, O Mazda (Lord of Wisdom), Thou wilt come with Thy Holy Spirit, Spenta Mainyu, with Xshathra, Thy Might and Majesty, and with Vohu Mana, Thy Good Mind, through whose workings living beings progress in Thy Law. Meanwhile Aramaiti shall instruct them, the Prophets, in the divine purpose of Thy Creation which no man may gainsay."(1)

This theme was taken up again by Jesus Christ, and made the supreme object of the only prayer of his that has been recorded, as well as of the vast majority of his parables; but mainly that of the Lord of the vineyard.(2) To administer the affairs of his estate, and collect his dues, the Lord sends successive messengers. He even dispatches his own son. But every time, the envoy is persecuted and killed. Until at last, he comes in person, and judges his tenants, and punishes them for their iniquity. In other words, there is the advent of a series of prophets, or messengers, before the dawn of the Day of the Lord. Jesus was, however, more explicit when he said: "But the Comforter, which is the Holy Ghost, whom the Father will send in my name, he shall teach you all things, and bring all things to your remembrance, whatsoever I have said unto you."(3) "Nevertheless I tell you the truth: It is expedient for you that I go away: for if I go not away, the Comforter will not come unto you; but if I depart, I will send him unto you."(4)

(1) Songs of Zarathustra tr. by Dastur Framroze and Ardeshir Bode p. 72. Published by George Allen & Unwin Ltd., London.
(2) Mark 12:11.
(3) John 14:26.
(4) Ibid. 16:7.

32

In the early centuries of the Christian era, the return of Christ, or the coming of the "Comforter," as Jesus had designated him, was referred to by the Greek speaking believers, as "Parousia." The term meant literally the divine presence, or "Shekinah," of the Old Testament, and referred to the presence of the Spirit of Christ amongst men, in order "to complete the messianic work and usher in the final judgment."(1) The advent of Parousia, as well as the establishment of the Kingdom of God on earth, which formed an outstanding feature of the teachings of Jesus, was a source of infinite hope and faith to his early followers. It was only when Christianity began to lose hope in such "return," that it started to consider the Kingdom of God a state of inner consciousness, and "Parousia" a divine presence, felt inwardly as a sort of mystic experience; and thus stripped them both of their original meaning and significance, as the advent of a new prophetic cycle, and a rebirth of the spiritual and cultural life of man.

Tertullian, who was born about the middle of the second century after Christ, wrote considerably about "Paraclete," which in Greek meant "consoler," "comforter," "helper" or "intercessor," terms which fully apply to the function the prophet plays. What Tertullian says on the subject, supports the belief that the early Christians looked to the "Paraclete" as another exponent of "Wisdom," or the Word of God, another revelation of the Spirit of Truth. And such a belief implies the principle of progressive revelation; of the principle that no religion can be absolute and final.

"The Paraclete," says Tertullian, "has many things to teach which the Lord reserves for him, according to his pre-arranged plan. First, he will bear witness to Christ and our belief about him, together with the whole design of God the Creator; he will glorify him and remind us of him; and then when the Paraclete has thus been recognized in the matter of the primary rule of faith, he will reveal many things which relate to discipline. These revelations will be attested by the consistency of their proclamation; although they are new, in the sense that they are only now

(1) Ency. of Religion and Ethics, Art. on Parousia.

33

revealed, and burdensome, because they are at the moment being born: but still they are the demands of the same Christ, who said that he had many more things which were to be taught by the Paraclete." (1)

It is true that Jesus Christ foretold the coming of the Comforter, but he also warned his followers of false prophets, or anti-Christs, who will appear in his name, but will try to lead the Christians into error and perdition. To put them on their guard, however, and help them distinguish between the genuine and the false: to enable them to appreciate and follow only the true messenger of God who shall "comfort" their soul, he said: "Beware of false prophets, which come to you in sheep's clothing, but inwardly they are ravening wolves. Ye shall know them by their fruits. Do men gather grapes from thorns, or figs of thistles? . . . Wherefore by their fruits ye shall know them." (2)

If the fruit of a prophetic message, or dispensation, is the cultural values, and life, it imparts to humanity; if it is the spiritual regeneration it effects, and the universalism it ushers into human society and its institutions; then the history of the last two thousand years clearly distinguishes between who acted as Paraclete, or "Comforter," on the one hand, and imparted "Shekinah" to mankind; and who were the false prophets of whom Jesus warned his disciples. Many heretics sprung in Christianity from its very early days. They divided the ranks of the believers, introduced pagan beliefs and practices, gave wrong interpretations of the sacred writings to support their syncretic tendencies, tarnished the purity of the Faith, broke up the ranks of the believers, and weakened their unity of purpose. None of these heretic movements created a healthy cultural life, that stimulated the spiritual growth of mankind. None produced fruits that would vindicate their divine origin. None resuscitated Christianity which through internal dissension, and rising pagan influences, was fast deteriorating spiritually. And because they produced "evil fruits," they were hewn by the hands of adversity

(1) De Monogamia 2, in "The Early Christian Fathers," by Henry Betterson, p. 181.
(2) Matthew 7:15-20.

34

and destroyed. It was Islam that regenerated the perennial religion of God, Jesus had served and promoted; brought true "comfort" and "Shekinah" to mankind; combatted paganism in all its forms; established a universalistic society covering the major part of the world: all, characteristics peculiar to very early Christianity, which had inspired the disciples of Jesus. In other words, it was Mohammed that, in the words of Tertullian, "bore witness to Christ and our belief about him, together with the whole design of God the Creator."

24. THE PRINCIPLE OF PROGRESSIVE REVELATION IN ISLAM: The idea of "Shekinah," or "Parousia," acting as a source of "comfort" to mankind, was carried forward into Islam. "Shekinah" was interpreted by the Jews as a divine presence in human society, acting as "an intermediary between God and the world."(1) The Christians of Greek origin used the term "Parousia" to convey that conception. The Koran states that "Sakinah," or "Shekina," was sent down by God upon Mohammed and his faithful followers; (2) in other words, that through him "divine presence" in the world was effected. The word "Sekinah" is also used in the Koran, to mean the "comfort" imparted by God. In fact this is its literal meaning in Arabic, though the Koran adds its original Jewish interpretation, as the "divine presence," that was believed to exist in the Ark of God, (3) and hence, venerated by the Jews. In other words, the principle of the "divine presence" in the world, through the prophet, and his laws, which was basic in Judaism and Christianity, constituted the fundamental conception of the Koran as well.

Furthermore, Mohammed presents Islam, not as a new independent Faith, which he conceived and promoted, but as the ancient perennial religion of God, all the prophets, in turn, reformed and regenerated.(4) These prophets of perennial religion, are not only those of Israel and Jesus, mentioned in the

(1) Encyclopaedia of Religion and Ethics, Article on Shekinah.
(2) Koran 48:4, 26.
(3) Ibid. 2:248.
(4) The Koran 3:84.

35

Koran, but others as well, whose story has not been told, and whose name has not been recorded. (1) Being himself the latest of these prophets, his advent was expected and foretold in the Torah and the Evangel. (2) In fact, he calls on Jews and Christians, to consider what he is revealing as a reversion to basic principles they already possess in their Sacred Scriptures. (3) He defines his task as, clarification of points they have come to misinterpret, and misunderstand; and which had become the source of controversy and dissension. Yet the interpretation he gives to those sacred Scriptures, and the new principles he advocates, should be considered to over-rule, and prevail, over them. (4) For they constitute a fuller revelation of the truth, of aspects of reality that Jesus had explicitly stated, humanity in his own age could not grasp, and the future revelation of the Spirit of Truth will impart to mankind.

But the unfoldment of the divine Purpose will not end with Mohammed, the perennial religion of God will not cease to be progressive with his advent. The Christians had been eagerly awaiting the coming of the Kingdom of God, and referred to it as "the great event," or "glad tiding." The Koran has a chapter under that title (5) and stresses the advent of that day as fast approaching. It is significant, however, that Mohammed does not identify that "Great News" with his own mission, but as an event to be expected in the future. Asked when that hour will strike, he answered that only the Lord knows, and when the time comes He shall reveal it. (6) It shall come suddenly, he said, when heaven and earth will be heavily laden—words that recall to memory the words uttered by Christ, depicting the circumstances of his return.

By the end of the sixth century, most of the pagan values that early Christians had combatted, and succeeded to eradicate, began to reassert themselves. Interest in pagan thought was revived;

(1) Ibid. 4:16.
(2) Ibid. 7:157.
(3) Ibid. 16:64.
(4) Ibid. 5:48.
(5) Ibid. 78.
(6) The Koran 7:187.

primitive Christian moral standards were no more practiced; meakness, which had been characteristic of the early Christians had given way before that insatiable thirst for power, and domination, that was specifically pagan; even pagan themes and symbols began to reappear, and influence Christian artistic expression. With such resurgence of pagan values, and their adoption by Christianity, came Islam as a contrast and a reversion to the ancient religion of God revealed to Christ, with its twin principles of spirituality and universalism. In opposition to the rise of pagan principles, the Koran reasserted the principle uttered by Jesus in his sermon of the mount, that man is essentially a spiritual being, and true culture is what promotes spiritual values. In opposition to race consciousness, and tribal affiliation, the pagan Germanic tribes began to introduce into the universalistic Christian Empire; the Koran stressed that humanity constitutes one people,(1) and called on the faithful believers to establish universal peace.(2) In other words, the Koran contained the spirit of the Evangel, and spread its principles a step further, unfolding more fully the divine truths, that the Scriptures had taught. And this was the very task that Jesus promised the "Comforter" will fulfil.

Mohammed was not preoccupied only with his own age, and its spiritual rebirth. Just as Isaiah visualized the coming of the Lord,(3) Zoroaster referred to the appearance of Mazda (the Lord of Wisdom), and Jesus spoke of his return in the "glory of the Father";(4) so Mohammed speaks of the day when humanity will arise to receive "the Lord of all the world," "the Lord of the judgment day," referring thereby to the words of Jesus Christ who, at his return, shall sit on the judgment seat, separate the sheep from the goat, the faithful from the faithless, the good from the evil, send the one to eternal bliss and the other to damnation.(5) In short, Mohammed, like the prophets who preceded him, looked to an ideal state of society, and that made

(1) Ibid. 10:19.
(2) Ibid. 2:208.
(3) Isaiah 52:12.
(4) Matthew 16:25.
(5) Ibid. 25:31 ff.

37

his conception of religion, and of revelation, essentially progressive.

25. THE CULMINATING POINT OF THAT PROGRESSIVE REVELATION: Thus, though the principle of progressive revelation is universally maintained by the prophets of the past; nowhere is it put in as arresting and unequivocal terms, as in the Persian Bayan of the Bab. And the outstanding point, in his exposition of the theme, is that "He whom God will make manifest," that is, he whose advent he was sent by God to usher, constitutes the one foretold and awaited by all the prophets of the past.

An infinite number of Adams, The Bab states, preceded the one whose advent is recorded in the Old Testament. Every one of them ended an old cycle, and started a new one, in the process of man's spiritual and cultural evolution. This last Adam, the Bab says, (1) appeared only 12,210 years before his own advent. With him started our cycle, which has been developing on an ascending scale of revelation, like the sun rising above the horizon, with an ever more resplendent light and potency, for the earth to receive. That gradation of the ascending scale of divine revelation had to be, to suit the slow spiritual and cultural growth of man; which, by its very nature, necessitates that, God's infinite light, should not exceed his own capacity to receive and assimilate profitably. The zenith, the culminating point, in this cycle of man's spiritual and cultural evolution, the hour when humanity will have attained maturity, both individually and socially, with the highest receptivity for God's revelation, will be under the aegis of "He whom God will make manifest," says the Bab. The coming of the Lord, the return of Christ in the glory of the Father, the advent of Mazda, the Lord of Wisdom, the day of resurrection, when all humanity will arise from spiritual death, to receive life from the Lord, all these which have been promised by the prophets of the past, will be fulfilled with the advent of "He whom God will make manifest."

Inasmuch as the Divine Essence is a reality absolutely inaccessible to human thought and understanding, the expressions: the

(1) The Persian Bayan, by The Bab, 3:13.

"presence of the Lord," his coming to the world as "Spirit of Truth," or "Lord of Wisdom," or as a "Judge" to sit on the judgement seat, and separate the good and faithful, from the evil and the faithless, all these expressions are meaningless if applied to the divine Essence. They obtain meaning and significance only if referred to the supreme manifestation, namely, "He whom God will make manifest," who will appear at the culminating point of the cycle started by the latest Adam. For, the Bab says, the divine Essence cannot be the object of human understanding. It cannot be described, qualified or even praised. It cannot constitute an object of vision, or intuition, though all things are created by It, are made the object of understanding through the outpouring of Its light, and acquire meaning and value through the rays It sheds.(1) It is only the divine nature revealed in the prophets, the Primal Purpose, the creative defining Point, the Word, or Wisdom vouchsafed through these messengers of God, and culminated in the advent of "He whom God will manifest," which constitute the supreme attainment of man upon this earth. At the culminating point, when "He whom God will make manifest," will reveal himself, shall the "divine Presence" be fully realized, the "Kingdom of God" become finally established, universal brotherhood and peace reign over all the earth, and the goal of man's spiritual and cultural evolution attained. That would be the summum bonum man has been trying to reach, the paradise in which he has sought to dwell, while yet on earth.(2)

Referring to "people of 'danesh' and 'binesh',," which literally means "of understanding and vision," and is taken to apply to philosophers who seek the way of intellect, and the mystics who try to apprehend reality intuitively, Baha'u'llah says in his Persian Hidden words: "O Son of Desire! The learned and the wise (men of understanding and vision) have for long years striven and failed to attain the presence of the all-glorious; they have spent their lives in search of Him, yet did not behold the beauty of His countenance. Thou without the least effort didst attain thy goal, and without search hast obtained the object of thy quest. Yet,

(1) The Persian Bayan, by The Bab 3:7.
(2) Ibid. 2:16.

39

notwithstanding, thou didst remain so wrapt in the veil of self, that thine eyes beheld not the beauty of the Beloved, nor did thy hand touch the hem of His robe, Ye that have eyes, behold and wonder." (1)

The supreme object of philosophers and mystics has been to understand the divine nature and attributes of perfection, and attain to the Presence of the Lord. During the darkest hours of human history, at the beginning of the last century, when Europe was in turmoil, discarding cherished ideas and beliefs, and destroying strong and well established institutions, The Bab and Baha'u'llah appeared. Their mission was to reveal to humanity that divine nature, and call mankind to their "presence." They ushered the Day of the Lord, so long and anxiously awaited. But neither philosophy, nor mystics heeded their call. Even that had been expected by the early Christians; for we see Paul say: "For yourselves know perfectly that the day of the Lord so cometh as a thief in the night." (2) "But the day of the Lord will come," said Peter, "as a thief in the night; in which the heavens shall pass away with a great noise, and the elements shall melt with fervent heat, the earth also and the works that are therein shall be burned up." (3) Revelation says: "If therefore thou shalt not watch, I will come on thee as a thief, and thou shalt not know what hour I will come upon thee." (4) Like thiefs also both the Bab and Baha'u'llah were beaten, persecuted and put in prison. And the Bab was executed like a thief. Our task is to show that they both possessed the answer to the predicaments philosophy and mysticism confronted in that age, and under which they have been ever since labouring.

26. REVELATION IS TO REESTABLISH LAW, NOT TO BREAK IT: Revelation is generally qualified as miraculous, and a break into the law and order which prevails in nature. It is truly miraculous in the sense that it overcomes through divine interposition, a recession of society, brought about by reversion

(1) The Hidden Words, by Baha'u'llah, 22.
(2) 1. Thessalonians 5:2.
(3) 2 Peter 3:10.
(4) Revelation 3:3.

to the natural instincts of man. It is a creative act of God which checks, and directs into new channels, the current and steady sequences which develop from the materialistic and naturalistic trends of events. But it is not miraculous in the sense that it is a unique and unprecedented event, in the long and eternal process, of man's spiritual and cultural evolution; or that it is in utter violation of universal law and order. The principle of progressive revelation, which we have stressed, shows how recurrent, periodic and purposeful the process is; and how it conforms with an eternal and everlasting law, which governs the spiritual and cultural life of man.

For example, physical, social and natural forces, which then prevailed, cannot explain the reason for the appearance of Jesus Christ, at that specific period of human history; nor why his message, pursued with utter meekness, soon acquired ascendancy, in spite of Roman might and bloody persecutions. Nor can contemporary natural social events explain why the inflow of Germanic tribes from the North, brought about the Dark Ages in Europe; while the spread of the Arabs from the desert in the South, inaugurated one of the greatest cultures history records. These were contemporary events that transpired in the same cultural field. The Germanic tribes, and the Arabs, were both primitive and uncultured, compared to the Romans; and their potentialities can be regarded the same. There can be no other explanation, but that a spiritual force was driving the one, which the other completely lacked. Thus, these two events, namely, the appearance of Jesus, and then of Islam, constitute miracles in the sense that they were intervention in the course of prevailing social forces; but they were far from miraculous, in the sense that they were contrary to law and order. For the eternal and ever abiding spiritual and cultural law, as stated in the Koran, is that God starts creation, and periodically gives it a new birth; (1) that He raises the living from the dead, and quickens the earth whenever it droops to die. (2)

Therefore, the revelation of the Primal Purpose through Jesus

(1) The Koran, 30:27.
(2) The Koran, 30:19.

Christ, and later through Mohammed, was unique, and hence, miraculous, in the sense that it was characteristic of certain specific junctures in the gradual process of human history, that it was not due to the operation of a natural phenomenon then prevailing, that it was the action of a force, other and higher, then dominating the cultural field. But nevertheless, this intervention of the Primal Purpose was periodic, and in pursuance of law and order. It operated in conformity with a spiritual law and order, emanating from a Creator; and its object was to establish law and order in the spiritual and cultural life of mankind.

We considered divine illumination, vouchsafed by the Primal Purpose, or the divine nature revealed in the prophets, as the supreme type of polarisation. The intervening force which polarises the individual atoms in a magnetic field, and directs them to a specific goal, is not immanent and ingrained in the field itself. It constitutes a higher force, hitherto beyond that field. Can we, on that ground, consider its operation, and sudden activity, unique and miraculous? We could, if we were to limit our understanding to that one incident and occasion, and disregard others; but not if we study similar phenomena, and observe the same force and purpose operating.

In other words, there is a cyclic and periodic polarization of the field of the spiritual and cultural life by a force beyond man. It operates through the recurring advent of prophets, revealing the Primal Purpose of God to man. That Purpose sets the goal of human evolution, individually and socially, and directs the attention, love and longing of man towards its realization. Coming from a transcendent source, that activity is miraculous. But whenever the effect of this positive and dynamic force, wielded by the Primal Purpose, through the instrumentality of the prophet, dies out, or is discarded by man; and as a result the atoms of the human heart get diverted and dissipated, and lose their inner unity of consciousness, and as a result, a cultural void prevails; that Primal purpose operates again to reestablish law and order in that cultural field. This law has eternally operated in the past, and will eternally operate in the future.

42

27. DURATION OF THE PROPHETIC CYCLES: The duration of these propetic cycles, that is, from one dawn to another, has been considered by all sacred Scriptures to extend about one thousand years, depending ultimately upon the spiritual and cultural needs of man, and the forces operating in the age itself. We find such references in Hebrew, Zoroastrian, Christian and Muslim Scriptures, as well as in the writings of the Bab and Baha'u'llah.

Zoroastrian eschatology maintains the existence of such cycles, or "world-ages, each of four periods of 3000 years. Towards the beginning of the final 3000 years Zarathustra is born. Towards the beginning of the second millennium of this period, evils increase, there are signs in heaven and earth, and now Hushetar is born. Religion is restored, and he brings back the creatures to their proper state. Towards the beginning of the final millennium Hushetar-mah is born. In his time creatures become more progressive and men do not die. But now evils again increase . . . at the close of the period Soshyans, the Persian Messiah, 'who makes the evil spirit impotent and causes the resurrection and future existence,' is born; now begins the new order of things. All mankind . . . are raised from the dead. Then follows the great assembly, in which each sees his good and evil deeds. The righteous are set apart from the wicked; the former are taken to heaven, and the latter cast back to hell."(1) In this context we can appreciate the significance of the Book of Revelation when it says: "And I saw an angel come down from heaven, having the key of the bottomless pit and a great chain in his hand. And he laid hold on the dragon, that old serpent, which is the Devil, and Satan, and bound him a thousand years. And cast him into the bottomless pit, and shut him up, and set a seal upon him, that he should deceive the nations no more, till the thousand years should be fulfilled: and after that he must be loosed a little season. . . . This is the first resurrection. Blessed and holy is he that hath part in the first resurrection: on such the second death hath no power, but they shall be priests of God and of Christ, and shall reign with him a thousand years. And when the

(1) Encyclopaedia of Religion and Ethics, Article on Eschatology (Parsi).

thousand years are expired, Satan shall be loosed out of his prison. . . ."(1) The first resurrection after Zoroaster, when mankind was spiritually reborn, was the one realized through the advent of Jesus Christ, who can be identified as "Hushetar" of Zoroastrian eschatology. And his spiritual and cultural empire lasted about a thousand years. Then Satan was loosened again, and evil became rampant throughout the world another time. But with the second millennium Mohammed appeared. He thus corresponds with "Hushetar-mah." We might take Revelation as referring to him when it says: "And I saw a great white throne, and him that sat on it. . . . And I saw the dead, small and great, stand before God; and the books were opened: and another book was opened, which is the book of life: and the dead were judged out of those things which were written in the books, according to their works. . . . And death and hell were cast into the lake of fire. This is the second death. And whosoever was not found written in the book of life was cast into the lake of fire."(2)

After this second cycle of human regeneration, or as it is called "resurrection" and death, Revelation proceeds to say: "And I saw a new heaven and a new earth: for the first heaven and the first earth were passed away; and there was no more sea. And I John saw the holy city, new Jerusalem, coming down from God out of heaven, prepared as a bride adorned for her husband. And I heard a great voice out of heaven saying, Behold, the tabernacle of God is with men, and he will dwell with them, and they shall be his people, and God himself shall be with them, and be their God."(3) And that would constitute the Messianic age, of Zoroastrian eschatology.

The principle of spiritual and cultural cycles of a thousand years is also affirmed in the Koran, where Mohammed says: "And they will bid thee to hasten the chastisement. But God cannot fail His threat. And verily, a day with thy Lord is as a thousand years, as ye reckon them."(4) "From the Heaven to the earth He governeth all things: hereafter shall they come up to him on

(1) Revelation, 20:1-7.
(2) Revelation, 20:11-16.
(3) Ibid. 21:1-3.
(4) The Koran, 22-47.

a day whose length shall be a thousand of such years as ye reckon."(1) In short, all these sacred Scriptures maintain the principle of periodic revelation; every cycle of which lasts about a thousand years. The Bab and Baha'u'llah reaffirm that principle and consider it eternal and everlastingly recurring.

Thus at the dawn of every new day, or cultural springtime, the Primal Purpose, or the divine nature revealed in the prophets, sheds its illumination upon the spiritual and cultural life of man. And nothing short of such repeated cyclic revelation, can maintain perennial religion progressive, and a constant source of inspiration and guidance. Nothing short of such a principle of progressive and periodic revelation, can preserve religion as the factual source of the primary premises, and dynamic force, that the spiritual and cultural life of man demands. For a progressive culture necessitates a religion that is progressive.

28. REVEALED RELIGION IS ESSENTIALLY PROGRESSIVE: Pagan philosophies distinguish between matter and mind; and when they speak of spirit, they consider it as identical with thought. Revealed religion, on the other hand, regards them both —matter and mind—as essentially natural faculties of man; and distinguishes the natural from the spiritual, which it considers as transcendent to both. It considers the physical and the rational as mere instruments of the spirit. The task of revealed religion is to make man conscious of this transcendent spirit, trace the road, and provide the necessary values, to achieve its gradual development and perfection. The result is, that while pagan thought and culture attempt to maintain man on the level of nature, and develop his physical and mental faculties; revealed religion seeks to muster all the forces of nature, physical, social and intellectual, to raise man to an ever higher level of being, develop in him spiritual characteristics, and make him acquire spiritual perfections. If we apply the principle of polarization, the task of religion would be to direct every atom in man and galvanize his energy towards the same transcendent purpose, and thereby establish unity and coherence in his thought and

(1) Ibid. 32:5.

45

activity. It would be to muster all human energy, to ensure the gradual evolution and perfection of man, individually and socially.

But to reach up to the realm of the spirit, which transcends mind and understanding, man needs guidance from above. He needs knowledge of the nature of those characteristics he has to acquire to achieve perfection, faith in that guiding hand, and assurance of his ultimate purpose and goal. Such knowledge, guidance and purpose, however, should be imparted by a higher reality; just as a polarizing force should proceed from a higher source than the atoms to be polarized. This is the basis of the principle of divine grace, the reason why self-revelation of God, is considered prior to, and sine qua non of, man's spiritual and cultural evolution. Left alone and unguided, with no understanding and love of divine characteristics, and perfections, man may secure mental and physical development and well-being; but he cannot rise to the realm of the spirit, acquire attributes which are essentially spiritual, or create a culture which serves, not merely his mental and physical requirements, but stimulate the growth of his complete personality, which is primarily spiritual in nature. Just as the transcending force polarizes the atoms resident in its field, and directs them towards a goal beyond them, which is in line with its own operation; so does the Primal Purpose, by inculcating the principle of "thy will be done" in man, guide his capacities towards a level of being other and higher.

But such a notion necessitates, that this self-revelation of God, or divine grace, should be a periodic and recurring process. For man's inveterate tendency, and moved by his free will and choice, is apt to fall back repeatedly to the level of nature, especially when the person of the prophet recedes into the past and his dynamic power ceases to operate; just as the atoms gradually cease to be polarized, when the polarizing force stops to operate, and extraneous forces set in to disturb their harmony and direction. Human salvation, once achieved, does not abide eternally. Human society is the cradle in which the individual is born, nurtured, and schooled. And history shows that its tendency has been to fall back, to the level of nature, and to adopt naturalistic values, whenever the dynamic force of the Primal Purpose, revealed by the prophets, receded into the past, and its unifying uplifting and stimulating influence became less. This is not positive sin, as theology is wont to qualify it. It is mere absence of virtue. Nature is not a state of sin. There is no primordial sin in man, an evil he has to uproot. As the Bayan states, it is a state of "non-divine," when attributes of God do not dominate. Man is born in a state of untutored innocence, not of positive perversion and sin. This inveterate tendency of man, to fall back to the level of nature, is the reason why whenever revealed religion, with its uplifting influence, ceases to operate, culture falls back to the level of nature, and its values become essentially naturalistic. It ceases to be polarized, loses its unity and harmony, and as a result chaos begins to set in.

29. PAGAN CULTURE WAS THE RESULT OF A SPIRITUAL RECESSION: Greek pagan thought came into existence, when such a spiritual recession prevailed on the Eastern and Western shores of the Aegean. In the age of Pericles there was a striking contrast between the Greeks, on the one hand, and the Achaemenian Empire, on the other. The Greeks were heirs to the materialistic and naturalistic philosophies that had appeared in Hellas, and had gradually been reduced to Sophism, and its skeptic attitude towards the basic conceptions of culture. The Persians were Zoroastrians, with a culture and set of values, that were believed to be prophetic, and revelational, in origin. The one considered man as the measure of all things, and human thought the source of all cultural values, that is, of truth, goodness, justice and beauty. The other regarded the revelation of God, vouchsafed through Zoroaster, as the source from which they were all derived, and the standard with which they were to conform. The Persians followed that religious outlook with hope and faith; while Greek thought, under such eminent thinkers as Plato, seemed uncertain, and fervently questioned the validity of Sophism and its materialistic point of view. These were dissatisfied with the moral and cultural implications that materialism entailed.

They were, unlike other Greeks, lured by the seeming luster, that material prosperity had brought about, and political independence secured. It was the prevalent cultural values that caused their misgivings and aroused their apprehensions. And the subsequent deterioration of Athenian power proved that their forebodings were not unfounded. But though Plato was staunchly opposed to materialism, he did not divest himself of naturalistic tendencies. He did not discard the basic assumption of Greek thought that the "All" was God, that the universe was divine in substance and reality. He merely reserved paramountcy for mind. He did not distinguish qualitatively the creator from the created, but included them both under the same category of "being," a principle that is in absolute contradiction to that of religion as interpreted by its prophets. Greek culture thus remained naturalistic, until Christianity appeared and redressed that basic error of Greek thought.

Another recession into pagan tendencies occurred, when early Christianity started to spend its original force and vitality, and gradually discard its twin principles of spirituality and universalism. As we have already observed, by the sixth century after Christ, Greek pagan values began to reassert themselves in all fields of cultural life: in the intellectual, moral, social and aesthetic. For example, when viewed in the light of early Christian ideals and principles, such as the significance Jesus attributed to the spiritual life in his Sermon on the Mount, and the meekness with which it should be advocated and served; the wars of conquest that Justinian waged in the name of Orthodoxy, and with the pretext of destroying Arianism, these stand in striking and revolting contrast. Spirituality was identified with an Orthodoxy, that had already succumbed to pagan influences, and meekness had been completely discarded in favor of political domination, and military crave for power and conquest. Similarly, universalism and complete detachment from national, racial, class, and even religious affiliations in social dealings, stressed in the parable of the Good Samaritan, were fast giving way to tribal considerations, that the Germanic peoples introduced into Europe, and which in time gave birth to the spirit of nationalism, which

48

undermined the unity of the Christian Empire. In other words, with the weakening of Christian universalism, which had forged the Roman Empire into one community, giving it a basic common consciousness; separatism, both racial and national, which were pagan in origin and spirit, began to reappear and reassert themselves. And ever since they have remained the dominant considerations in shaping the political life of Western Europe. Thus, the recession of Christian spirituality and universalism, left a void which pagan naturalism and separatism could easily fill. And the result was that Europe entered its Dark Ages.

This recession of Christian spirituality and universalism was more than an occasion for the outflow of another wave of divine grace, another self-revelation of God to man. It called for it. It put into operation the eternal law, that everytime human consciousness starts to languish, and the social environment in which it is to be nurtured and developed, deteriorates beyond repair; divine love and mercy surges, and the dawn of a new spiritual and cultural era breaks. Islam appeared and reinstated spirituality and universalism over a vaster region of the earth. The Koran, when adequately studied, especially in the light of contemporary Christian controversies and practices, will be found to act as a reversion to the spiritual interpretation of the religious life, stressed by Jesus and the ancient prophets of Israel. And wherever Mohammedan dominion reached and exerted its influence, national, racial and class hatred, and distinctions, were obliterated, or appreciably reduced.

And when, in turn, Islam began to lose its spiritual dynamic, that is, by the fifth or sixth centuries of its era, which corresponds to the eleventh and twelfth centuries after Christ, in other words, when recession began, Pagan thought and culture started to awaken interest in Mohammedan countries. A great controversy began between the supporters of the revelational conception, on the one hand, and students of pagan thought on the other. In Europe, where revealed religion was in a state of greater recession, pagan thought found fuller reception; while in Islamic countries it remained confined to the few intellectuals. Orthodoxy here remained supreme.

The result of the spread of pagan principles, ever since the Renaissance, has tended to eliminate the significance of the mission of the prophets, in shaping the spiritual and cultural life of man. Religion has been stripped of revelation, thinking that it can survive alone. The task before us is to show, that the many problems that have confronted philosophy, and encouraged skepticism, have arisen from this very fact; from discarding the Primal Purpose, the defining Point, and the Word as source of knowledge and understanding, all revealed through the instrumentality of the prophets, as source of the spiritual and cultural life. The principle that a Primal Purpose animates religion, as a phenomenon in history, has ceased to awaken interest. The idea that as "Point" it defines the spiritual and cultural values, is utterly discarded. The notion that the Word of God constitutes the source of truth, upon which human reasoning rests, is denied.

30. GOD'S PRIMAL PURPOSE ABHORS A SPIRITUAL AND CULTURAL VOID: In this universe, which is both physical and spiritual, where the Primal Purpose of God is dominant, and as a result, there is constant and eternal generation and regeneration; in such a universe, there can be no abiding void, no field where the atoms of being can remain discordant, depolarized and erratic for long. Just as a field in which the atoms, either individually or as a group, through some inadvertent event, get momentarily depolarized and lose their order, is immediately constrained to abide again by law, and resume its function in an orbit, through the physical effect of the rays of the sun; so human society, and the consciousness of the individual, cannot live long in a spiritual and cultural void. That very void calls on the source of the creative energy to operate, to direct again its Primal Purpose, regalvanize human consciousness and environment, and polarize them again in the direction destined for them. The unity of the universe, and the purposeful activity of God entail such readjustment.

It is on this ground that Zoroaster considered Asha, or Law and Order, one of the emanations of Ahura Mazda. It constitutes a supreme Form, to which all things both physical and spiritual have to submit. Mohammed says in the Koran (1) that every thing moves in an orbit. And there is an orbit for physical being, as well as for the spiritual and cultural life of man. And in neither field can the individual or the group move long erratically. His freedom of choice and activity is within certain limits. He can bring about his own destruction, as well as that of the community he lives in; or merge himself in a higher orbit purposed and willed by God, and thereby achieve a higher destiny. Similarly the Bab stresses the principle of law and order, which he says, reigns "in heaven, on earth and in between." This law and order would not permit void to prevail. That very void, which is discordance in the field of the spiritual and cultural life of man, presents the occasion and longs for God's creative Purpose to operate, regalvanize it and restore order in human consciousness and social environment.

31. SUMMARY: In short, we saw in this introduction, how Empiricism, Idealism, and Mysticism, cannot impart certainty to man, to establish his spiritual and cultural life upon a secure foundation. The reason is that these schools of thought are essentially naturalistic, employing physical senses, intellect, or intuition, to unravel spiritual and cultural values and conceptions, which, by their very essence, transcend the field of nature. Furthermore, they constitute the points of view of an observer, not of a creator who desires certain reality and actually produces it. The cultural life, we say, is a super-structure created and built upon natural foundations; or acting as matter seeking form. Hence the essentially natural faculties of an observer, cannot grasp its nature and needs. In contrast to these schools of thought, we found the divine nature revealed in the prophets, acting as the Primal Purpose, the defining Point, the Word, or Wisdom. While those schools of philosophy approach reality as an observer, or contemplator; the prophets view it as creators, who visualize the object desired, and then generate it, in accordance with a definite plan and project. The disclosures of these prophets,

(1) The Koran, 21:33.

51

therefore, regarding the nature and destiny of the reality they have created, are truths which inspire certainty and command faith.

When the persons of these prophets recedes into the past, and their influence on human consciousness wanes, their function as instruments of the Primal Purpose, the defining Point, the Word, and the source of Wisdom, ceases to be fully appreciated by man. Pagan systems of thought, which try to dispense with revelation, then find ready reception. But with pagan values dominating the spiritual and cultural life of man, peculiar problems appear. Such predicaments at present confront man. We undertake to show, taking the Bab and Baha'u'llah as our guide, how these predicaments could have been averted if human thought had remained true to the primary premises, all the Sacred Scriptures of the past stressed.

Chapter

I

REVEALED RELIGION AND THE DICTUM OF DESCARTES

1. PHYSICAL GENERATION AND SPIRITUAL REBIRTH:
We said in our introduction that man, as conceived by revealed religion, is first born on the level of nature, and then reborn in the sphere of the spiritual, which is identical with the cultural, life. He constitutes a seed planted in that earth, but whose trunk, branches, foliage and fruits, rise above it, and far transcend it, in value and significance. And he achieves this by acquiring attributes that are divine, and which his spiritual and cultural environment provide. This is the reason Jesus Christ constantly urged his followers, and among them Nicodemus, to be born again. "Jesus answered and said, 'Verily, verily, I say unto thee, Except a man be born of water and of the Spirit, he cannot enter into the kingdom of God. That which is born of the flesh is flesh; and that which is born of the Spirit is spirit.'"(1) The Koran considers this rebirth, or regeneration, a new creation, and confirms what Jesus said, exclaiming, "have we been tired by the first creation!"(2) Compared with the spiritual and cultural life destined for man, physical being is lifeless regidity, from which he has to be raised, and resuscitated. "Shall the dead," says Mohammed, "whom we have quickened, and for whom we have ordained a light whereby he may walk among men, be like him, whose likeness is in the darkness, whence he will not come forth?"(3)

The mission of Jesus Christ, and the purpose for which the

(1) John 3:3-6.
(2) The Koran, 50:15.
(3) Ibid. 6:122.

Koran was revealed, were to help the rebirth of man, to regenerate him, raise him from the dead, and gradually nurture him, until he becomes a faithful image of God, revealing His many attributes of perfection. Their purpose, like that of the other prophets, was to impart to humanity that higher life, which raises the individual, and humanity at large, above the sphere of physical nature, in which he is born, and which he shares with animals, into a realm exclusively his own: into a sphere of culture, where his spirit grows, and gradually unfolds its infinite capacities. It is true that the human body needs all the nourishment physical nature affords; but man also requires elements that far transcend that nature, if he is to cultivate his spiritual and cultural life as well. The "light" he needs, is divine illumination; the "water" is the shower of blessing that the spirit of Christ pours upon all mankind.

It is in the same sense that the Bab attributes to every soul a "grave" in which it is buried. But all these dead souls, he says, are destined to arise, when "He whom God will manifest," shall appear. For his day of "resurrection," "regeneration," and "new creation," will affect them all. All will arise from their spiritual and cultural "grave" at his bidding.(1) The process, whereby man is thus reborn into the spiritual and cultural life, constitutes religion.

2. THE PRIMAL PURPOSE IS THE SOURCE OF PERENNIAL RELIGION AND CULTURE: Religion is the revelation of God's Primal Purpose, to guide and stimulate the spiritual growth of man. The culture generated by revealed religion, which is periodically reformed by the prophets, provides the necessary elements for that growth, namely, the guiding values, the inner impetus and desire, the objective goal, as well as the social environment necessary for it. Hence, the different revealed religions and cultures, the prophets have established throughout the ages, are identical in their basic nature, values and purpose, and together constitute one perennial religion and culture periodically reformed. In other words, we should consider the

(1) The Persian Bayan, by The Bab 2:9.

religion of the ancient Hebrews, Zoroastrianism, Christianity and Islam, as successive revelations of God's spiritual and cultural purpose, to impart to man that rebirth, which leads him into the higher life of the spirit, he is destined to acquire. We should accept this principle, and realize the unity of their basic teaching, and the spirit of their laws; namely, the stress they lay on the paramountcy of the human spirit and its needs, and the universalistic environment they seek to establish throughout the world. We should acknowledge the unity of the Primal Purpose, which animated these successive dispensations; and view these different cultures, they have produced in recorded history, as one single perennial culture, inspired by the same perennial religion. Moses, Zoroaster, Jesus, Mohammed, the Bab, Baha'u'llah, the infinite prophets that went before them, and the infinite ones that shall succeed, all are missioned by God to afford man the means to attain his spiritual destiny. And with the advent of every one of them, religion and culture are reborn. And the acme of that universal regeneration of the individual, and his social environment, constitutes Paradise on earth.

Paradise in heaven, the Bab says, is a state of being which is absolutely beyond human understanding and expression; hence, it cannot be considered the supreme object of thought and of human attainment on earth nor can belief in it be made a criterion of his religious understanding. Therefore, Paradise, or the Kingdom of God, is "on earth," as Jesus said. It constitutes the attainment of social perfection, for it will be the reign of universalism throughout the world. It will be the perfection of man's individual state of being, for he comes in the presence of the manifestation of God, which is the "presence" of God Himself. As the Bab further says, the Paradise of every dispensation is the perfection, or culminating point, in the cycle of that dispensation,(1) hence, it is the appearance of the subsequent messenger of God, when man will be judged, and the faithful fully recompensed. The paradise of the Jews, for example, was the advent of Jesus; and the Paradise of Christianity the return of Christ in the glory of the Father. The period between the two manifesta-

(1) The Persian Bayan, by The Bab, 3:13.

tions, or culminating points of human attainment, constitutes, according to the Bab, the Purgatory.(1) For, he adds, Purgatory, like Paradise, could not constitute a state of being in the other world, and at the same time be considered foundational in human belief. For a state, or reality, that is by its very nature unknowable, cannot be made by God the object of man's intelligent quest and attainment, and belief in it criterion of his sincerity.

To every springtime, and period of fruition, there are wintry days of desolation. When religion ceases to impart illumination, when it gradually spends its galvanizing and polarizing power, man is left with no other alternative but to fall back on his own resources, however meager they may be. If he can no more rely on revelation, he possesses no other alternative, but to follow his reason, in satisfying his inner urge for growth and culture. This is the state of man in Purgatory, as defined by the Bab: when the twilight of the previous day is fast receding, and the dawn of the new one has not yet come. The history of every one of these revealed religions affords ample example of such spiritual recessions, such wintry days of desolation and uncertainty. During such recessions, and as characteristic of its nature, pagan culture surges and starts to dominate human thought.

3. THE RISE OF PAGAN CULTURES: The outstanding feature of perennial culture, we have observed, is the principle that, the divine nature revealed in the prophets, constitutes the Primal Purpose, the creative and defining Point, the Word of God, and the source of all Wisdom. The outstanding feature of paganism is to set aside this claim of the prophets, and assert instead one of the natural faculties of man, whether sense perception, human thought or inner intuition, as the source of all wisdom and understanding, as well as of moral, social and aesthetic values. It considers the spiritual and cultural life, not as an act of grace from a transcendent God, vouchsafed through the instrumentality of a prophet; but the product of natural forces immanent in man himself.

(1) The Persian Bayan, by The Bab, 2:8.

56

Thus, Greek pagan thought appeared during such a period of spiritual recession, and as the result of such human endeavour and natural powers, Socrates was charged by Meletus to be an "atheist," and was condemned to death by the Athenians on the ground that he believed "in gods other than what the city recognized." (1) In his Laws, Plato, referring to certain religious writings, says: "Whether these stories have in other ways a good or bad influence, I should not like to be severe upon them, because they are ancient; but, looking at them with reference to the duties of children to their parents, I cannot praise them, or think that they are useful or at all true." (2) In other words, paganism as a religion, had no intellectual, moral or social values to inspire thinkers and establish a healthy cultural atmosphere for the Athenians. If it influenced art considerably, it was because it was naturalistic, worshipped natural gods, and tried to represent them through idols. The representative art paganism developed, and stimulated, was through the influence of its naturalism and idolatry, neither of which revealed religion could endorse. But an art which is so naturalistic and idolatrous, cannot help man transcend nature, and attain the spiritual life. Religious art ought to be uplifting, and stimulate the soul towards spiritual perfections, not to direct it to the satisfaction of natural desires as an ultimate goal. To religion beauty is primarily spiritual, not naturalistic.

In short, Socrates was condemned to death because he regarded the naturalistic gods of Greek mythology, as bereft of cultural values; and tried instead to teach his pupils the conception of a God who acts as source of goodness, justice, and of the intellectual life of man; a conception of God more in line with that of Zoroastrianism and Judaism at that time. But if we are to take the Republic of Plato as a guide to the basic thoughts of Socrates, he failed to consider God as absolutely transcendent, as these two revealed religions understood Him to be. He merely shifted his position from the physical and Empirical to the Idealistic conception, which we said, is also essentially naturalistic.

(1) Apology by Plato 26.
(2) The Laws by Plato, 886.

But if Greek mythology had no cultural values to impart to Socrates and Plato, neither could Judaism and late Zoroastrianism in that stage of their development. Judaism had lost its universalism and spiritual outlook, and become at the hand of its priests particularistic and ritualistic. Its own prophets had condemned and disowned it. And Zoroastrianism was fast losing the spiritual purity and vitality which characterised its early days. In such a spiritual vacuum, there was no alternative left for Plato, but to hold to the principle of pagan philosophers: that man is the measure of all things, and that the source of all values is his own mind.

The genius of Socrates, as we have observed, was in accomplishing just this task, namely, of making the transcendent God he conceived, the source of cultural values, a task which cost him his life. That task which led him to Idealism and Rationalism inspired his student Plato, who received it as an intellectual legacy, and upon it as a foundation, built his philosophic system of thought. And this system eventually became the one, human thought has adopted, whenever confronted with similar predicaments. In other words, the genius of the Greeks was to create a rational foundation for cultural values, when the light of revelation was obstructed, or momentarily obscured. Philosophy is a noble and venturesome intellectual enterprise on the part of man. It is an earnest quest for truth. For what else can man do, when the light of revelation does not reach him: when religion has lost its spirituality and universalism, and on that ground, has ceased to inspire confidence, and impart high cultural values?

When early Hebrew religious thought, such as expressed in the Psalms, or the writings of the pre-exilic prophets of Israel, considered the revelation of God, the source of all truth, goodness, justice and beauty, and proclaimed spirituality and universalism as the twin basis of cultural life; human understanding could, with full justification, look up to it and feel confident, satisfied and adequately guided and informed. But when its spirituality gave way to strict formalism at the hands of its priests, and its universalism relapsed into separatism and particularism; Hebrew religion lost its cultural mission, and the convincing power of its thought. The same was true of Zoroastrianism. Philosophy, as love of wisdom, could no more be attracted, and made to regard religion as source of cultural life, which it considered its task to strengthen and promote. Religion no more possessed those ultimate truths, philosophy required, to use as basis of its reasoning; nor did it contain spiritual and universalistic principles regarding the reality of man and his destiny, to employ in advocating the regeneration of the individual and the rehabilitation of society. It was because of that failure on the part of religion, or rather of religious leaders, that philosophy reverted to human reason, and tried to seek cultural values in man's own natural powers and potentialities. But in seeking these values, from man's natural faculties, as ultimate sources; culture receded to the level of nature, and thereby lost its transcending tendencies and uplifting power.

But Greek culture itself, bereft of that spiritual outlook, and universalism, had no special message to offer to the Jews and Zoroastrians. Its own religion was naturalistic and formalistic; and its social principles were firmly founded on particularism, that is, on class distinctions, racial arrogance and national loyalties. And such principles, which are intrinsically of much inferior value and scope, could hardly inspire peoples bearing the tradition of spirituality and universalism; though they had discarded its actual practice. It is for this reason that Hellenic culture failed to permeate the rank and file of the Jews and Persians, in the period prior to the rise of Christianity. The orthodox element in both communities felt, that the traditions they already possessed, were much superior, and that Hellenism offered to them no higher principles of culture, which they could adopt in preference to their own.

4. HELLENISM AND EARLY CHRISTIANITY: With the rise of early Christianity, and its spiritual and universalistic outlook; Hellenism with its naturalism and race, class and national consciousness and prejudices; had no superior cultural values, to carry conviction. Hence, we observe its gradual deterioration. On the other hand, because Christianity offered more

convincing truths, higher moral precepts, wider social outlook, and expressed beauty in a manner that stimulated the spiritual growth of man, it won the cultural conflict, that then raged between them. And Christian values remained dominant until the fourth century; when it, in turn, began to succumb to man's natural and inveterate tendency towards ritualism and particularism. But though Hellenism, by that time, had begun to reassert itself in Christian thought and art; the masses remained orthodox, and true to their religious traditions. Just as previously, among the Jews and Zoroastrians; here only a group of Christian scholars were won over to Greek thought; and that to a very limited extent. Greek learning was unearthed, Greek naturalistic symbols were adopted; but to express Christian themes. Similarly, the universalistic Empire, which Christianity had established and maintained up to the time of Justinian, began to be dismembered; and the Germanic tribes, which had remained partly pagan in tendency, started to assert their own principle of racial and national separatism. Only a semblance of universalism lingered, and that in the institution of the Holy Roman Empire, and the spiritual domination of a universalistic Church. In other words, Greek culture was revived, but it never obtained the paramountcy it acquired in much later ages. And it did not fully succeed, because the spiritual and universalistic traditions of Christianity were still strong enough to withstand that onslaught.

5. HELLENISM AND EARLY ISLAM: In the fourth century of the Mohammedan era, that is about the tenth century after Christ, through Arab scholars of Jewish and Christian faith, Hellenism was introduced into Islamic thought. Its first influence was exerted to make religious belief, that is revelation, conform with logical thinking, that is, human thought. How could revelation of the Word, which is the manifestation of the source of all truth; within the field of human understanding, turn out to be irrational, and maintain doctrines that intellect cannot endorse? How could Wisdom, which provides the basic premises of all thought, lead to conclusions that are contradictory to human experience, science and reasoning? The doctrines of creation in

60

time, and of the resurrection of the body, were striking examples of such anomalies. These questions had been confronted by Jewish and Christian thinkers, and were based upon Sacred Scriptures that were deemed to be revealed. Islamic thought, as heir to that intellectual heritage, had to face them and find a reasonable answer. For both led to irrational conclusions. To the philosopher it constituted a predicament that had to be confronted, to the religious devout it was a doctrine to be accepted on faith, no matter how unintelligible were the conclusions it entailed. Their validity could not be questioned, for the Scriptures revealed it.

To appreciate the significance of the term "rising from the dead," or breaking out of the "grave," mentioned in the Koran, and which thinkers in Islam tried to reconcile with logical reasoning; to understand them, we should refer to the words of Christ, from whom we receive those conceptions, or terminologies, as part of our spiritual legacy. Jesus said: "Verily, verily, I say unto you, He that heareth my word, and believeth on him that sent me, hath everlasting life, and shall not come into condemnation; but is passed from death unto life. Verily, verily, I say unto you, The hour is coming, and now is, when the dead shall hear the voice of the Son of God: and they that hear shall live. . . . Marvel not at this: for the hour is coming, in which all that are in the graves shall hear his voice." (1) "And the graves were opened; and many bodies of the saints which slept arose." (2) These verses definitely show that rising from the "dead," means to enter the spiritual life offered by Jesus; and that the saints who, at the resurrection of Christ, arise from the "grave", are the ones who hearken to his voice and are thereby regenerated. These, and the many other references to the "dead" and their "grave," mentioned in the Scriptures, were applied by Jesus, to a spiritual conversion achieved by man when still on earth; and hence, during the span of his physical existence in this world. It does not apply to life after death, into which he proceeds as an ordinary natural phenomenon. But the fact that it

(1) John 5:24, 25, 28.
(2) Matthew 27:52.

transpires during this earthly life, does not mean that the rising is a physical phenomenon, that it is a reassembly of our dismembered body, or the reintegration of our disintegrated bones and flesh. It constitutes a purely spiritual and cultural rebirth. And it is in this sense that we have to interpret similar verses of the Koran, such as: "And when the graves shall be disturbed."(1) "And God shall resurrect those who are in the graves."(2) "But they to whom knowledge and faith have been given will say, 'Ye have waited, in accordance with the book of God, till the day of resurrection': for this is the day of resurrection—But ye knew it not."(3) Elsewhere Mohammed asserts that God created and resuscitated man, as one spirit,(4) meaning with one single fiat, directed to mankind as a whole. Following this spiritual and universalist interpretation of the rising from the grave, the Bab adds that, the supreme day of resurrection shall be the one that will attend the coming of "Him whom God will manifest."(5)

Christianity had, by the seventh century, gradually given up hope in the return of Christ, the resurrection of the dead, and the advent of the Kingdom of God on earth, as this-worldly events. It had began to consider it, either as a purely mystic experience, enjoyed by the individual human consciousness; or a physical rising from the grave, or as an event that would transpire in the world to come. Perhaps these latter interpretations, were given priority after the rise of Islam, when Mohammed claimed to be another messenger of God, quickening the dead with the spiritual and cultural life he imparted; for that would make his dispensation unimpeachable. In other words, Christianity was caught between three possible alternative interpretations, of the conception of the rising of the dead from their grave. The first was to take it as a physical phenomenon, which would entail acceptance of conclusions that human intellect could not possibly endorse. Secondly to consider it as a mystic experience applicable

(1) The Koran 82:4.
(2) Ibid, 22:7.
(3) Ibid. 30:56.
(4) Ibid. 31:28.
(5) The Persian Bayan, by The Bab, 2:9.

to the individual consciousness; and in that case it would not be a universal phenomenon as visualized by Christ and characteristic of his return. And the third was to regard it as a spiritual and cultural reawakening attendant to the appearance of a new divine dispensation, which would fully apply to the advent of Islam. The Christians could not endorse this last interpretation, because it would logically rob their attitude towards Islam, of all its justification. They would have to accept Mohammed, if the phenomenon of rising of the dead from their grave, was a spiritual and cultural rebirth of mankind. For it was this interpretation that Jesus had meant, when foretelling the event, and the one on which the claim of both Islam, as well as his own, rested.

In short, what the Koran tried to assert was that resurrection, or rising of the dead from their grave, was first, an earthly historical event; secondly, that it was spiritual and cultural; thirdly, that it was a universal awakening, and not an individual mystic experience; that it was more in the nature of a mass rebirth of mankind. Thus, the advent of every prophet, including that of Jesus and Mohammed, was attended by such regeneration and reawakening; and in the Day of the Lord, humanity shall experience its fullest realization; for it shall comprise all mankind.

Islam, in the fourth century of its era, had ceased to give such a spiritual and cultural interpretation to the phenomenon of resurrection, or the rising of the dead from their graves. It had ceased to consider it a cultural and universal reawakening, such as the one Moses, Zoroaster, Jesus and Mohammed had brought about; and considered it instead as a rising of the individual from physical death and bodily deterioration, as the Jews and Christians of the day interpreted it to be. Philosophy, however, could not accept that physical bones turned to dust and dispersed, could be reassembled and revived, or the human soul that had passed to higher realms of being, and attained the blessings of the hereafter, would care to return to this earthly plain, much as it would desire to behold what shall transpire in the Day of the Lord, and partake of its many blessings.

Similarly, the problem of creation could be given an interpretation that would be in full conformity with both human reason and the principles established by the Koran. The account of creation, given in the first chapter of Genesis, makes it an act done in time; and this raises the very plausible question as to what happened before. Was there no act of creation before that date? If not, then God could not have been creator before that specific period. In such a case, the creative power was not an eternal attribute of his being. It was a faculty He acquired. It was a mere potentiality hidden in His nature that was only in time actualized. In that case He was not eternally perfect actuality. And if He was not eternally perfect, how could He become so? Christian thinkers could not answer these questions, because the interpretation they gave to the verses of Genesis was physical; and the Gospel had thrown little light on that subject. And the Mohammedan thinkers received the Scriptures, together with this physical interpretation of Genesis, as part of their heritage, and were baffled by its logical implications.

Plato and Aristotle could not subscribe to the principle of creation, because they considered reality to reside in the universal, that is, in the idea or form. To them the individual, and the changing could not be real, for they were not abiding. Furthermore, Plato and Aristotle distinguished between the intelligible and the sensible; and considered both as constituting together the All, or Universe. In other words, God was identified with the Universe, or rather, with the intelligible element which was considered essentially unchanging and abiding, admitting no creation.

In the Koran, however, the distinction is made, not between the intelligible and the sensible; but between the creator and the created. The universe, which is the objct of sense perception, and intellectual understanding; together constitute the world of creation. And God transcends it, as a creator does his creation, or handiwork. Hence, He is neither sensible, nor object of human thought. And such a distinction between the Creator and the created, brings out the principle of creation and renders it foundational. Furthermore, as the principle of creation is stressed; reality is attributed not to the universal conception, but to the individual and particular. For physical creation, and spiritual and cultural recreation, are both of the individual. The Koran traces the growth of the child, for example, from the time it is first conceived by the mother, and is born, to the stage when it is reborn into the life of the spirit (1). All the process is the result of God's creative will and purpose; and its fruit is the individual, adding to its concreteness and distinctiveness and as the result of the characteristics he acquires. The created reality, therefore, resides in the individual, concrete child. Spiritual and cultural rebirth is of the individual person, even though that person is subject to constant change and evolution. In a dynamic universe reality resides not in the unchanging, but in the reality which changes, and is constantly reborn. And the individual does proceed from non-existence into being, that is created.

The masses in Islam might have retained the physical, and literal, interpretation of the first chapter of Genesis, held by the Jews and Christians of that age; but the Koran itself presents a conception of creation which is constant, eternal and everlasting. The creation in time, is the spiritual and cultural creation and rebirth of man, through the periodic appearance of prophets and messengers of God. Al-Ghazali tried, in his dissertation against the philosophers, to defend, not the principle of the Koran, namely the existence of an eternal and ever abiding process of creation, both in the physical universe and in the spiritual life of man; but a wrong interpretation of it, which had been bequeathed by Judaism and Christianity, and accepted unquestioningly by the masses of Islam. And this view led to logical conclusions that were rightly unacceptable to philosophy serving the paramountcy of logic and reason.

In short, the prevalence of traditions, sometimes wrongly claimed to be based upon divine revelation; and materialistic and physical interpretations of essentially spiritual principles; together created such a disturbed intellectual atmosphere, that Greek critical thought could easily find prevalence, and obtain facile reception by dissatisfied minds. Again reason, finding no

(1) The Koran 23:12-16.

65

comfort in what was represented as revelation, fell back on independent human thought as source of the basic values it sought. That there was actually such a religious recession at that period in Islam, is evidenced by the title of the voluminous book which Al-Ghazali, as mouthpiece of orthodoxy, wrote, namely, "The Revival of Religious Learning", which stands as his outstanding work. In his introduction he laments the low level to which Islamic thought had reached, and tries to readjust it. But notwithstanding such a recession, the twin basic principles of spirituality, and universalism, were strong enough to withstand the naturalism, and particularism, that Greek thought advocated. Political power, backed by the masses, joined forces with orthodoxy, and the influence of Greek thought was checked in Islam.

6. THE INABILITY OF THE CHURCH TO WITHSTAND THE TIDE OF NATURALISM AND SEPARATISM IN EUROPE: But meanwhile ritualism and separatism had sapped the spiritual vitality of Christianity in the West. By the end of the Middle, and Dark, Ages in Europe, little had been left of the universalistic and spiritual outlook that characterised early Christianity. Jesus Christ, the true source of revelation, had been too much identified with the Church; and the Church had ceased to operate as the actual source of spiritual and cultural values: of truth, goodness, justice and beauty, as it had been in its earliest days. Just as the priests, as distinguished from the prophets, had brought ritualism and separatism in Jewish thought and life; so did the Church bring about ritualism and separatism into Christianity. And that trend was accentuated by the sectarianism that had appeared in it. In its internal administration, the Church claimed universality of outlook; but it was too weak to withstand the tide of nationalism, and racialism, that was fast asserting itself in Europe.

Claiming infallibility, the Church considered itself the medium of revelation and its interpreter; but it could not vindicate it in fact. Here was a much stronger spiritual recession than the one which prevailed in Islam. And this complete spiritual relapse, opened a large gap in human thought and consciousness, for Greek critical thought to penetrate and secure a firm hold. With true and authentic revelation, which was vouchsafed by Jesus Christ, overshadowed, Europe had no other alternative but to fall back on independent human reason as source of guidance, and of cultural values.

We have observed the Bab maintain that, the basis of all thought, is the principle that, "all else other than God is His creation". In other words, God projects His Primal Purpose, or Word, that is, His attributes of perfection, through the divine nature of the prophets, acting as a primary mirror of His light. All else is God's handiwork, and this includes even the human nature of the prophets themselves. For as the Bab says, (1) while the divine nature revealed in the prophets represents God and His attributes, their other nature, which is human, is His servant, doing His bidding, and standing in adoration before Him. The Church in Christianity, which corresponds to the "vilayat" in Islam, would thus be a secondary mirror, reflecting the divine light shed by Jesus Christ. It is the creative fiat of Jesus that brought the Church into being, and conferred upon it, its authority. (2) But notwithstanding that authority the Church is part of the world of creation, and not an emanation of the divine Essence. Hence, absolute infallibility, which is characteristic of the divine nature revealed in the prophets, is not shared by the Church. For the Church does not constitute the Primal Purpose, the Word, and Wisdom, with which the Christ in Jesus is identified. Its authority is derived from Him as a secondary mirror receives its rays of light from a primary one. And this is the principle confirmed by Baha'u'llah in the opening passages of his Ishrakat. The Church, like the human nature in Jesus, the Vali in Islam, or even an ordinary man, has a personal freedom of choice; and that freedom opens up to it the possibility of error. It can act as a secondary mirror, and reflect the light of God, which is shed by the divine nature revealed in the prophets; or to deviate from that source of light, and

(1) The Persian Bayan, by The Bab 4:1.
(2) Matthew 16:18.

67

cease to reflect it. It can pursue the divine Purpose, or disregard it. That there is such a possibility to error, is borne out by the fact that Jesus himself was tempted by Satan; (1) but refused to deviate from the mission that God had set for him. Similarly before his crucifixion the human nature in Jesus showed signs of weakness when he said: "O my Father, if it be possible, let this cup pass from me: nevertheless not as I will, but as thou wilt." (2) Such freedom of choice, and the possibility of error, rendered the obedience of Jesus to God's will and purpose, a free moral act, and an example to the rest of mankind. For, as the Bab says, (3) while the divine nature revealed in the prophets represents God and His attributes, their other nature, which is human, is His servant, doing His bidding, and standing in worship before Him. That the Church was not infallible, in the manner conceived by the Christians, its subsequent history shows. Its most flagrant error, according to the Bab, was that it failed to recognize in Mohammed the reality of Jesus Christ; and in the Koran the very essence of the Gospel. Through that very act, the Church shut itself from God's spiritual and cultural purpose; and instead of remaining a source of guidance to mankind, led Europe into the dark ages. When the element of freedom of choice exists, divine appointment alone cannot explain or support authority. The question becomes one of fact as well. Was that freedom of choice adequately employed, as it was in the case of Jesus, when tempted by Satan, or when confronted by crucifixion? The secondary mirror should, through the light it reflects, prove that it is fully directed towards that center of divine illumination: that the Church is factually following the divine Purpose, and dominated by its values, and laws; before claiming infallibility.

Referring to "supreme infallibility", claimed by some sects of Shia Islam for Ali, Baha'u'llah states in the introductory section of his Ishrakat, and also in his letter addressed to Sheikh Salman; that this supreme station is reserved by God for Himself, as creator of all things. Hence, it cannot be claimed by any

(1) Matthew 4:10.
(2) Ibid. 26:39.
(3) The Persian Bayan, by The Bab 4:1.

one, save the revealer of His divine nature. To say otherwise, Baha'u'llah says, is to impair the principle of divine unity. It is to introduce dualism. Only this divine nature revealed in the prophets, the Primal Purpose of God, possesses absolute sovereignty. For, no man, or institution, can question Its authority; while It can question theirs. All, Baha'u'llah says, are subject to the Primal Purpose revealed in the prophets, and should abide by it. If they deviate to the extent of hair's breadth, from that source of illumination, that Primal Purpose, they will cease to reflect that Light. These manifestations of God, he says, have no associates or partners in their sovereignty. Baha'u'llah further states that Mohammed had no partner, associate, or equal in that infallibility. The "Valis", who succeeded Mohammed, were creatures of his command. These were after the prophet, the most learned men; but in utter subservience to him.

In other words, the Church came into being through the creative Word, uttered by Jesus; with the specific mission of furthering the Primal Purpose of God, and regenerating mankind spiritually and culturally. It is a question of fact, whether the Church, like a pure mirror, reflected that light, and fulfilled that function. Therefore, to assert that Jesus founded the Church, is not sufficient. The point is to prove that it in fact reflected divine Light, and pursued that Purpose; that it served that mission, free from all other motives. The historical fact is, that after the advent of Islam, or even prior to it; the Church had ceased to pursue that task. It had ceased to further the twin principles of spirituality and universalism throughout the world. And the reason for it, was that it had itself succumbed to pagan formalism, and was torn by internal dissension.

7. THE CONTROVERSIES OF THE 17th. and 18th. CENTURY WERE THE RESULT OF THE ADOPTION OF PAGAN PRINCIPLES: Thus, the controversy which characterized seventeenth and eighteenth century thought in Europe; was not on the spiritual and cultural interpretation of religion; and the reality and destiny of man, presented by Jesus; nor the universalism which he advocated; which are cardinal principles prophets have

advocated down the ages. The controversy was the result of naturalistic and ritualistic tendencies of Greek thought, that had permeated Christian belief and practices, on the one hand; and the empirical criterion of understanding, and values, on the other. In other words, the struggle was between two aspects of paganism: pagan elements that had been introduced into Christian doctrine; and pagan criteria of knowledge. It was the same type of struggle that prevailed during the time of Plato; namely, the pagan principle of knowledge, which considered human faculties as the measure of all things; and the primary premises of thought, which were hypothetical in nature: both basically pagan in origin. And whenever thinkers referred to the Gospel for enlightenment; they interpreted its principles in the light of pagan systems of thought, they had already assumed to be true. Revealed religion was not considered as possessing a system of thought all its own, with a metaphysics, ontology, and epistemology, logically intertwined; and with cultural values characteristic to itself. While if we look back to past history, we observe, that the force which could withstand paganism, and its evil consequence on the spiritual and cultural life, was revealed religion, especially while it retained its original vitality and purity of thought. In recorded history, this was first achieved by Hebrew religion; it was then assumed by Zoroastrianism. Later Jesus Christ and his teachings, turned the thought of mankind away from pagan premises; and centered it around doctrines, that could secure spiritual and cultural unfoldment. The greatest force that assailed paganism, to which Christianity had succumbed in the sixth century, was nascent Islam. In other words, the predicaments that Idealism, Empiricism, and mysticism confronted were the conclusions of pagan naturalism, its physical interpretation of reality, and discarding of the prophets. Their method of procedure, and criteria of reality and being, have never been able to settle those anomalies, that naturalism necessarily entails. It has been the task of revealed religion to provide adequate premises of thought, clarify the truth, and elucidate the issues, and thereby stimulate the spiritual and cultural growth of man.

To elucidate the issue, let us take for example the two problems already dealt with in connection with Islam, namely, creation in time, and the rising of the dead from their graves. Taken spiritually and culturally, neither gives rise to insurmountable problems. They entail no anomalies, and present no predicament, for philosophy to try and settle. While, if considered as natural phenomena, they begin to bristle with anomalies. If creation is interpreted to be a spiritual rebirth, as Jesus and Mohammed conceived it, then it means mere conversion. Paul, for example, was reborn or recreated of a sudden, while on his way to Damascus. This event gives rise to no metaphysical problem. It constitutes a psychological phenomenon, of gradual conviction, achieved subconsciously, that suddenly merges into consciousness. It is a creative process, because through it Paul assumes a totally new personality, with totally new attributes, values and characteristics. This principle of creation gives rise to anomaly, if interpreted physically and naturalistically. In that case, creation becomes the appearance of physical being out of absolute non-being. Then the problem arises, as to why did God suddenly become a creative reality, how did being spring from absolute non-being, how this created universe, which has had no beginning and cannot possibly have an end, was suddenly formed, some few thousand years ago. All these predicaments arise because a spiritual and cultural phenomenon is given a wrong physical, and naturalistic, interpretation; on the false assumption that it constitutes part of a physical universe.

Similarly, the problems centered around the rising of the dead from their graves. If we take that doctrine as a spiritual and cultural phenomenon, as Jesus and Mohammed took it, it gives rise to no problem or anomaly. The life Paul was leading, persecuting the Christians, was spiritual death. The level on which he lived was that of a grave. With the acceptance of the spirit of Christ, and dedicating his life to the service of Jesus, he was reborn, resuscitated, and saved from the grave. He had a physical being, he assumed a spiritual and cultural life as well. Mary went to the grave of Jesus, but became suddenly conscious, that a spiritual reality such as the Christ, the divine

71

nature, which was the life-blood of Christianity, and was revealed in Jesus the man, cannot be entombed. That it repaired to the eternal realm of the Father, from which it had originally descended. That it had risen from the grave of the body, and of the physical life, and ascended to heaven. It is when the soul is considered, as Aristotle regarded it, to be a "form" of the body, and inseparable from it, that it becomes subject to natural phenomena. Then we are faced with the problem of how a specific soul or "form" can remain, or come again into being, when the body or matter, of which it was a form, has completely disintegrated, or through natural phenomena, become the matter of some other being. All such predicaments arise from a physical interpretation of an essentially spiritual and cultural phenomenon. And this is what pagan naturalism entails. These anomalies bear no relation with what prophets taught. They are anomalies that they have come to obliterate. A spirit that transcends both mind and matter cannot be deemed to be destroyed when freed from them.

8. SEPARATION OF THE PROVINCE OF REASON FROM THAT OF REVELATION: This movement back to Hellenism, started among the clergy; mainly because their class dominated thought, and its various centers, in Europe. Their relation on the one hand with Christianity, and the Church; and on the other, with education, and the interest of the age in Greek thought, made it incumbent upon them to delineate their respective limits. They could neither break away from the first, to which they belonged, and towards which they bore allegiance; nor disregard the findings of human reason, which was fast awakening. To try and reconcile the two was an impossible task; for Christian thought was encumbered by all sorts of superstitions and traditions, mostly of pagan origin; to which reason could not logically subscribe. Mohammedan philosophers with Hellenic tendencies, had tried to settle the issue, between misinterpreted revelation, on the one hand, and reason, on the other; by advocating the independence of each, within its own field of interest. Thomas Aquinas, who received his intellectual training

at their hands, followed that course, and adopted that principle. To him, religion was to remain the exclusive domain of the Church; and science of human reason and research. The first could accept its cherished traditions and beliefs through blind faith; the other, pursue its course in the light of independent reason and investigation.

But such theoretical delineation of fields of interest, could not be easily enforced in pursuit of objective truth. And truth was what both claimed to desire and possess. Objective truths however cannot be contradictory, no matter what constitutes their angle of approach. Human reason cannot be cut into separate compartments, each allotted its own object of interest, its own method of understanding, and its own standard of truth. The separation might serve the temporary interests of philosophy, and scientific research, by giving them more freedom of operation in their respective fields; but the results achieved, and the objective truths verified and established, were bound to have implications that affected traditional beliefs, cherished by the Church, and accepted through blind faith. The early Fathers of the Church, such as Justin Martyr, and Clement of Alexandria, could profess Christianity, and teach philosophy at the same time; because they found the two complementary. Philosophic thought, sought ultimate premises that Christian revelation fully supplied; and the principles of the Gospel on the reality and destiny of man, contained nothing which human reason could not conscientiously advocate. As students of Greek thought, they found in Christianity, the elements the former lacked; and on that ground they embraced the new Faith. But after the accumulation of tradition, in the course of fifteen centuries, and the inclusion of pagan beliefs, into the tenets of the Church, the condition was totally different. What the church wrongly considered as revelation, and supported with its authority; could not all be endorsed by reason, especially when awakened and liberated, free to search and criticise.

Furthermore, when human reason is permitted to pursue its subject of interest unrestrained, it cannot be limited to a certain field; and denied the right to encroach into others. It could not be stimulated and encouraged to study physical science, and held back from entering the field of cultural values: of finding for itself what constitutes the criteria of truth, how goodness should be defined, the manner social justice could be ensured, and what are the norms by which man can assess beauty; all ultimate questions foundational to the spiritual and the cultural life of man.

With Descartes, this method of convenience, agreed upon between the students of science, on the one hand, and those of theology, on the other, and confirmed by Thomas Aquinas, broke down. For the method adopted by Descartes in his study of mathematics and physical nature, could apply as well to theological discussions, on the existence of God, and the nature and destiny of man. He attempted to break through into the field of religion, and find out the validity of its principles, in the light of the methods he had devised for physical science; but the task was too venturesome for him to undertake. The power of the Church was supreme, both in the intellectual field, and also in the political life of Europe. His fears increased, when Galileo was condemned to death, on the ground which the indirect implications of his scientific discoveries, entailed. It was due to such apprehensions; to the fear of treading on dangerous grounds reserved for the Church, that his language on the subject is mainly apologetic. But the step he took, though timid, was far reaching in its consequences. A new epoch started with him in European thought. A striking contrast was thus made explicit, between the early Christian doctrine that, revelation is the source of all Wisdom; and his own basic principle that, an inner experience of man, the phenomenon "I think", constitutes the criterion of "I am", that is of objective reality. It was the rebirth of the old pagan principle that, man is the measure of all things, confronting the principle of revelation.

9. MAN IS THE MEASURE OF ALL THINGS: There can be only two possible pivots on which human thought and understanding can stand: either human faculties of understanding or divine revelation. We say "divine revelation" in preference to

"God"; because all revealed religions have maintained, as we have already observed, that the divine Essence is inaccessible to human senses, thought and intuition. Revelation is the sole source of the truth man can seek. This is why Jesus said: "I am the way, the truth."(1) The Koran repeatedly states that God imparts "Wisdom" to His prophets. The Bab says: "The Book is true"; and he means by "The Book" the revealed Word; for whatever is written or uttered by "the Point of Truth", meaning the prophets, is written or uttered by God Himself.(2) It is God's self-revelation in what is termed "Purpose", "Wisdom" or "Word", that can constitute the pivot, on which human understanding and knowledge can stand. And these, we have observed, are identical with the divine nature revealed in the prophets. This constitutes the true foundation of Christian thought. Descartes discarded it, and in preference, reverted to the ancient Greek principle that "man is the measure of all things"; by starting his process of reasoning with the dictum: "I think, therefore, I am". Upon this basic principle, he tries to study, not only objective physical phenomena; but also prove the existence of God, and the nature and destiny of man: two themes reserved to religion and theological discussions.

10. ELIMINATION OF UNCERTAIN ELEMENTS IN THOUGHT: To build a system of thought, that would comprise truths concerning nature, man and God, Descartes had to clear the ground, reach bare solid rock, and upon it lay the foundation he deemed secure. But this process of eliminating uncertain elements, is by nature negative. It can start only by discarding beliefs that are not certain. Therefore, he begins by laying down maxims to guide him. "The first," he says, "was never to accept anything for true which I did not clearly know to be such; that is to say, carefully to avoid precipitancy and prejudice, and to comprise nothing more in my judgment than what was presented to my mind so clearly and distinctly as to exclude all ground of doubt. The second, to divide each of the difficulties under

(1) John 14:6.
(2) The Persian Bayan, by The Bab 2:15.

75

examination into as many parts as possible, and as might be necessary for its adequate solution. The third, to conduct my thoughts in such order that by commencing with objects the simplest and easiest to know, I might ascend by little and little, and, as it were, step by step, to the knowledge of the more complex, assigning in thought a certain order even to those objects which in their own nature do not stand in a relation of antecedent and sequence. And the last, in every case to make enumerations so complete, and reviews so general, that I might be assured that nothing was omitted."(1) Descartes thus starts with "the simplest and easiest to know," namely, mathematical propositions; and then proceeds to what is more complex, such as the nature of the soul, and the existence of God. For in all these subjects of understanding we find common principles applying. "All agree in considering only various relations or propositions subsisting among those objects."(2) Having undertaken that procedure, Descartes for nine years "did nothing but roam from one place to another, desirous of being a spectator rather than actor in the plays exhibited on the theatre of the world."(3)

11. THE PROBLEM OF THE AGE WAS RELIGIOUS AND CULTURAL: As E. Gilson says, the main controversy of the age was religious;(4) and to that we can add, was for its cultural values. But we have further to observe, that the principles involved were essentially pagan. Revelation was disregarded and even tabooed, by intellectuals such as Descartes. The principle that man is the measure of all things, was pagan; and the conception of the human soul, and of God, as the supreme objects of understanding; were of pagan origin. To neither of which revelation subscribed. For this latter considered the creator, and

(1) Discourse on Method, part II, p. 15 by Descartes, tr. by John Veitch, in Everyman's Library Edition No. 570.
(2) Ibid. p. 16.
(3) Ibid. Part III, p. 23.
(4) Descartes se trouve plonge de 1623 a 1630 dans un milieu dont la preoccupation dominante est la refutation du scepticism, athee, deiste ou Chretien, de l'atheism naturaliste et du materialisme epurien. (Role de la Pensee Medieval, par, Gilson p. 261.)

not the "observer," the criterion of the nature, and being, of the created; and the human soul and God, absolutely transcendent realities that human understanding cannot reach. Revelation presented no such predicaments.

Value, the "ought", is experienced when a purpose dominates human activity. It is relative to the realization of that purpose that an object, whether intellectual, moral, social or aesthetic, obtains value and significance. The purpose of cultural values, is to attain the goal of human development, namely, to acquire perfection for man's many capacities. And this, we have maintained, is the province of religion. It was the task of Christianity ever since its inception. The first step, and adequate approach, therefore, would have been to go back to the source of the religious life, to the revelation of Christ himself, and discard the traditions that had gradually accumulated, and the pagan elements that had been incorporated into Christian doctrines, and which were hiding its light, and preventing it from functioning as source of illumination. To diagnose the ailment that had befallen European culture, and to find a method to remedy it, was not by choosing an angle of approach, which might be suitable for the understanding of physical nature; but by going straight back to the source of illumination, to Jesus Christ, who was the initial founder and creator of Christian culture, and discriminate between what was authentic revelation, and what was added later, through syncretic tendencies that it gradually developed. And that was what Descartes failed to do, and would not venture, as his apologetic remarks here reveal.

12. THE ASSUMPTIONS IMPLIED IN THE DICTUM OF DESCARTES: There are two basic assumptions, implied in the dictum of Descartes, which demand consideration. The first is that, immediate apprehension is a criterion of being. Secondly, that we can eliminate all uncertainties—meaning all that is not directly and clearly apprehended,—and still maintain thought. Just as conceptions unify, and impart significance, to individual sense experiences, so does the creative cultural purpose, and its assertions regarding the nature and destiny of man, impart unity

77

and meaning to conceptions empirically acquired, and makes them serve the same goal. But these basic conceptions of culture, which state the nature and destiny of man, like all basic premises of thought, transcend the senses, and all conceptions inductively derived from them, as well as intuition, which Descartes defines as direct apprehension of things. The fundamental premise of Greek thought, and of modern philosophy, in so far as it has received that heritage, and propagates it; is based upon the principle, dogmatically asserted, that the physical and intellectual realms of being, that is, the sensible and the intelligible, constitute one Universe, one "All", and that there is nothing beside. God may be identified with the intelligible, or Mind alone, as did Plato or it may be identified with both, as maintained by pantheism. In any of the two cases, this conception of God is dogmatically asserted, but constitutes the primary premise of Greek thought. It is not a truth directly apprehended by man. Apprehension can, at best, detect an inner psychological experience, a phenomenon within human consciousness. It cannot project itself beyond the consciousness of the individual, grasp the object outside, and establish whether there is correspondence between the two. How can it, therefore, authenticate the "All", as an objective being, and assert further, that there is nothing else beside. In short, this pagan conception of God, is not an object of direct apprehension; and yet is foundational to Greek thought.

When we consider the dictum of Descartes, we observe that, in fact, he did not attempt to eliminate this metaphysical assumption from his process of thought. For his dictum, "I think therefore I am", stands squarely upon the immanental principle maintained by Greek thought. It is based upon the pagan assumption that the universe comprises the sensible and the intelligible; and that individual human thought is a particle divided from that intelligible reality, but one with it in essence and substance. The thought, which Descartes tried to study, was considered as the attempt of this fragment of the universal mind, to discover a ground for asserting the existence of objective reality, using its own direct apprehension as criterion of its being.

In contrast to this dogma, that the sensible and the intelligible realms of being constitute one Universe, one "All", and identical with God; is the primary premise of all revealed religions as expressed by the Bab, namely, that this universe, which includes the sensible and the intelligible, constitutes the created universe; that beyond it is the Essence and being of the Creator Himself, Whom neither the senses, nor human thought and intuition, can possibly grasp and express. These two dogmatic assertions, stand in absolute contrast one to the other. Both are beyond man's direct apprehension, and yet without the adoption of one of them there can be no thought. Sense perception, direct inner apprehension, inductive reasoning that leads to universal conceptions, all demand a principle, and purpose, to unify them and impart to them meaning and significance.

Values have a worth, and contain a meaning, in so far as they are related to a purpose. It is the goal in view, and its attainment, that impart worth and significance to a value, or principle, and guide activity. The ultimate goal of human development, can never be considered as constituting an object of direct possible apprehension. It is a future state of being that requires a long process to attain. Just as the spiritual reality of man is unknowable, and unintelligible; his ultimate destiny is far beyond his grasp, far beyond his power of intuition, as well as his understanding. And yet they constitute the purpose, and state of being, that impart value and significance to the intellectual, moral, social and aesthetic life. We can have no culture without them, just as we can have no principle of culture without some conception of God. And yet both the conception of God, and the conception of the reality and destiny of man, are far beyond human understanding and intuition. Their assertion might be dogmatic, but they cannot be dispensed with.

Descartes tried to attain a tabula rasa, before attempting to collect data, that would build up his thought, and establish the validity of objective reality: natural, human and divine. But his very attempt at that process was in pursuance of a unifying purpose, and a system of thought, that dictated his procedure, and unified his individual experience. The very philosophical questions he confronted, his very attempt to attain a tabula rasa, the very predicament he tried to overcome, were the result of his dominating purpose. Without it, and the pre-established systems of thought he was familiar with, and the problems that each involved; his individual experiences would not have been even recoded by his mind; much less made to serve a continuous process of thought, aimed at a specific goal.

13. REVERSION TO REVELATION: The way of purgation, which constitutes the first step to the spiritual life and the first stage in man's cultural growth, is not as the mystics conceive it. It is not in mortifying the flesh, or denying man physical comforts, amenities of life, or objects of beauty, which God has in His loving kindness spread out in nature before him, or made the fruit of his cultural achievements. Purgation is the purification of human understanding from things that hinder man from appreciating God's cultural purpose, and bar him from attaining his spiritual end. It is the revelation of the Primal Purpose, freed from pagan, and man-made, accretions that have gradually accumulated around it and thus shut out its illumination from reaching human consciousness. As Jesus said: "Howbeit in vain do they worship me, teaching for doctrines the commandmentts of men. For laying aside the commandment of God, ye hold the tradition of men, as the washing of pots and cups: and many other such like things ye do"(1). Purgation is to free the "commandments of God", from the defiling effect of "traditions of men". For it was such traditions, such doctrines added by the prieshood to divine revelation, that held back the Jews from accepting Jesus, and the spiritual and cultural rebirth he inaugurated in the world. It was such spiritual and cultural purgation that Europe of the age of Descartes required, to set its intellectual, moral and social life aright. In the opening passage of his "The Kitab-I-Iqan", Baha'u'llah quotes and then expounds a passage of the Bayan by The Bab, saying: " 'No man shall attain the shores of the ocean of true understanding

(1) Mark 7:7, 8.

80

except he be detached from all that is in heaven and on earth. Sanctify your souls, O ye peoples of the world, that haply ye may attain that station which God hath destined for you and enter thus the tabernacle which, according to the dispensations of Providence, hath been raised in the firmament of the Bayan.'" The essence of these words is this: They that tread the path of faith, they that thirst for the wine of certitude, must cleanse themselves of all that is earthly—their ears from idle talk, their minds from vain imaginings, their hearts from worldly affections, their eyes from that which perisheth. They should put their trust in God, and, holding fast unto Him, follow in His way. Then will they be made worthy of the effulgent glories of the sun of divine knowledge and understanding, and become the recepients of a grace that is infinite and unseen; inasmuch as man can never hope to attain unto the knowledge of the All-glorious, can never quaff from the stream of divine knowledge and wisdom, can never enter the abode of immortality, nor partake of the cup of divine nearness and favour, unless and until he ceases to regard the words and deeds of mortal men as a standard for the rue understanding and recognition of God and His prophets.

14. DESCARTES' FIRST PRINCIPLE OF PHILOSOPHY: After ridding his mind of all prejudices, and taking great care "scrupulously to withhold our assent from opinions we have formerly admitted, until upon new examination we discover that they are true"; (1) Descartes starts his positive search for a first principle, upon which he could base his system of thought. Just as Archimedes, he says at the beginning of his Meditations II, needed a point from which he could move the earth; so he requires a point to stand on, to displace the prevailing systems of thought, and then build up a true and stronger system instead. And he discovers that fulcrum in man's direct apprehension. "Seeing that our senses sometimes deceive us," he says, "I was willing to suppose that there existed nothing really such as they

(1) The Principles of Philosophy, by Descartes. Principle LXXV, t. J. Veitch.

presented to us; and because some men err in reasoning, and fall into paralogisms, even on the simplest matter of geometry, I, convinced that I was as open to error as any other, rejected as false all the reasonings I had hitherto taken for demonstrations; and finally, when I considered that the very same thoughts (presentations) which we experience when awake may also be experienced when we are asleep, while there is at that time not one of them true, I supposed that all the objects (presentations) that had ever entered into my mind when awake, had in them no more truth than the illusions of my dreams. But immediately upon this I observed that, while I thus wished to think that all was false, it was absolutely necessary that I, who thus thought, should be somewhat; and as I observed that this truth, *I think, hence I am,* was so certain and of such evidence, that no ground of doubt, however extravagant, could be alleged by the sceptics capable of shaking it, I concluded that I might, without scruple, accept it as the first principle of the philosophy of which I was in search." (1) Thus, in contrast to the first principle of revealed religion, namely the dictum: "I am God, and there is no other God but Me. All other than Me, is My creation. O My creation, worship thee Me"; in contrast to this we have Descartes' first principle: "I think, therefore, I am." The first makes God, the Creator, the source of all Wisdom; the second makes the direct consciousness, or apprehension, of the actor, or thinker, that fulcrum: the observer in observing.

15. THE REALITY CONCEIVED IS COEXTENSIVE WITH INDIVIDUAL THOUGHT: The outstanding problem confronting philosophy, as we have already observed, has been to prove the existence of objective reality, namely, natural objects, moral values, and God. The method has been empirical, idealistic, or mystic. Through his dictum, Descartes follows the rational and idealistic. His reality is the rational, as experienced by the individual in his act of thinking. This constitutes the fulcrum, upon which reality rests. But does this solve the problem, and prove the existence of the objective world?

(1) Discourse on Method, by Descartes, Part IV, tr. by J. Veitch.

82

First, it is necessary to stress, that it is his reason, not senses, which constitutes the point, upon which his whole intellectual edifice rests. For, he says, he has a body with which he is closely "conjoined"; "yet since on the one hand I have a clear and distinct idea of myself, in so far as I am only a thinking unextended thing, and on the other hand a distinct idea of the body, in so far as it is only an extended unthinking thing, it is certain that I am truly distinct from my body, and can exist without it."(1) He thus considers the distinction between body and soul, distinct, clear, and hence, true.

But thinking is not limited by Descartes to simple cognition. What then is the soul? "It is a thing that doubts, understands (conceives), affirms, denies, wills, refuses, that imagines also, and perceives."(2) In short, Descartes sees in the "cogito," the basic reality of the soul, with its entire functions, acting as observer of objective being. And the ground of his certainty, is that he is a thinking thing, that is, a purely rational entity, separate from the body; supported by the fact, that the experience is "clear and distinct." For, as he says, "all the things which we clearly and distinctly conceive are true."(3) Thus, Descartes' object of understanding, the method he uses, and the criterion he employs to verify truth, all are essentially rationalistic.

But this rationalism does not serve his main purpose, namely, to break away from solipsism which confronts every philosophic system that is not based on the principle of creation, which alone joins the source of knowledge, and of being, in the same transcendent reality. Descartes fails in that. He limits thereby the experience to the observer and his reactions. He limits reality, and makes it less objective and independent of the observer. For "I think, therefore I am," implies that my being is coexistent and coextensive with my act of thinking in time. "I am, I exist. This is certain, How often? As often as I think; for it might indeed be that if I entirely ceased to think, I should thereupon

(1) New Studies in thhe Philosophy of Descartes, by N. K. Smith, p. 289.
(2) Meditations II, by Descartes, tr. by J. Veitch.
(3) Discourse on Method, Part IV, by Descartes, tr. by J. Veitch.

cease to exist. . . . I am then a real thing, and really existent. What thing? I have said it, a thinking thing."(1)

16. THE CREATOR IS THE MEASURE OF THE EXISTENCE AND REALITY OF HIS CREATION:

The principle of Descartes, which considers the individual human soul, or his consciousness, the measure of existence and reality, suffers from a basic metaphysical flaw, which vitiates all his system of thought, and gives rise to insurmountable problems. The flaw is that it separates the epistemological and the ontological source of objective reality.

When the individual human soul is made the measure of the reality and existence of all things, the sole point of view man can take, at least as regards the realm of physical science, and natural phenomena; is that of an observer. His stand is that of a person who beholds the phenomena of nature enacted before him, tries to understand them, and upon his sense perception, builds the universal conceptions, his mind requires. Or, who looks to ideas, he deems innate in his soul, contemplates them, and reacts towards them, as objective realities. The angle of approach of both, the empiricist and the idealist, is that of an observer. In his Discourse on Method, Descartes says: "And in all the nine following years I did nought but roam hither and thither, trying to be a spectator rather than actor in all the comedies the world displays."(2) This statement was not made figuratively, but with its full philosophical import. As N. K. Smith explains, "he has explicitly formulated one all-important tenet, central in all his teaching, early and late; that the mind, qua cognitive, is purely contemplative, 'patient' in the reception of what the 'objects' of knowledge disclose themselves as being, having no power of producing ideas in and by itself, not even those of the imagination and memory."(3)

When the point of view assumed is that of an "observer," a separation is made between the being of an object, and the

(1) New Studies in the Philosophy of Descartes, by N. K. Smith, p. 280. Russel & Russel, N. Y.
(2) Discourse on Method, by Descartes, Part III.
(3) New Studies in the Philosophy of Descartes, by N. K. Smith p. 22.

mind that tries to understand it; between that reality, and the one who seeks to know its nature and purpose. The inevitable result is the gulf generated between the thinking subject on the one hand, and the object of understanding on the other; which no ingenious philosophic manipulation can overcome. And thought is, thereby, led to solipsism. For necessity of thought would not entail necessity of being and existence; and the ground for a basic skepticism is thereby generated. If, on the other hand, the subject is at the same time the creator of the object; that is, the mind that generates the object, is also the one which initially conceived the idea or form, sketched the process of its generation, purposed its existence, and brought it into being; then no gulf is permitted to cut between the ontological and the epistemological aspects of that being. The idea, or form, in the mind of the creator would necessarily and logically entail the existence, and being, of the objective reality. The form, which is the object of his knowledge, would be the same form which he chooses, and moulded into its being. In other words, when the object starts as a conscious thought, or form, in the mind of the creator, and then through his purpose, and activity, comes into being, preceded at every stage of its formation with further conscious planning; when the existence of the object is the direct result of a conscious ontological purpose, then no gulf is left to justify any skepticism. The ontological, and the epistemological, aspects of the objective reality will then be centered in the same mind. And here lies the strength of the Bab's dictum, when contrasted with that of Descartes. God's Primal Purpose, which is the creator of the physical as well as the spiritual and cultural life of man, is at the same time the defining Point, and the Truth and Wisdom, from which is derived all understanding.

17. MAN IS A PARTICIPANT IN THE CREATION OF THE SPIRITUAL AND CULTURAL LIFE: In the sphere of natural science, man is presented with no alternative but to assume the point of view of the "observer." But in the field of the spiritual and cultural life, he positively partakes in the creative activity. He helps in discovering, expounding, and verifying, truth in

developing his moral life, and social institutions. He helps to create the aesthetic environment that would stimulate his spiritual growth. It is true that he does not create his nature, or trace fully his own destiny; but having obtained those ultimate notions and values, he can choose to participate in their realization. And in so far as he is creative, and freely pursues that cultural purpose, he combines in his consciousness the ontological and the epistemological aspects of that objective reality. The stand that he takes is not that of a mere "observer," contemplating the fulfilment of that cultural purpose; but that of a creator as well, who actively participates in its realization.

Kant was, therefore, justified in distinguishing between the field of physical being, and that of the moral life, and considering the source of the latter immanent in man, not as an observer, but as an active participant and creator. It was on this ground that he termed the method of the latter, "practical reason," in contrast to "theoretical reason" which he reserved for the former. But human creativeness is not limited to the field of morality. It comprises all the field of culture: the social institutions he helps to develop, the objects of art he creates, the physical implements he invents, to raise the level of his existence beyond the one nature initially provided from him.

The flaw in the reasoning of Descartes, was in applying the approach of an observer, and the method he is constrained to follow, in studying physical nature; to the field of culture and the spiritual life. In the field of physical science, man is interested primarily, not in the substance and nature of the object, but in its attributes, properties, functions and reactions, with the laws that dominate them; factors that define the manner he can employ them to his own use. His approach as an "observer" fully provides him with the necessary knowledge of those phenomena, if he diligently pursues his researches and discoveries. But in the field of the spiritual and cultural life, a knowledge of the substantial nature and destiny of man is paramount. We have to know the substance of which he is made, and the purpose that underlies his being and becoming. For it is the nature and destiny of man which determine whether he is part of nature, or beyond it, the course of development he has to undergo, and the values he has to employ in attaining his end. And this constitutes a creative process. The truth regarding his existence, substance, and nature, and the destiny he has to attain, determine the premises of his thought, the moral attributes he has to acquire, the type of social environment he needs, and the aesthetic values he has to adopt. And it is his creator alone who can reveal what that substance, and that destiny, are. These ultimate premises are far beyond his reach as an "observer." And the fact, that the method of physical science does not fulfill the needs of the spiritual and cultural life, is amply proven by subsequent history of thought in Europe, which adopted the method of Descartes. It failed to achieve for the spiritual and cultural life of man, what it accomplished in understanding nature. It failed to be spiritually creative.

18. THE NEED FOR REVELATION: But in the field of culture, human creative power is restricted in scope, and limited in extent. Man can act only as a participant in that creative process. He needs prior knowledge and understanding of his nature and destiny. He has to acquire a knowledge of the values he has to adopt. He cannot formulate them independently. For these derive their nature, form, and purpose, from the nature and destiny he has to serve; and these are beyond his grasp. His creativeness, therefore, is dependent upon the knowledge he can acquire from the reality that made him, and set the purpose of his being. In other words, man's creative purpose is derived from the supreme Primal Purpose. It is derived from God as his creator, and the prophets as instruments of His revelation. These alone can impart to him a knowledge of his substantial nature and destiny.

Plato admits that God is the real source of absolute knowledge. The reason he did not subscribe to it as a principle to be worked upon, and advocated that man is the measure of all things; was that, as a pagan, he did not believe in revelation. "And if," he says, "there be such a thing as participation in absolute knowledge, no one is more likely than God to have this most exact knowledge." (1) "Now God ought to be to us the measure of all things, and not man as men commonly say (Protagoras): the words are far more true of Him." (1) The difficulty, as Plato proceeds to say in Parmenides, is to find the way of obtaining a knowledge of God's will, and purpose: how is man to obtain access to God's mind, to learn of His creative Purpose, Will and Wisdom. The answer of revealed religion is that, that knowledge is imparted to man, through a divine act of grace, through the self-revelation of God in the prophets, as Primal Purpose, Wisdom, the Word, and the Truth. This Wisdom revealed through the prophets, and their authentic Scriptures, acts as the source of man's cultural life, and constitutes the fountainhead of his values. Descartes' source of error was to follow in the foot-steps of Plato, and disregard the divine Wisdom revealed through Jesus Christ, and the other prophets; and attempt to establish European thought, and cultural values, upon the pagan principle, that individual human consciousness, is the pivot and criterion of all understanding, as did the Greeks during a similar recession of revealed religion.

19. DESCARTES' RATIONALISM IS THE RESULT OF HIS STAND AS "OBSERVER"; There are two further points that Descartes attempts to establish through that act of the intellect, or "cogito"; first, the existence of the soul; secondly, that it is a thinking thing, or mind. Granting the validity of the first point, some reservations should be made as regards the second. And this will prove to be foundational when we shall discuss the nature of the soul.

What "I think" determines, is that "I am"; that is, my existence. It does not tell of the substance of which this "I" is made, or the purpose for which it is made, and the destiny it has to attain. It stresses only one of its many functions, namely, that it thinks, that it is a "thinking thing." But, that the soul possesses other characteristics besides intellection, or understanding, is borne out by Descartes himself when he says, that it also feels and

(1) Parmenides, by Plato, 134 D.
(1) The Laws, by Plato, 4:716 D.

wills. In other words, the soul cannot be identified with "mind" alone, if mind is mere cognition. Mind is a mere function of that unknowable reality, we term soul or spirit. Therefore, rationalism which tends to identify the two, mind and soul, distorts our conception of the ultimate reality in man; it tends to reduce all other functions of the soul to understanding, and theoretical knowledge; and identify these functions with the substance of the soul itself.

With the doctrine of creation, however, cognition or intellection, becomes a means for creative activity. And that creative activity will maintain the supremacy of the soul over its many functions, as a substance to its many attributes or phenomena. It will constitute the complete personality of man, while mind, like will and emotion, will be considered as functions, serving that paramount reality, and pursuing its purpose. Furthermore, in the light of the doctrine of creation, the "cogito" will obtain a new significance. For "I think" can be interpreted as an activity of the soul, and as such entail "I am." It need not be necessarily intellectual activity. Any conscious activity will do as well. A creative activity will be its supreme form, with the advantage that it will not entail the difficulties of rationalism. It will not establish the paramountcy of theoretical, abstract, thought over other forms of activity. And in a dynamic universe, ever created, and recreated, reality can better apply to the moving and the constantly moved, than to the formal, the abstract, and the unchanging, which rationalism and idealism imply.

But this rationalism of Descartes, is a direct outcome of his stand as an "observer." To an observer, the unknowable substantial reality, possesses no significance. His interest is directed mainly to the formal and phenomenal; not to the substantial nature of things. In other words, to the fact that the "I" thinks, not to the stuff of which it is made; or the purpose it pursues. This stuff, or substantial nature, is of interest to the creator, who generates and regenerates it, with a set purpose and specific aim.

20. CLARITY AND DISTINCTNESS AS SIGNS OF TRUTH.
We further observed, Descartes maintains that clarity and distinct-

ness, are criteria of truth and ground of certainty. For to him, as a general rule all things which man perceives very clearly and distinctly are true. To an observer, with a rationalistic frame of mind, a conception is deemed true, when it is clearly defined and distinctly apprehended; such as a definition is required to be. Its highest form is observed in mathematical formulas. For they are definitions, which reason constructs as purely formal realities. And being such, mind can grasp them clearly and distinctly. In the sphere of the formal, therefore, clarity and distinctness are signs of truth. In fact, in the field of history, and considered against the background of prevailing formlessness, there is no phenomenon as arresting, and strikingly clear and distinct, as the appearance of prophets, revealing the supreme forms of man's spiritual and cultural life. The landmarks, in the history of mankind, have been the appearance of Moses, Zoroaster, Jesus and Mohammed; every one of whom started a new age, and cultural cycle.

But only to an observer, and within the realm of the formal, distinctness and clarity, are signs of reality. Forms are rational entities, and the more clearly and distinctly defined, the more formally true they become. But a form is an inchoate reality. Forms become real when moulded into existence, as part of an individual, concrete being, that is, when made to operate as project in a creative process. A medical prescription, for example, is a distinct and clear formula, but it acquires full reality when prepared into a specific medicament, and acquires physical existence. As a medicine its ingredients are not as clear and distinct yet they are more real and true. Hence, in a creative process clarity and distinctness are not signs of truth and reality. Furthermore, the creator, or the reality that defines and generates, is more real than the one which is defined; even though it is utterly indistinct, and unclear, to the latter. God is infinitely more real than His creation, even though He is utterly inaccessible to the senses and understanding. Clarity and distinctness are attributes of the reality defined, not of that which defines it. They are qualities of the limited, not of the one that limits, of the created not of the creator.

Furthermore, clarity and distinctness, being attributes of formal being, they are applicable only to the phenomenal, to the attributes a reality reveals, the properties it possesses, the functions it fulfils; they do not apply to the substance of things. The divine Essence, according to revealed religion, absolutely transcends human senses, thought and intuition; even though as Primal Purpose, defining Point, Word and Wisdom, revealed through the thought, words and deeds of the prophets, is the most manifest reality, clear and distinct. The medicament prescribed is infinitely more real than the prescription itself, even though its ingredients which render it effective, are unclear and indistinct. In short, even though, in the field of the formal, clarity and distinctness are signs of truth; they utterly fail in the realm of existence and substantial being.

We saw that, according to the creative principle, maintained by revealed religion, the source of the ontological being of things, is also the fountain head of its truth: that the creative Primal Purpose is also the Word, and the Wisdom, that define the reality of things, for human thought, to grasp. As the Bab says, the Word of God is true whenever it is uttered, and creation is thereby effected.(1) In other words, truth is enclosed within being. Any creator, or artisan, when he produces an object, encloses the truth regarding its nature and destiny, within that object. For its truth is the intelligible aspect of its being; that ontological process of becoming is itself the source of its epistemological significance, irrespective of whether it is "clear and distinct" or not. The sure way to a knowledge of that truth, is its revelation by the creator. When a prophet appears in the world, and regenerates the spiritual and cultural life of mankind, he creates the necessary capabilities in the individual human soul, as well as its environment, but also discloses the truth regarding them.

(1) The Persian Bayan, by The Bab, 2:1.

Chapter

II

DESCARTES' DOCTRINE OF FORMS

1. THE THREE POSSIBLE SOURCES OF FORMS: In Plato we can trace two conceptions regarding the source of Forms or Ideas. The one is discussed when dealing with creation in "Timaeus"; and the other when defining goodness, justice and beauty in dialogues such as the "Republic." When dealing with creation, he unconsciously assumes the role of a creator, and the Ideas become to him patterns of creative production. "Which of the patterns," he asks, "had the artificer in view when he made the world—the pattern of the unchangeable, or of that which is created? If he be indeed fair and the artificer good, it is manifest that he must have looked to that which is eternal." (1) As the soul is the repository of eternal, unchanging and intelligible reality, Plato proceeds to say, the Creator "put intelligence in soul, and soul in body, that he might be the creator of a work which was by nature fairest and best." (2) Then "he made the soul in origin and excellence prior to and older than the body to be the ruler and mistress, of whom the body was to be the subject." (3) These Ideas or Forms are thus considered as "patterns" pre-existent in the mind of the Creator, and then moulded in the nature of the soul, to render it the fairest and the best. Being woven into the fabric of man as innate aspects of his soul, they become, like the good and the just, universals which he can contemplate and understand. And that contemplation and understanding constitutes his supreme virtue, and the goal of his

(1) Timaeus 29-29.
(2) Ibid. 30.
(3) Ibid. 34.

spiritual life. Thus, though the forms start as "patterns," they end by being the supreme objects of understanding and contemplation.

There is no contradiction between these two Platonic views of Form: of their immanence in the divine nature, on the one hand, and their innate nature in the human soul, on the other; if we go deep in his metaphysics. For he considered the human soul as a fragment divided from the Universal Soul, or God. Therefore, the distinction between the two is not formal and qualitative, but numerical and quantitative. In other words, when Plato speaks of creation, he does not mean adding a new form, upon a reality that was utterly deprived from it; but a sort of segmentation of a reality which already possessed all forms ingrained in its nature and substance. Thus, the individual human soul, though divided from the soul of the Universe, or God; is considered by Plato as containing all the Forms as innate and ingrained in its very nature. The task of education, therefore, is merely to awaken the consciousness of the student to its realization, it is merely to make him "recollect" it. Furthermore, these Forms, or Ideas, being unchanging, are eternal and everlasting. They had no beginning and will have no end.

Plato's philosophy was dualistic in the sense that it considered the realm of the intelligible separate from that of the sensible, and dominant over it. To him mind transcended matter. Therefore, these Forms were regarded as ingrained in the intelligible element of the Universe. Aristotle parts company with that definition, and favours the monistic conception, namely, that the intelligible is immanent in the sensible, and not separate from it. Mind is the intelligible element in the physical universe; forms are aspects of physical nature. God alone, being the Form of all forms, is free from all matter.

As we have already observed, in revealed religion, as interpreted by the Bab, the basic distinction is not between the intelligible and the sensible, between mind and matter; but between the Creator and the created. All else other than God, the Bab says, is His creation, and that includes all Forms; even the Primal Purpose, the Word and Wisdom. Therefore, the universe with both its aspects, the physical and the intellectual, constitutes the world of creation, and is created by God. Creation is not merely numerical and quantitative; but formal and qualitative as well. It is giving form to the formless, or adding a new form, to an individual reality, to raise it to a higher level of being.

We can thus distinguish between three conceptions regarding the source of Ideas or Forms: First, the Platonic one as intelligible "patterns" ingrained in the Universal Soul, and transmitted to the individual human soul, when the latter is divided and separated. Secondly, the Aristotelian conception that Forms are intelligible aspects of physical being, and hence, not separate but immanent in nature. Thirdly, the religious conception that they are "patterns" of thought and behaviour, revealed by the prophets, for man to acquire in his process of regeneration and rebirth.

With the introduction of Aristotle, through the works of Thomas Aquinas and others, the Aristotelian conception of Form had become dominant in Europe, and gradually permeated Christian thought, which the Church, at first, reluctantly sanctioned, but then gradually adopted as one of its own. It was a departure from the old Platonic Idealism which Augustinian tradition had established. Descartes' conception was a sort of reversion from the prevailing Thomistic, to the old Augustinian tradition.

Notwithstanding the basic difference between the Idealistic and Platonic conception, on the one hand, and the immanental and Aristotelian conception, on the other; the real contrast and diversion was between the pagan idea of the real source of Forms, which disregarded the principle of revelation, and the religious one, which was squarely based on it. For the pagan, which discarded the principle of creation, rendered the Forms the supreme objects of thought, understanding and contemplation; while the religious, being essentially creative in purpose, considered them as mere patterns for the regeneration of both the human soul and his environment. The one led to contemplation of the Forms, as the supreme object; the other stressed creative activity in acquiring them. The one conceived God as merely a formal Cause; the other primarily an Efficient Cause of being. The one implies a mere passive contemplation and receptivity of a so called divine light; the other demands active participation on the part of man in a creative activity. As Descartes considered the consciousness of man, the measure of reality and being, and had to accept its necessary corollary, namely, the point of view of a mere "observer"; he was forced to adopt the pagan conception of the source of Ideas, and disregard the creative religious one. These three conceptions are not in the least contradictory; but only in revealed religion do we find them adequately presented as elements of a systematic creative system of thought.

As we shall observe, the divine attributes of perfection, that is, the supreme Forms, originate in God, but they may be considered innate, and ingrained, only in the divine nature revealed in the prophets; not in the generality of mankind, as Plato conceived it. They are observed diffused throughout physical nature, and the moral life of man; but they are there because God, as Creator, moulded them into their being. And when so considered, Forms become the very "patterns" of creation, physical as well as spiritual, serving the cultural purpose of the prophets.

2. IDEAS OR FORMS ARE CREATED: We should, however, clarify one point, which Plato seems to leave obscure, in his exposition of the doctrine of Ideas, as "patterns," in the creative process, namely, that though they are universals, unchanging and eternal; they are originated in the mind of God as parts of His Primal Purpose, if we are permitted to use that expression. Plato seems to exclude that characteristic to his Ideas. He refers to them as if they are eternally pre-existent, and ungenerated. His identification of God with the Universe, especially its intelligible element, and his avoidance of the principle of creation, as imparting form to the formless; or imposing a new form, upon an existent reality, to raise it to a higher state of being; makes the Forms co-existent with the Universe, not only in time, but also in causality. With his conception of God such causal priority

had no sense; but with the principle of creation it acquires a basic one. The Creator is causally prior to His creation, even if this latter is eternal and everlasting in time.

For example, a chemist decides to produce a certain substance with specific properties. He starts his research and experiments, until he comes across a formula answering all his requirements. That formula is intelligible, universal and unchanging; but is far from being ancient and pre-existent in the sense of being ungenerated. In fact, its origin is in the creative mind of the chemist. Similarly, if we consider the mind of the prophets, as revealing the mind of God; then the conception of the Kingdom of God on earth, would be a Form originated by it, and destined to be superimposed upon human society after attaining a certain degree of evolution. That supreme Form of human society, had an origin in the mind of the prophets; but once formulated it became eternal and unchanging.

It is on this ground that in the book of Proverbs, Wisdom is presented, on the one hand, as "set up from everlasting, from the beginning or ever the earth was"; (1) and on the other as "brought forth" (2) by the Creator. In other words, as creation is eternal and everlasting the Wisdom of God is eternal and everlasting; but that does not preclude the principle that it was "brought forth," or generated by God as an attribute is by the one whom it qualifies. God acts as the source of attributes, as the sun is of its rays. This is why the Bab stresses that all other than God is His creation. All Forms, even if they are divine, such as goodness, are created in the sense of being generated by God. Thus the Word, as source of illumination, is as ancient as God and His creative power; but never-the-less it is projected by Him as a ray of light proceeds from the sun as its source.

3. DESCARTES CONCEIVES THE IDEAS AS INNATE IN MAN: Descartes disregards the conception that ideas, as presented by revealed religion, originate in the divine nature revealed in the prophets; and maintains the pagan idea advocated by Plato. N.

(1) Proverbs 8:23.
(2) Ibid. 8:24.

K. Smith says that "the only reliable, trustworthy foundation upon which a philosophical theology can be built is, he (Descartes) holds, a doctrine of innate ideas conceived as divinely implanted in us by our Creator. Man finds himself in inalienable possession of these innate ideas, and imperatively summoned to judge of truth and to pursue the good in accordance with them."(1)

These ideas stand as objects of understanding and direct apprehension; and impose themselves as values upon human intellect, and the moral, social and aesthetic life. Like Plato, Descartes considers them as eternal essences, moulded by God in the mind of man. These eternal essences, or truths, are established by God as a king establishes the laws of his land. They are not emanations of his nature, as the rays of light are of the sun; He is their author.(2) He has decreed them; and man is endowed with the natural light to seek them, and obtain access to them, through his power of intuition.

4. IDEAS ARE INTUITIVELY GRASPED: "By intuition," Descartes says, "I understand, not the fluctuating testimony of the senses, nor the misleading judgement that proceeds from the blundering constructions of imagination, but the conception which an unclouded and attentive mind gives us so readily and distinctly that we are wholly freed from doubt about that which we understand. Or what comes to the same thing, intuition is the undoubting conception of an unclouded and attentive mind, and springs from the light of reason alone."(3) In other words, three factors operate in intuition. First, a direct apprehension of the idea; secondly, clarity and distinctness; thirdly, it is grasped as a single and complete whole. It does not constitute a succession of individual mental experiences linked together through memory. In fact, intuition differs, according to Descartes, from deduction proper, in that the latter is a combination of successive intuitions, joined together by reason. This direct apprehension, clarity and

(1) New Studies in the Philosophy of Descartes, by N. K. Smith, p. 168.
(2) Ibid. p. 181.
(3) Rules for the Direction of Mind, by Descartes, Rule III, tr. Haldane and Ross.

wholeness, are deemed to make intuition free from all possible error.

5. KNOWLEDGE IS RECOLLECTION: If ideas are innate, that is, moulded by God in the very nature of the mind; then knowledge cannot be a new acquisition. It is a mere recollection of truths already possessed; but of which the mind is not fully aware. Through the intuitive process, man is considered to unravel its existence, and make it part of his consciousness and understanding. In his example of the slave-boy, Plato tries to explain this principle. He attempts to show that the basic and general truths of mathematics, which are formal, are innate in the mind of the slave-boy, even though he seems completely unconscious of it. Starting with the same premise regarding innate ideas, Descartes comes to the same conclusion, and regards knowledge as mere recollection. "I discover," he says, "an infinitude of particulars respecting numbers, figures, movements, and other such things, whose truth is so manifest, and so well accords with my nature, that when I begin to discover them, it seems to me that I learn nothing new, or recollect what I formerly knew—that is to say, that I for the first time, perceive things which were already present to my mind, although I had not as yet applied my mind to them." (1)

6. JACQUES MARITAIN'S CRITICISM OF DESCARTES: In an essay on Descartes, Jacques Maritain takes the former to task for attributing to human intellect such innate ideas with intuitive means of knowledge. He rightly sees in such innatism an intuitive way of attaining truth the independence which man will possess in asserting his consciousness as measure of all reality and existence—an independence that will completely free him from the restraints of religion, the faith it tries to inspire, and the authority it claims to assert on human behaviour and thought. Maritain takes Descartes to task for attributing to man such characteristics, possessed exclusively by the "intelligences," or "angelic realities."

(1) Meditation V, by Descartes, tr. by J. Veitch.

"According to St. Thomas's teachings," Maritain says, "the human intellect is the last of the spirits, and the most remote from the perfection of the divine Intelligence. . . . Above it, crowded like sea sand, rise in countless multitudes the pure spirits in their hierarchies. These are *thinking substances* in the true sense of the word, pure subsistent forms, who certainly receive existence and *are* not existence, as God is, but they do not inform matter and are free from the vicissitudes of time, movement, generation and corruption, of all the divisions of space, all the weaknesses of individuation by *materia signata;* and each concentrates in himself more metaphysical stuff than the whole human race together. . . .Transparent each to his own glance; each with full perception of his own substance by that substance, at a single leap naturally knowing God also . . . their intellect always in act with regard to intelligible objects, does not derive its ideas from things, as does ours, but has them direct from God Who infuses them into it when He creates it. . . . That is the model on which a son of Tourraine (meaning Descartes) set out one day to reform the human mind." (1)

7. NATURE OF THE INTELLIGENCES: The absolute transcendence of God that Hebrew religion maintained, a transcendence both to thought and being of man, necessitated the belief in an intermediary. What is definite in the Scriptures, in that regard, is that God appointed Moses to bear His Commandments to the Israelites, and to guide them from a life of servitude, to a much nobler spiritual and cultural state of being. To use the terminology of the Koran, God imparted to him "Wisdom" to fulfill His divine mission in the world. It was a wisdom that was revealed in the thought, words and deeds of Moses, but primarily in the Ten Commandments he carried to the people of Israel. During his own life time he acted as the mouthpiece of the Lord. After his death it was the Tablets, on which the Commandments were written, that symbolized the divine Presence among them. It was a spiritual "Presence" of the Lord, dominating the spiritual and cultural life of mankind.

(1) Descartes, by Jacques Maritain, p. 55.

We have the same conception of an intermediary in the Gatha hymns of Zoroaster. This prophet fulfilled at his time the same function fulfilled by Moses in his age. Both were instruments used by God, to reveal His will and purpose to the world. But all during this period animism was rife among the heathens that surrounded them. In fact, the mission of these prophets was to fight, and overcome, this heathenism and its animism. For an essential element in that heathenism and naturalism was belief in the prevalence of spirits, associated with different objects and phenomena in nature. They were considered entities that pervaded nature, and thereby dominated the life of man, aroused his awe, and exacted worship. Thus, while in revealed religion divine "Presence" was through the existence of the prophet on earth, and after him, through his words and teachings; among the heathens divine "Presence" was deemed to be, through such imagined spirits, that were believed to dwell in, and dominate, nature. And a peculiar characteristic of the period of recession in revealed religion has been the gradual compromise with this naturalism and animism, which invariably led to their final domination over religious thought. An outstanding example of such reconciliation, between Zoroastrianism as a revealed religion, and animistic naturalism once the period of recession set in the former, is the manner the Amesha Spentas, namely, the Holy Spirit, Good Mind, Law and Order, Dominion, Perfection and Immortality, imparted by Ahura Mazda through the instrumentality of Zoroaster, gradually became a hierarchy of archangels and angels, associated with physical and natural phenomena.

Pagan philosophy, with its conception of the Universe, as constituting the sum total of all things, both physical and mental; the intelligible and the sensible; could well receive this animism, and incorporate it into its naturalistic teachings. All it had to do, was to term the spiritual or "mental," the pervading spirit; the all-encompassing "Reason." And such a process was especially easy for Platonism and Neoplatonism, which considered the realm of the intelligible separate and transcendent to the sensible, and dominant over it; especially if matter was considered as defiling to Form. These spirits, or intelligences were, according to them, mere segments divided from the Universal Soul or Reason possessing the same Forms, bearing the same attributes of perfection. The difference between the two was not formal, but merely in magnitude, and numerical. The individual human soul, being partly enmeshed in physical and material interests, was naturally considered to be of the lowest level, compared to the other intelligences.

The ancient animism that Moses, and Zoroaster, had condemned in their contemporary heathen environment, and which they had combatted, and tried to eradicate from human thought; made another come-back in the third century after Christ. When Gallienus (r, 260-268) the Roman Emperor, saw that all the persecution, and torture of the Christians, was unavailing to suppress the spreading faith, he sponsored the teachings of Plotinus (205-270), and tried to carry the struggle on the intellectual plane, by providing what he deemed to be, spiritual teachings, that would rival those of Jesus. The object of Plotinus, through his doctrine of "intelligences" was primarily to undermine the basic principle of Christianity; namely, that the divine nature revealed in Jesus Christ, was the sole repository of the supreme spiritual and cultural Forms, humanity was eagerly seeking. In contrast Plotinus held that divine emanation was a universal phenomenon prevailing in respect of all intelligences; that in principle it applied even to the individual human soul. But only, because this latter had lost its purity of form, by being associated with matter, and encased in physical being, it had to set aside this earthly element to become conscious of its true nature, and revert to its original purity. This process of purgation, or purification, demanded a renunciation of worldly and earthly interests; which is essentially mystic in nature. It is not an acquisition of supreme spiritual and cultural Forms which it lacks, an acquisition which entails a process of recreation and rebirth, as revealed religion deemed it to be.

Now, Jacques Maritain starts these remarks regarding Descartes by saying: "The sin of Descartes is a sin of angelism. . . . He conceived human Thought after the type of angelic Thought." Maritain maintains that angelic knowledge is "Intuitive as to its

101

mode, Innate as to its origin, Independent of things as to its nature." (1) By this he means, that intuitive knowledge of innate ideas, which is at the same time independent of objective physical things, is characteristic only of angels, who are pure intelligences, and free from earthly physical encumbrances; that man, while on this earthly level of being, cannot possess that form of knowledge. He might attain it only as a result of renouncing the life of the senses, and assuming that of angels, which needs effort and much renunciation. In short, the "sin" of Descartes as conceived by Maritain was to confuse between human, and angelic knowledge: it was to part company with Plotinus and his "intelligences," and yet stick to the doctrines of Plato expressed in his Republic. It was not a "sin," committed by Descartes, because he differed from what Jesus had taught. That point did not arise for Maritain; because reason and revelation had been relegated, each to its own autonomous dominion, each free in its own field of operation. In the whole of his discussion, there is not even a casual mention of Jesus Christ, and his claim to be the Truth, and the Light; that through the divine nature revealed in him, spiritual and cultural Forms can be understood and acquired.

The crucial point, according to revealed religion, is whether the human soul is an emanation of God; or a mere creature "made" by Him, as a work of art, is at the hands of an artist. Plato and Plotinus, both maintained that they are qualitatively the same; that in substance, nature and attribute, that is formally they are alike; that the one is a microcosm, and the other a macrocosm, that their difference is in magnitude and number. Hence, the human soul does not demand recreation, or acquisition of new forms, to achieve perfection. The Bab on the other hand, we have observed, definitely states, that the supreme principle of all thought, is that all other than God is His creation, and subject to rebirth and regeneration. (2) Hence, there can be no intermediate reality, in the nature of "intelligences," or angels. If "intelligences," or angels, in whom the forms are innate, existed, and their knowledge was intuitive, and absolutely inde-

(1) Descartes, by Jacques Maritain, p. 54.
(2) Persian Bayan, by The Bab, 3:6.

pendent of further acquisition, they would be similar in nature with God; and their difference would be, as Plato conceived it, that is, in number and magnitude. Their likeness, and similarity, would be essential and formal, not merely numerical. According to the preface of the Persian Bayan, however, there can be no similarity and likeness between the Creator and the created, between God and other than Him. In other words, neither such "intelligences" can be assumed to exist as intermediary realities between God and man; nor, if they did exist, could they possess the supreme Forms innately, ingrained in their nature.

Baha'u'llah states that, the angels mentioned in the Scriptures, are the saintly souls of departed individuals who, after death, continue to evolve in worlds to come. In every stage of that evolution, he says, they need God's guidance to proceed in their course. In other words, all the forms they have to acquire, in this eternal process of recreation and growth, they do not possess innately; but have to acquire them, by turning to God as their source. All other than God are His creation; hence, as the Bab says, no spirit can trespass the limits within which it has been created: a spirit related to a creature eternally remains subject to recreation,(1) and therefore, to becoming, and to the necessity of looking beyond itself, for the forms it has to acquire. If the human soul is, as the Bab considered it to be, a mirror reflecting the light of God, then the light is not originally in the mirror, but in the reality that radiates it. If it were in the mirror, and ingrained in it, then there would be no scope left for its acquisition of that light. The true Christian doctrine is that Christ in Jesus; the divine nature revealed in him, was the source of that Light. In his introduction to the Persian Bayan, the Bab states that all divine names and attributes, that is, all supreme spiritual and cultural forms, pertain to the Primal Purpose; and this is manifested through the divine nature revealed in the prophets. It is in contrast to this doctrine of Jesus Christ that Jacques Maritain ought to have weighed the value of Descartes' thought regarding innate ideas, before branding it as "sin."

(1) The Persian Bayan, by The Bab, 3:6.

8. JACQUES MARITAIN IS "TEACHING" FOR DOC-
TRINES THE COMMANDMENTS OF MEN: (2) There is a
great difference between the Spirit of Christ, which imparts the
divine "Presence" in the world, and the spirit of man which
partakes of it. The first is an emanation of God, revealed through
the divine nature of the prophets; the other is a created reality,
wholly reliant on the former, for its constant and eternal
regeneration and rebirth. The former is a self-revelation of God,
an outpouring of His grace, to regenerate the spiritual and
cultural life of mankind; the other is to be receptive, and thereby
regenerated and reborn. The one is in substance and nature
divine, and constitutes the source of all Forms: of truth, goodness,
justice and beauty; the other is utterly human, and seeks those
Forms, to partake of the life of the spirit. This constitutes the
basic doctrine of Jesus Christ, as well as all other prophets.
What Jacques Maritain presents, as criterion of Christian belief,
is Neoplatonism incorporated into it, through the influence of
Thomas Aquinas.

Jacques Maritain is fully justified in calling Descartes to task,
for confusing the intelligences and angels, on the one hand,
and the human soul, on the other. But the term "intelligences"
and angels has certain animistic and pagan associations, that
might confuse, rather than clarify, the issue. First, it confuses
between two basically discrepant realities: the Spirit of Christ,
which imparts divine Presence, and the spirit of man and angels
which partake of it, as already observed. Secondly the term is
apt to incorporate into Christian doctrine elements of Neoplatonism which was formulated purposely to combat early
Christianity in the field of thought, and set aside the principle of
revelation. For these intelligences were considered by Plotinus as
emanating from God, and therefore, as innately possessing the
same divine substance and attributes. Forms were considered as
ingrained and innate in that substance and nature. Thirdly, the
spirit of man, or the human soul, is represented as a further
projection or emanation of the intelligences, with all the formal
similarity and likeness that implies. To put it in the terminology

(2) Mark 7:7.

104

of the Bab, the doctrine of intelligences as presented by Neo-platonism, entails the principle that the "image," which constitutes the sum total of all the forms, is in the mirror, and not in the source of the light alone. For Neoplatonism did not regard the human soul as formally and essentially different from the intelligences; being a further projection of the latter, and possessing the same divine substance and reality. The human soul was not considered as a creature of God, and therefore, distinct in substance and nature from an emanation. This principle of creation was the dividing line, between early Christianity and Neoplatonism, which cannot be overlooked without endangering the whole of Christian belief, in the role of the prophets, as source of the spiritual and cultural values. Early Christianity stressed it, and Neoplatonism tried to discard it. And it is this belief namely, that the human soul is a created reality, which rendered the idea of innate Forms, and intuitive knowledge, inapplicable to man, and makes him fully dependent on an outside source for illumination and empirical experiences. For if the human soul were in substance divine, that is, if it were an emanation of God, or of the intelligences, then the ideas, or forms, would be innate in its very nature. It would obtain access to them intuitively, and would not depend on an objective reality to reveal them.

Furthermore, the very terms "intelligences" and "angels" render the whole principle of innate ideas, and intuitive knowledge, theoretical hypothetical, and mystical for a skeptical mind which seeks to be rational objective, and realistic. While if we limit the application of the principle of innate idea, and intuitive knowledge, to the self-revelation of God, that is, to the divine nature revealed in Jesus Christ, for example, then they acquire historical validity and become empirically verifiable. The innate ideas, which the prophets reveal, would then spring from the Primal Purpose they all are missioned by God to serve, the cultural purpose they all pursue—a cultural purpose that has been actually unfolding itself in history. Being untutored, their knowledge was innate, intuitively recalled to memory, as the occasion for their expression arose. The ideas and values they taught, were not principles they gathered from the objective environment in which they lived; they were spiritual and cultural values humanity lacked, and which sprung from the Primal Purpose they entertained, and the creative mission they undertook. And because the divine nature revealed in the prophets, was in substance one with God, constituted the source of the spiritual and cultural Forms, possessed their knowledge intuitively, and independently from the chaotic environment in which they were born; because of that, their teachings constituted the supreme standard, whereby all knowledge, and all values, have to be measured. This is why the Bab says: that the prophets who, like Jesus Christ, reveal the Truth, stand as the supreme standard whereby all things are measured. Their person, the order they establish in the world, the words they utter, the acts they perform, the proofs they advance for their mission, things that characterize them, all are standards with which all things have to conform. And were that standard to be discarded humanity would relapse into a cultural void. (1) Before incriminating Descartes, Jacques Maritain should decide with which standard of truth he has to conform: the "doctrine" of Christ, or the "commandments" of men.

9. THE PRIMACY OF INTELLECT: When man extracts himself from his environment, with which he constantly acts and reacts, and assumes the passive attitude of an "observer"; his power of understanding is bound to assume primacy over his will and desire. In such a case his mind becomes like a sheet of wax, on which objects of sense positively act, and impress themselves. The fact does not alter much when the objects that act on his mind, are ideas which he has acquired, or whether they were moulded in the very structure of his reason, and hence, are innate, and ingrained in it. In all such cases, it is his attitude as an "observer," which he assumes, that gives primacy to his faculty of understanding, and lays the emphasis on the ideas and forms. For example, it was his attitude as an observer seeking to understand, which led Plato to regard intellect as the highest

(1) The Persian Bayan, by The Bab, 2:13.

faculty of man, and the ideas, the supreme objects of understanding. Similarly, it was his assumption of the role of an "observer," which made Aristotle a rationalist, and consider form, the true nature, substance and reality of things. It was that perspective which made him consider God the Form of all forms; and His "contemplation" the end of the spiritual life.

But even thought, and understanding, are merely types of action and reaction, man can have with his environment. Reason is an accident of his being; for he can exist and yet not think and understand. This is a faculty endowed to man alone, and which he employs during his conscious hours. Activity in general is a more real and permanent feature of his being. And the chief form of activity, especially in the field of culture is the creative. In that field reason, or understanding, acts merely as a guiding light which illumines the path his cultural purpose has to pursue. It makes him aware of his end, and helps him find the means to attain it. Descartes limits his role to that of an "observer," and therefore, maintains that, "in man the intellect has primacy over the will." (1) In God, on the other hand, N. K. Smith says, "no such distinction between understanding and will, no such subordination of the will to the understanding can, Descartes argues, be allowed in respect of Divine Existence. In God neither faculty can have primacy over the other." (2) But this contrast between the primacy of intellect in man, and the unity of both faculties on God, which Descartes maintains, is not due to the fact that the one is human and the other divine. The difference is the direct result of the angle of approach peculiar to man as an "observer," on the one hand, and to God as "creator," on the other. This basic distinction between the perspective of the "observer," and the role of the "creator," or actor, should, therefore, be stressed to appreciate the reason why intellect is either given primacy over the will, or the two faculties are associated on equal terms in a common pursuit.

Action and reaction, we have observed, is not purely or always

(1) New Studies in the Philosophy of Descartes, by Norman K. Smith, p. 268.
(2) Ibid. p. 268.

rational. Physical objects, for example, do not act and react to each other intellectually. Neither is there a rational force in plant and animal life. The distinctive feature of intellect, in contrast to the senses, is that it can retrace its steps into the past, project itself into the future, and scan them both in one and the same experience. In other words, to become intellectual, and rational, an activity has to be purposeful and creative. It has to visualize an end to be attained in the future, at the completion of a successful creative project. And in the pursuit of a purpose, mind and will have to proceed abreast. To an inventor, acting as a creator, in contradiction to a philosopher playing the role of an observer; intellect has to proceed hand in hand with a conscious will and purpose. Vision and understanding of the idea and end, should be accompanied by a compelling will and desire to attain it. That visualization of the idea or end, the constant search for adequate means and measures to actualize them, together with the determined will and purpose to pursue that course, make the activity planned and creative. Therefore, in so far as man, especially in the field of culture and spiritual life, is creative, intellect and will are equally significant and necessary. For him neither should have primacy over the other: neither should function alone. It is only when man restricts his role to that of an observer, his intellect acquires ascendancy. And when the intellect obtains primacy, ideas as abstract universals, become the supreme form of reality, and hence, considered as having independent substance and nature. The best proof that such rationalism could not serve the best and highest interests of the spiritual and cultural life, is the fact that the age which produced both, the rationalistic religious movement designated as Deism, and the school of thought called Enlightenment, to which Descartes belongs; was soon closed, and followed by the age of Mysticism and Romanticism, which laid stress on human emotion and natural instincts, as source of spiritual and cultural values.

10. THE RATIONAL AND THE EMOTIVE ELEMENTS OF THE PRIMAL PURPOSE ARE PRIOR TO EXISTENCE: To the creator, an idea is a mere sketch or plan for activity. It is a

reality his mind generates, and then, tries to actualize. The idea thus becomes the ideal or formal cause of a purposeful activity, and the end which it seeks. For example, to Plato in the Timaeus the primacy of the idea is due to both its unchangingness and eternity, as well as to its nature as a sketch for creative activity. Because to a creator the significance of the idea is the end pursued. It constitutes the rational and intelligible element prior to, and preceding, every step of a creative process as well as the goal it seeks. These originate in the mind of the creator, whether he be human or divine. And that sketch might be modified as the creative process develops, and new conditions, with new requirements, arise.

To a mere observer, the Good and the Just possess priority in being because they are universal, eternal and unchanging. To a creator they are values which promote a creative purpose. Hence, their priority resides in that they are universal characteristics with which a creative project has to conform. It is the nature of the dominating purpose which determines what the principles of goodness and justice entail, what form of thought, words and behavior they dictate. And at different stages of that creative process, that principle of goodness and justice requires different interpretations to promote the selfsame purpose. For, as Paul observed, the requirements of a person in childhood differ from his needs in maturity.

The Bab says that all things were created by the Primal Purpose, and the Primal Purpose by God Himself.(1) But the rational element of this Primal Purpose, that is, thought and understanding, is not the only factor that possesses priority of being. The emotive elements are just as prior to the existence of the created. The will and desire, the Primal Purpose possesses; the love for the created, and for his perfection, it displays; the sovereignty and dominion it exerts in mustering all the forces of nature in pursuit of its goal: all these are equally prior to the existence of the object created. Without them the created cannot come into being. For example, the love of Jesus for the sick, was prior to the actual healing of the spiritually ailing. His dominion

(1) The Persian Bayan, by The Bab 3:6.

and sovereignty were prior to the universalistic state of society, termed the Kingdom of God on earth. Hence, to state that only forms are prior, is to disregard these other equally important factors in a creative process. In the purely rationalistic approach of an "observer," the forms alone seem prior in existence; but in the light of the principle of creation, all these emotive elements, involved in the conception of "purpose," are equally indispensable and significant, acting as prerequisite to all creative activity.

Thus, Descartes, assuming the role of an "observer," was confronted with the problem of how are ideas found in the mind: how it happens that the definition of a triangle, for example, is stored there. His conclusion is that they are innate. But a triangle has no priority over any other figure, whether plain, solid or spherical. Are there, therefore, an infinite number of formulas, each defining one such figure, and all ingrained in the mind. Descartes admits the existence of such a predicament when he says: "I am able to form in thought an innumerable variety of figures with regard to which it cannot be supposed that they were ever objects of sense." (1) But does this imply that all these figures have eternally existed in the mind, whether of God or of man? It is part of the creative genius of the creator to "produce" one such figure, possessing such specific characteristics, defined by such a specific formula, when the need for it arises. To Descartes, who assumed the role of an observer, such a third alternative did not present itself; for to an observer, if the formula does not exist in the world outside—and it cannot, because it is not subject to change, as physical things are—then it has to be considered as innate and ingrained in the mind itself. To the creator there is a third possibility; namely, that the formula is a thing he determines, as part of his creative activity, and prior to the process, and then, accordingly, generates the figure. Furthermore, inasmuch as he is the sole determining factor in the generation of the nature and being of that figure; he can at any stage of its development, revoke his decision, discard his plan, or modify it to suit new conditions. And this is the element that renders his mind ever on the alert, resourceful and inventive.

(1) Meditation V, by Descartes, tr. by J. Veitch.

And what is true of the rational element, is also applicable to the emotive ones. Love is an outpouring of the divine nature revealed in the prophets. It is not ingrained and innate in man; nor is it necessarily found in the surroundings, in which he is born. Man acquires it from the prophets, and his supreme task is to reciprocate it, and also diffuse it in turn on his environment.

The prophets of perennial religion were missioned by God, not only to transmit to man ideas and forms, innate and ingrained, in the divine nature revealed in them; not only to shed upon the human soul the regenerating power of their love; but to pursue a dominating spiritual and cultural purpose. Their idea, or notion, or definition of man's nature and destiny provided the formal and final causes of man's cultural evolution. It set the purpose he has to pursue: the end he should attain. Of all the so called spiritual and otherworldly, or natural and earthly, definitions of man, they set before him the one they generated, and according to which they fashioned him; and bid him realize it. There can be infinite forms of human behavior, infinite variety of moral systems of conduct; but only one can help the unfoldment of the spiritual reality of man as the prophets conceived it; and that they termed "good." There can be many definitions of social justice, a variety of social institutions; but only one system—a universalistic Kingdom of God on earth—can afford man an optimum environment wherein the human soul as the prophets conceived it, could grow and unfold its potentialities. There can be many forms of artistic representation; many interpretations of the nature of beauty; but only one type stimulates the soul and urges it on to the attainment of the ideal, the prophets have prescribed. In short, the definition and integration of goodness, justice, and beauty are derived from the creative Primal Purpose, the prophets reveal. And the driving force, which can guarantee their ultimate realization, is the love and devotion they awaken in the human soul.

11. THE LOCUS OF THE IMAGE: Creation is to impress a new form upon an individual being, to raise it to a higher state of existence. As spiritual and cultural rebirth and regeneration,

creation is to impart a new and higher form to the human soul, and thereby raise it to a higher level of being. It is an eternal and everlasting process, which has had no beginning, and will have no end. It is constant, cyclic and recurring. With such a conception of creation, we are led to the fundamental distinction between the Creator and the created, stressed by the Bab, in his basic premise of all thought; namely, that "all other than God is His creation."(1) This absolute distinction leaves no ground for any intermediate reality such as "Forms," "Intelligences," or "Angels." Not even an "eternal Rome," such as Maritain conceives.

The Bab says that "God has been eternally God; and other than Him, His creation. There has been, between God, and His creation, no third (reality). The third has been His creation. There is no God but Him. We all worship Him."(2) We should take the Bab to mean here by "the third," the Primal Purpose, revealed in the prophets.(3) And the Primal Purpose, as stated elsewhere, constitutes God's first creation, an effulgence of His light upon all things acting as mirrors, and acquiring illumination. On such ground, there is no occasion for an "intermediary," other than the Primal Purpose, either in the world of the spirit, as "Angels" and "intelligences"; or on earth, as human institutions, such as the Church. It is on this ground that the clergy in Islam does not constitute an institution which can dispense saving grace; and claim thereby special prerogatives. It is also on this principle that Baha'u'llah states in the Ishrakat, that all political questions fall under the jurisdiction of the House of Justice; while all devotional matters, should conform with the Book revealed.(4) In other words, he leaves no ground for an institution to claim spiritual jurisdiction, by interfering in devotional matters; and thereby claiming to proffer divine grace.

Forms are universal characteristics, or modes of activity, in a creative process. They constitute universal conceptions of moral, social or aesthetic values. According to the Bab, they proceed

(1) The Persian Bayan, 3:6.
(2) Ibid. 4:1.
(3) Introduction.
(4) Ibid.

112

from the Primal Purpose, as revealed by the prophets.(1) Divine "Wisdom" and "Sovereignty" are attributes prophets reveal, in pursuing their divine mission.(2) In Timaeus, however, Plato locates these forms, as "Ikons" or images, in the human soul. For it is considered part and parcel of the Universal Soul. The one is the microcosm of that macrocosm. With such a major premise, the two become substantially, and formally, the same. This became the primary premise of Neoplatonism, and bequeathed to later thinkers, among them to J. Maritain.

But the principle does not apply, when the distinction between the one and the other is both formal and numerical: when the one is the creation of the other; when the Creator and the created are substantially and formally different; the one actually generating and sustaining the other. The Bab says: "the sea of the world of creation cannot enter the sea of the divine substance; nor the sea of the divine substance enter the sea of the world of creation."(3) And when the difference between the two is both formal and numerical, the one cannot be considered the actual "image" of the other. The "image" of God is, therefore, the divine nature revealed in the prophets. It is the spirit of Christ which animates them all, that represents the divine attributes in full actuality. For this divine nature constitutes the outpouring rays of the divine Essence, the overflow of that infinite Sea, the offshoot of that eternal Tree. Formal unity prevails between the divine Essence, and Its rays or revelation; not between It and the human soul, which has merely the capacity to receive that light. And it is in this light, that we can appreciate the words of the Bab, when he says: "the 'image' is in the image, not in the mirror."(4) For if it were in the mirror, he adds, men who play the role of mirrors reflecting the light revealed by the prophets, would have to be considered as already containing the "image," even before the appearance of the prophets in the world. In other words, if the "image" is already ingrained in the human soul; even if it be considered "potentially," then there can be no

1) The Persian Bayan, by The Bab, 2:5.
2) Ibid. 2:8.
3) Ibid. 4:1.
4) Ibid. 4:1.

acquiring of higher forms, and hence, no true rebirth and regeneration. The conception of "potentiality" here intimates an immanence which we must avoid; to stress the necessity of "acquiring" perfections, as the true process of re-creation and rebirth.

Chapter

III

DESCARTES ON THE REALITY
OF THE EXTERNAL WORLD

1. THE REALITY OF THE EXTERNAL WORLD: We have observed how Descartes considered the apprehension, or direct inner experience, of both, the self as a thinking being, and also of ideas in the mind, immediate, clear and distinct, and hence, certain. But this certainty is not limited to these two objects of thought; for they do not constitute the only direct rational experiences. All forms of ideas, even if they are empirical in origin, and derived from external phenomena as representations, are equally certain; for they are the rational elements in the nature of things, immediately conceived, and unchanging. To quote Descartes: "If these (ideas) are considered only in themselves and not referred to any object beyond them, they cannot properly speaking be false . . . nor need we fear that falsity may exist in will or affections." (1) Such ideas, will, and affections, being immediate to human awareness, and having clarity and distinctness, are bound to be certain and admit no ground for error. Even inference, which depends on the laws of identity and non-contradiction, being an immediate experience, cannot be subject to error. (2) For these are functions fulfilled by the mind, in accordance to universal laws inherent in reason itself and common to all individuals. The possibility of error arises only when we refer these rational inferences to objects, external to thought, which are not immediately apprehended, are not distinct and clear, and hence, are not certain. The ground of uncertainty

1) Meditations III, by Descartes, tr. by J. Veitch.
2) New Studies in the Philosophy of Descartes, by N. K. Smith, p. 72.

is that we trespass the limits of immediate experience and apprehension, and make assertions regarding objects beyond the bounds of our own consciousness. The incorrect and insufficient data we gather, the manner we interpret them and classify them, to draw our conclusions: such factors in the process of thought are sources of error, in our inductive reasoning. And the reason for such error is the admixture of purely rational, immediate apprehensions, which are clear and distinct, and hence, certain; with mediated, indirect objects of perception which are not clear and distinct, and hence are uncertain. In other words, it is the external reference to physical objects in the world outside, which vitiates thought, and lends itself to uncertainty. This fact is specially marked in childhood, for example, when the requirements of the body are dominant, and the rational powers still undeveloped. Furthermore, concentrated rational life is tiring and demands relapse into physical activity. All such sensual experiences breed error and lead to doubt. These constitute a "veil of sense" which shut out the natural light of reason.

These factors, together with the gulf that seems to separate the inner rational life of man, from external objects of sense, Descartes maintains, should not be considered as sufficient ground for skepticism; nor permit it to vitiate the basis of understanding. Because, he says, God Who is the creator of all things, and the source of all law and order, would not act as such an evil spirit, to confound our understanding of things, and permit diversion between the ideas we apprehend, and the external objects they are deemed to represent. Being good, he has established some measure of conformity between the two, and laid the ground, that can justify the efficacy of the external objects of sense.

2. THE TENDENCY TO SOLIPSISM: It is a fact of history that the Academy, which Plato founded in Athens as a center of learning, and to which he bequeathed his Idealism as an intellectual heritage, gradually deteriorated and produced Cynics and Solipsists. The trend towards those extremes of skepticism was logical, and we might add, inevitable. For these were the direct consequences of the doctrine that ideas have supreme reality, for

they are the highest objects of knowledge and understanding, apprehended through the immediate experiences of the mind of the individual himself, acting as sole measure of reality and being. When ideas are considered substantial and real, when the individual mind is regarded the measure of all things, when clarity, distinctness and immediate apprehension, are valued as sufficient ground for efficacy and truth, when there is no logical and necessary entailment between individual inner experience and the nature and being of the external object, then the validity of external reference may become subject to doubt. External reference then becomes hypothetical, and a question of mere analogy, and based upon some principle of universal law and order, such as Descartes resorts to, to establish the existence of the external world. For we saw him advance the principle that God, Who is a benevolent spirit, and the creator and sustainer of law and order in the universe, would not permit human senses to misguide and deceive man. In other words, that a pre-existent harmony prevails between the senses and the external objects. But the existence of both: such a benevolent God, and such a universal harmony, is itself the point in question. For these constitute objective realities in the external world, the existence of which has to be proven as a prelude to all reasoning. In other words, clarity, distinctness and immediacy of apprehension, which Idealism considers as criteria of existence and truth, can operate only in the private intellectual life of the subject, that is, between the self, on the one hand, and the ideas presented to it, on the other. And it is immaterial whether these ideas are presented to consciousness as innate, or as universal features empirically gathered by the senses as data. It is the individual and subjective and private criteria of truth and existence which give rise to solipsism and cynicism. For external objects, being external, cannot possess the immediacy of ideas, which are the constructions of the mind itself. Neither can they reveal that clarity of definition, and distinctness of limits, which mathematical figures and equations, for example, manifest. What can eliminate skepticism, solipsism and cynicism, is a firm ground that would establish sufficient reason for the existence of the external world, and that, through a logical and causal process of entailment, leads to necessary being.

3. THE DOCTRINE OF CREATION ELIMINATES THE TENDENCY TO SOLIPSISM:

We have observed that the substantial nature and existence of an object is determined by the creator, and to the extent that he is its creator. This is a field of reality which is a closed book to the observer. For this latter, with the passive attitude of mere understanding which he takes, and which is peculiar to his role, lives in the world of mere appearance, or properties and attributes of things. As Descartes says, mind is like a sheet of wax on which sense data are impressed. His immediate apprehensions, which provide his data, do not extend beyond these, that is, beyond the affections of his peripheral nerves. Even his vital practical interests do not extend beyond those properties and attributes. It is immaterial to the observer what the stuff or substance of the external object is, or even whether it is, as such, existent so long as he can ensure the permanence of the characteristics or properties he desires for the pursuit of his purpose. In other words, his interest is primarily in the appearance, not in the nature and substance of the external object. It is otherwise with the creator, whose immediate purpose is, not the understanding of the properties, but the generation and existence of that individual object, which would reveal those properties. For only the existence of that object, possessing that specific nature and substance, in the external world, and as a product of his creative purpose and activity, is what he wills and desires. Furthermore, inasmuch as his creative purpose is originally planned, and set as an intelligible end to be pursued, and he proceeds in its realization with full knowledge of the means he employs, he knows the stuff, or substance, of which the object is made, and the properties it is meant to reveal. Later, for added assurance, he may use the process of verification to ascertain whether the purpose he originally entertained has been fully realized. In other words, his original creative purpose together with the intelligent process he pursues, entail the existence of the object he desired, with the nature and characteristics he initially planned. The subsequent verification of his results merely adds to his certainty.

Before nature, man is constrained to take the stand of a mere "observer." He has no alternative. It is the sole role he can play when the object of his understanding is some other's handiwork. He can assume the point of view of a creator only when he has actually participated in the creation of that object. The physical objects man invents to use as instruments, the moral perfections he strives and acquires, the social institutions he plans and establishes, the artistic objects he produces, in short, all his different cultural achievements, are fruits of his creative activity. In the production of all these, he traspasses the limits of his own inward awareness, and moulds the nature and destiny of an external object, and defines its objective being. These are individual, substantial, concrete existent objects, beyond his peripheral nerves, which he desired and produced. They are external objects in his environment which he has generated, and in a sense, added upon what nature had already put at his disposal. They are the direct and logical results of what he planned and purposed. Their substantial reality is what he willed and produced. Under such circumstances there is no justified ground for solipsism. Man might declare the sun as mere appearance; but the moral life, social institutions and artistic productions, are his own making and, therefore, of substantial validity. In other words, man overcomes his solipsism, to the extent he participates in the spiritual and cultural regeneration of himself and his surroundings. But man is a mere participant in this creative process. The Creator of the spiritual and cultural life, is the divine nature revealed in the prophets. It is the Primal Purpose. By participating in the realization of Its will and purpose, man can overcome the uncertainties that enshroud the nature and destiny of man, and dissipate solipsism, and skepticism.

4. THE NATURE OF UNIVERSAL HARMONY: We observed Descartes establish the necessary correspondence, between immediate sense experiences, and external phenomena of nature, on the universal principle of harmony. It cannot be maintained, he

says, that the benevolent spirit of God would leave such an incongruity, between the inner apprehensions of man, on the one hand, and external phenomena, on the other, that would lead the individual to an inveterate source of deception. The absolute harmony which prevails in the universe, does not operate only between the starts of heaven, but penetrates into the intricacies of all things, even the relation of the senses to what they claim to perceive. That such eternal, everlasting and universal law and order prevails in the physical universe, is incontrovertible; and in conformity with that principle we are justified to maintain, that sense perception cannot be, in the main, deceptive. Deceptions, if any, are exceptions and abnormalities, not the usual and normal.

But what maintains law and order is not only the absolute dominion of God, as Creator and sustainer of all things; but also the absolute determinism under which physical nature operates. Without this absolute determinism, law and order would not be as absolute as it, in fact, is. The essential difference between physical nature, on the one hand, and the spiritual and cultural life of man, on the other, is that the latter possesses the element of free choice which tends to thwart the reign of law and order. With the existence of that freedom, law and order becomes a state of being that "ought" to prevail, and not a condition that eternally, and universally, does.

Furthermore, the problem of correspondence between the subjective experiences of the individual, and the external phenomena of nature, does not confront Empiricism alone. As we have already observed, it is peculiar to all systems of thought, which assume for the individual the role of an "observer," who considers his immediate experiences, the measure of the nature, and destiny, of all things. Hence, the idealistic assertion that ideas are real, involves the principle that they are in absolute harmony with other ideas, and ultimately with the universal forms, or ideas, which dominate the external universe. In other words, the problem of correspondence between the private idea of the individual, and the public ideas which dominate the external universe, arises here as well. Hence the need for correspondence is a source of predicament to both, the Idealist and the Empiricist. They both would have to face solipsism, unless they solve the problem of correspondence. And the predicament exists, because they are both limited to the experiences of the individual, apprehended immediately within his field of consciousness, whether as innate ideas, or as affections of the senses. Now, is there a necessary correspondence between the form of law and order, as conceived and apprehended immediately by the individual, and the form of law and order as prevailing in the external world, whether conceived idealistically, or empirically, not only in the sphere of physical being, but also in the spiritual and cultural life, where the element of freedom of choice prevails?

There might have existed an absolute reign of law and order, which permeated even the consciousness of the individual, under the absolute domination of the Church, in the age preceding that of Descartes, and among the masses of Western Europe. That reign of law and order, might have maintained full correspondence, between the forms held by the individual, as part of his private religious and cultural heritage, on the one hand; and the public, intellectual, moral, social and aesthetic conceptions that pervaded the environment, on the other. But with Descartes, and the intellectuals of his day, that reign of universal cultural and spiritual harmony was coming to an end, and with an accelerating speed. The Church had been paramount, and its religious conceptions were supreme, and engraved upon the mind of the youth, through the colleges and universities it dominated. Values pervading public life, more or less corresponded with the conceptions that had sway over the private life of the individual, and constituted his immediate objects of understanding and apprehension. But the outstanding feature of that age, and its thinkers, is that at their hands this universal reign of law and order was being destroyed. And Descartes was an outstanding figure in that movement. It was the cultural dislocations, to which Descartes contributed, that ultimately led to the age of revolution that soon set in. Previously, the spiritual and cultural life of Europe was dormant, even stagnant; but a reawakening was taking place. There was a disintegration of one system of law and order, to help the subsequent integration of the world, on a higher plane of existence. Europe was seeking a law and order characteristic of life and growth, rather than of stagnation and death.

The autonomy reason had acquired, by separating its field of interest, from that of revelation and religion, was the first blow to that intellectual and cultural stagnancy that prevailed. For the individual established thereby his right, to entertain private notions and ideas, which did not fully correspond with those cherished by the public, as part of their religious beliefs. The dictum of Descartes, "I think, therefore, I am," was in utter contradiction with the absolute sovereignty, the Church claimed to possess, over human understanding. It constituted the basis of intellectual radicalism, and a blow to the harmony and authority, the Church tried to maintain. For there can be no harmony, or law and order, when every individual is the measure of the efficacy of truth and being, as the dictum implies. In fact, the dislocations that Descartes, and the thinkers of his age, brought about; have caused upheavals, and disruptions of law and order, in all the spheres of the spiritual and cultural life. And humanity has not yet been able to reintegrate on a higher plane, the forces that have been thereby let loose.

5. UNIVERSAL CULTURAL HARMONY IS A FORM ACQUIRED BY HUMANITY: God, says the Bab in the Persian Bayan, absolutely transcends all characteristics that render an object "a thing," both in the past and in the future. He is the ultimate Cause of all creation and the dispenser of "the order" we observe in the heavens, on earth, or in the world in between. (1) The Bab thus maintains, that the universal harmony we observe in the world, is the direct result of the creative power of God and of the law and order He establishes between all things. But in the field of the spiritual and cultural life of man, this law and order is the effect of the creative activity of the prophets, acting as the selfless instruments of God's Primal

(1) The Persian Bayan, by The Bab, 2:10.

122

Purpose, revealed through them. In the Iqan, Baha'u'llah uses the analogy of the sun. He says that just as the sun stimulates motion, and gives direction, to all physical objects, even plant life and animal growth; so does the prophet quicken human consciousness, and guide it to its spiritual destiny. In other words, just as the sun polarises all physical realities; so does the divine nature revealed in the prophets, polarize human capabilities, and direct them towards a certain spiritual goal. And that polarization is the basis of the harmony, and law and order, we observe in all things, including the spiritual and cultural life of man. It is, in view of such polarization of human consciousness, that Jesus made the words, "thy will be done on earth as it is in heaven," the central theme of his prayer.

When the intellectual, moral, social and aesthetic life of mankind becomes dominated by one supreme Primal Purpose, and when human thought, words and behavior become directed to one common aim, then law and order will prevail; then there will exist correspondence between the guiding principles private to the inner consciousness of the individual, and the universal forms that prevail in the external public environment in which he dwells. For both his private intellectual notions and the public social conceptions will be derived from the same Primal Purpose, established upon the same idea of the reality and destiny of man, and pursued to the same common end.

Under the sovereignty and authority of Jesus Christ, as revelation of God, such a harmony prevailed, and was fully effective in Christian countries. Being derived from a true conception of the reality and destiny of man, it operated for true human weal, and a true social regeneration. Revelation was then supreme in truth and in fact; and reason confirmed both, its validity, and authority. But gradually a syncretic movement set in. Compromise was sought between Christian belief and pagan thought, between two absolutely incompatible systems of philosophy. As a result, extraneous ideas were permitted to creep into Christian doctrine; and the consequence was the break up of that harmony, that law and order. And the two basic principles to bring about that dislocation were, first, mutual independence of revelation, and of human reason, and their absolute autonomy, each in its restricted sphere; secondly, the introduction of the ancient Greek principle, that, man is the measure of all things, in Descartes' dictum: "I think, therefore I am." This principle, that individual human consciousness, is the pivot upon which reality and truth stand was a major blow which depolarized human consciousness. For, to maintain that revelation is the criterion of all truth, is to establish universal harmony, both in the inner private consciousness of the individual, and in the public external world. And to declare, that the criterion of reality, and truth, is the individual's immediate apperception and conception of sense data or innate forms, is to atomize and depolarize all thought, and all spiritual and cultural values. And that was the role Descartes, and his contemporary thinkers, played.

The task of Baha'u'llah, and the Bab, was to reintegrate human consciousness upon a higher plane, and establish that spiritual and cultural law and order upon revelation, with its true conception of the reality and destiny of man, by declaring that, not man, but the prophets of God are the ultimate measure of truth. To this effect, the Bab says in the Bayan, that when a person observes his relation with that "measure," meaning the Primal Purpose revealed in the prophets, severed; he feels the disruption of the harmony, or law and order, which dominated his own consciousness. And that feeling waxes stronger, until he finds no more relations binding him to it.(1) In other words, the Bab attempts to revert to the early Christian belief, namely, to the purification of revelation, from alien pagan elements, that had vitiated its harmony and validity; and thus reinstate it as the supreme measure, and criterion, of truth and reality.

What is, by its very nature, utterly inconceivable and unknowable, says the Bab in the Bayan, cannot, in full fairness and justice, be made a cardinal doctrine of religious belief; upon which human salvation is to depend. No one, but God, can know the nature and existence of the Paradise which awaits man after death. Belief in it should be made the criterion of religious salvation. What constitutes the basis of human salvation, is

(1) The Persian Bayan, by The Bab, 2:13.

124

belief in the Paradise on earth, says the Bab; it is the belief in the Kingdom of God "on earth," as Jesus said. And the faith of every one is measured according to the extent he believes in its realization, and strives to establish it. The paradise of a period, or cycle of human regeneration, is the perfection of that period; it is the appearance of the manifestation of God then awaited.(1) The supreme Paradise, the highest felicity of man, says the Bab, is to acknowledge the prophet of God when he appears on earth. It is to listen to his words, believe in his teachings, contemplate the beauty of his countenance, which is the countenance of God. It is to follow his good will, and pursue his Purpose, which like a vast sea encompasses his Paradise, and thereby share of its bliss and joy.(2) In other words, the Paradise in which man has to believe firmly, as a cardinal principle of his faith, and upon which his salvation in this world and the next depends; is that state of human consciousness, and of the environment in which he lives, wherein God's supreme cultural dominion prevails. It is attained when the conception of the reality and destiny of man, as conceived by the prophets, operates as the sole source of human values; when absolute correspondence prevails between the basic conceptions, which the individual entertains and apprehends, in the ground of his own soul, on the one hand; and the universal conceptions that dominate his environment on the other; when every individual acquires the ideal condition wherein he can grow to his full stature, physically, culturally and spiritually, and thereby achieve the purpose for which he was created. This perfection of human consciousness, and of the social environment; this universal harmony, and law and order, is not a condition eternally prevailing. It is an ideal condition ardently sought, and to be finally realized.

6. THE PRINCIPLE OF THE EXISTENCE AND NATURE OF THE CULTURAL WORLD IS ALSO ESTABLISHED THROUGH THE DOCTRINE OF CREATION: If universal harmony, in the spiritual and cultural life, is a relation to be

(1) Ibid. 3:13.
(2) The Persian Bayan, by The Bab, 2:16.

acquired and realized, especially between the inner consciousness of the individual man, and the external cultural phenomena, then it cannot constitute the necessary basis upon which correspondence between the two actually stands. The forms and values, the individual entertains, may not at all correspond with the ones that dominate the universal consciousness of the rest of mankind, or even of the restricted group to which he belongs. Such was the case with the early Christians. And if these two sets of forms and values differ, all individual events would be differently interpreted and valued. In other words, even if the principle of universal harmony, and law and order, may, on the level of physical nature, constitute a fairly strong basis of inference and correspondence; it surely does not apply to the sphere of the spiritual and cultural life, where there is constant change and evolution. For this realm of being necessarily includes two disturbing elements: first, the freedom of choice, the individual possesses, to adopt certain forms of thought and behavior, or to disregard them, and follow his own desires. Secondly, the constantly changing spiritual and cultural conditions, and requirements, of the social environment in which he comes to live. For, as the Bab says, God is eternally acting under new conditions, effecting a new creation and regeneration, and spreading a new law and order.(1)

Furthermore, the lack of an unchanging universal harmony, and the constant appearance of a new law and order, and the consequent divergence between the inner private consciousness of the individual, on the one hand and that of society, on the other; this divergence generates the necessary field in which the principle of obligation and duty can operate. If absolute harmony, and undisturbed law and order, prevailed in these two spheres of the spiritual and cultural life, namely, the individual and the social, then there would be no ground left for a sense of duty. And this would amount to spiritual and cultural stagnation and solipsism. For values would be limited in sphere within the bounds of individual consciousness. The individual would not have to go beyond his own self to attain the source of his values,

(1) The Persian Bayan, by The Bab, 2:15.

126

nor would he have to undertake a transformation of the consciousness which is public and other than his own. It is the divergence between the individual, and the public consciousness, which generates a field for creative purpose to operate. All intellectual, moral, social and aesthetic values would become subject to mechanical conformity, and hence, devoid of any virtue. The inner, individual resolve expressed in the words, "Thy will be done on earth as it is in heaven," arises only when man feels the duty of regenerating his own life, as well as that of the group, of which he is a part.

In short, human reason is freed from the clutches of stagnation and solipsism, in the field of the spiritual and cultural life, only when two basic aspects of the doctrine of creation operate. First, when the creative agent is considered to be the Primal Purpose, revealed by the prophets; secondly, when the individual willingly participates in that creative process, by dedicating his life and services to it. For then, the forms and values he makes his own proceed from a transcendent source, higher and other than his self; and he tries to reform and recast the prevailing social consciousness. In the one case, he is himself reborn and regenerated; in the other, he does not act as a sheet of wax, merely awaiting to be impressed upon; but actively participates in remoulding, and refashioning, the cultural environment which surrounds him.

7. THE PROCESS OF CREATION IS ETERNAL AND EVER-LASTING: The literal interpretation of the principle of creation, as recorded in Genesis, has involved human thought in insurmountable difficulties; both in ancient days, and also in modern times. Perhaps aversion to that interpretation, was what led Greek thinkers to deny the principle of creation, and develop in its stead the idea of the eternality of being, which seemed sounder philosophically. The creation of nature and man, out of an absolute void, at a certain period, when time also was made to start, contradicted some basic notions, even in the field of religion itself. For, as Abdu'l-Baha says: a God who is infinite, His creation also should be deemed infinite. Finiteness

of creation, entails finiteness of its creator. To say, therefore, that at a certain period, no matter how distant in the past, creation started, entails the limitation of God's creative power to that extent; and hence amounts to a denial of the efficacy of His creativeness before that event and period. It is in this light that the Bab says, in his preface to the Persian Bayan, to the effect that at no time God was, and there was no servant to worship Him, that He was from all eternity in the full light of His glory; while all other than Him were in abject servitude to His will and pleasure.(1)

8. THE OBJECT OF CREATION IS THE GENERATION OF THE INDIVIDUAL MAN AS THE SUPREME FORM OF CREATED REALITY: Greek thought was essentially rationalistic; for it maintained the paramountcy of mind, as faculty of understanding and knowledge. And as the function of thought is primarily to seek the universals in individual phenomena; rationalism aimed at discovering the universals, and making them the supreme objects of its attention and study. Furthermore, if these universals, that is, ideas and forms, are pure intelligible realities, and hence, the supreme objects of knowledge and understanding, they should be considered as possessing priority of being over matter which is unintelligible, and of the individual which contains an admixture of it. Moreover, an essential feature of absolute reality is that it is unchanging. Inasmuch as these ideas or forms are eternal, they ought to be considered uncreated and in nature divine. It is on such rationalistic grounds, that Plato, for example, considered "the good" as divine; and Aristotle regarded God as the Form of all forms; the supreme Form, free from any vestige of materiality, and utterly intelligible in nature and substance.

To the very extent that rationalism lays stress on the universal, and gives it priority of being; to the same measure, and in contrast to it, the doctrine of creation emphasizes the individual, and regards it the supreme reality in the world of creation, irrespective of whether it is intelligible or not. Under the doctrine

(1) The Persian Bayan, by The Bab, in the Preface.

of creation, forms and values, are significant as universals, only because they trace a general path for the progress of the individual; thought is valued in the measure it guides and directs human evolution. In other words, just as to the rationalist triangularity is the supreme object of knowledge and understanding; to the doctrine of creation it is the individual triangle that is traced, with its definite angles and sides, and the material employed, as an object of art. Even though that admixture of matter is unintelligible, and the individual triangle traced, or formed, is subject to destruction and change. Angels are supreme beings in the world of creation, not because they are intelligible —in fact, to human intellect they are not—but because they are the souls of individual human beings, that have been reborn, acquired higher perfections, and attained thereby to a nobler state of being after death. Under the doctrine of creation, that reality is supreme and possesses priority of being, which has been more fully subjected to the process of creation and rebirth, and hence, acquired a higher form, and attained a greater degree of progress and evolution. The Bab says, that all other than God are His creation. With such a dynamic conception of created reality, there is no place for immobility, such as ideas and forms represent. Movement is life and being; immobility death. In the world of creation the supremely real, is the individual object which is supremely active, and hence, changing; it is that individual man who has covered a fuller course on the road to perfection.

9. NEED FOR CERTAINTY IN CULTURAL VALUES: In Meditation IV, Descartes distinguishes between two mental faculties: "intellection," which he identifies with the act of conceiving and "imagination" which he defines as "a certain application of the cognitive faculty to a body," or sense-impression, as when he imagines a triangle. The difference between these two, is that whereas "intellection" is wholly dependent on mind, "imagination" has reference to an external physical object. But Descartes admits that "I do not find that, from the distinct idea of corporeal nature I have in my imagination, I can neces-

sarily infer the existence of any body." He, therefore, takes recourse to the religious belief, in the "omnipotence" and benevolence of God, in the assurance, that His universal reign of law and order, would maintain correspondence between private sense-impressions, immediately apprehended, and external objects to which these refer. "For by nature, considered in general," he adds, "I now understand nothing more than God himself, or the order and disposition established by God in created things; and by my nature in particular I understand the assemblage of all that God has given me." But notwithstanding this reign of law and order established by God, the fundamental flaw, caused by the physical element, persists. "Whence it is quite manifest," Descartes says, "that notwithstanding the sovereign goodness of God, the nature of man, in so far as it is composed of mind and body, cannot but be sometimes fallacious."

One fundamental feature of Descartes' reasoning here is that he takes the attitude of an "observer," and tries to establish the existence of material things through "perception," which he considers "a passive attitude" of the mind, acting as a sheet of wax, merely recording impressions received from outside. This attitude, we have observed, leads logically to solipsism and skepticism. And because these tendencies are the direct consequences of the role, the "observer" plays, they also apply to what Descartes considers the field of "intellection," or the conception of intellectual ideas and forms, such as "goodness," "justice" and "beauty" which constitute spiritual and cultural values. For even in relation to these, the individual assumes the attitude of a "contemplator," rather than of a "creator," pursuing a purpose; which generates the nature, and sets the end, of these supreme values. The same solipsism and skepticism dominate the nature of these values; while, what man in fact requires in this field, is absolute certainty. Uncertainty regarding the substance and destiny of physical nature, might be easily overlooked, if we possess assurance as to its properties and attributes; but the nature and destiny of man, is the source, from which all his spiritual and cultural values, spring. We cannot define the latter, without knowing the former, first. Uncertainty regarding the first, will absolutely vitiate our understanding, moral standards, social institutions and aesthetic appreciation.

Furthermore, taking for granted, that the prevailing law and order, will guarantee correspondence between individual private conceptions, and imaginations, and universal harmony; we have to ascertain with which set of law and order it should be; for according to the Bab, this is constantly being changed and modified. Should it be, for example, in harmony with a socialistic or an individualistic form of culture; or with the type that prophets of revealed religion establish in the world; should it be parochial, nationalistic and racial, or world-wide and universalistic: the type ancient Athens and Sparta possessed; or the one early Zoroastrianism, Christianity and Islam tried to establish? The only answer to such a contention, is that conformity should be with a law and order, based upon a true understanding of the nature and destiny of man, which is known with certainty only to his creator.

We need not restate The Bab's point of view. But it is the divine nature, revealed in the prophets which, as Primal Purpose, creates the spiritual and cultural life; as Primal Point it defines it; as a source of Wisdom and Truth, it imparts that knowledge to mankind, and inspires assurance and certainty. By accepting the primary premises, these prophets reveal, and interpreting his own thoughts and experiences in their light, man can attain the certainty his spiritual and cultural life demands.

Chapter

IV

DESCARTES' CONCEPTION OF GOD

1. THE BASIC PREDICAMENT OF RATIONALISM: In Timaeus, Plato presents the conception of creation as giving form to the formless, that is, of impressing a pattern existent in the mind of God, upon matter at hand, to generate a new being. But such a notion of creation is not in full conformity with the requirements of rationalism. For the supreme Artificer would, in that case, not be necessarily an "intelligible" reality; though the idea or pattern He employs is such. But if God, the supreme Artificer, is not necessarily "intelligible," then the requirements of rationalism will not be fully satisfied. For rationalism demands that the supreme Being be, both "intelligent," and "intelligible"; to act both as Reason and the ultimate object of reason. It is on this ground that rationalistic systems of thought have tended to identify God with the Universal Soul, and the Universal Soul with Mind; and on that ground have considered human intellect the measure of all things. For should that supreme Reality be considered unintelligible, then reason would not be able to claim, that it constitutes the measure of all reality and existence. In other words, the God of Timaeus represents a supreme Artificer, acting as the ultimate Efficient Cause, which is "unintelligible." God generates form, but is not considered Himself formal, to constitute the supreme object of understanding at the same time. That conception expresses the reasoned religious outlook, which considers the Creator as unknowable; but it fails to satisfy the requirement of rationalism, which demands a "knowable" and "intelligible" God.

In other dialogues, such as the Republic, where he tries to stress the priority of forms in reality and being, Plato tends to identify God with "the Good," that is, with the supreme "Idea" or "Form." This supreme Being, thus becomes essentially "intelligible," and the requirement of his rationalism becomes fully satisfied. For God, being considered the Universal Soul; becomes also the supreme Idea, the highest object of understanding.

In his Metaphysics, and also in his Physics, Aristotle tries to reconcile these two trends in Platonic thought, and make them more coherent and logical. He felt such need pressing, when he discovered that all basic values, such as truth, goodness, justice and beauty which are essentially formal, must needs trace their origin to a source that is necessarily "knowable" and "intelligible." For otherwise, how can man justly claim to attain an understanding of them. If God, the source of all cultural values, is essentially "unintelligible" and "unknowable," then man would have to confirm the contention of Parmenides, as expressed by Plato; (1) that even if God is the source of all values, how can man obtain an access to them, to understand them? An insurmountable gulf would then divide, Divine knowledge, from human understanding. To overcome that gulf, Aristotle advocated the principle, that God is the Efficient Cause of all being, the Unmoved Mover; by being the Formal Cause at the same time; that is, by acting as the supreme object of contemplation and understanding; and thereby attracting the human soul to itself through love. In that manner Aristotle tried to solve the problem of rationalism and overcome its basic predicament. For being the Formal Cause, as well, God would be justly considered both the source of all cultural values, which are essentially intelligible, and also the supreme object of understanding. But such an identification of the Efficient, and the Formal Causes, of being, tends to make the creative process, less in the nature of compulsion, and more in that of attraction; less of a dynamic drive, and more of an urge of love; less of a creative force, and more as source of illumination and understanding.

(1) Parmenides, by Plato, 134 D.

We find this tendency to identify the Formal with the Efficient Cause in Thomas Aquinas as well, when, for example, we see him try to establish the existence of God on the conception of goodness, truth, nobility and other attributes of perfection. For these are formal in nature; and to attribute them directly to the Efficient Cause, is to make it Formal as well. As we shall observe, in revealed religion, the Formal is distinguished from the Efficient Cause, by considering the first as a revelation, or appearance, of the second. But with the principle of separating the field of reason from that of revelation, and giving each its full autonomy within its own restricted domain, philosophy could not deal with the station of Jesus Christ, which the principle of revelation would have entailed. And this sidestepping of the principle of revelation has vitiated European philosophic thought ever since. It has confronted the discussions of the conception of God, with problems, and difficulties, that it has not succeeded to overcome. And it is symptomatic of that tendency, that Descartes does not even mention Jesus Christ in his discussion of the conception of God, when he actually professed Christianity, and seemed to maintain the divinity of Christ.

2. ARISTOTLE'S ANALOGY OF SEED, TO EXPLAIN POTENTIALITY, MAKES THE FORMAL AND THE EFFICIENT CAUSES COINCIDE: The metaphysics of Plato, we have observed, was based upon the basic principle that God constitutes the Universal Soul, and that the individual human soul is a mere miniature image of it, produced through a process of division and fission. Accordingly, the difference between the two is a question of magnitude not of form. For both possess the same forms, though the one in an ever active state, and the other potentially. Aristotle modified this basic Platonic conception, by maintaining that the Universal Soul is not separate from physical nature, as Plato had conceived it; but is immanent in it as snubness, for example, is immanent in a nose. It constitutes the shape it takes. This principle of formal similarity, and numerical difference, made Aristotle take up the analogy of a seed, to explain potentiality. For a seed is a potential plant, with similar forms, but

different magnitude. Should we provide that seed the necessary warmth and moisture, it will produce a similar plant. Furthermore, the forms that define the growth of the seed are inherent and ingrained in it, not in a separate reality. This principle necessarily entails the belief, that the formal is coincident with the efficient cause, and may be identified with it. For the mother plant both generates the seed, and also imparts to it the nature and direction of its growth. This coincidence and identity of the efficient with the formal cause is dominant in Aristotle's philosophy and permeates its many spheres.

3. DESCARTES FOLLOWS ARISTOTLE'S PRINCIPLE IN THAT REGARD: In his discussion of the Idea of God, Descartes follows this Aristotelian trend, by making God, and His attributes of perfection, innate in human thought. "I am thus," he says, "clearly taught by the natural light that ideas exist in me as pictures or images." "But, among these my ideas, besides that which represents myself, respecting which there can be here no difficulty, there is one that represents a God." Further he says: "The idea, I say, of a being supremely perfect, and infinite, is in the highest degree true; for although, perhaps, we may imagine that such a being does not exist, we cannot, nevertheless, suppose that his idea represents nothing real, as I have already said of the idea of cold. It is likewise clear and distinct in the highest degree, since whatever the mind clearly and distinctly conceives as real or true, and as implying any perfection, is contained entire in this idea."(1) In this last quotation Descartes confirms the truth of the idea of God, and of His infinite perfections, on the ground that they are immediately and clearly and distinctly apprehended; even though they may constitute private notions, with no corresponding reality existent in the external public world. Further on, Descartes, following Aristotle maintains, "But perhaps I am something more than I suppose myself to be, and it may be that all those perfections which I attribute to God, in some way exist potentially in me, although they do not yet show themselves, and are not reduced

(1) Meditation III, by Descartes, tr. by J. Veitch.

135

to act." But he adds, "Yet, on looking more closely into the matter, I discover that this cannot be"; and the reason why the human soul cannot be considered divine, is that being essentially potential in nature it cannot be fully actual. "I am not, therefore, induced to think that it will ever be actually infinite, since it can never reach that point beyond which it shall be incapable of further increase."(1) This cautious language of Descartes, betrays his fear of offending the Church, which did not endorse full immanentism; but the whole reasoning shows how deeply he was influenced by the analogy of the seed in explaining human potentiality, and the coincidence of the efficient and the formal cause.

4. THE BAB'S EXAMPLE OF THE MIRROR DISTIN-GUISHES BETWEEN THE EFFICIENT AND THE FORMAL CAUSES: Descartes might have shied from the idea that God, as Universal Reason, is immanent in the human soul; but to maintain that His idea as well as His attributes of perfection, are innate and clearly and distinctly apprehended, and hence, true, is to go very far along that line. In any case, his conception of potentiality gradually becoming actual, is akin to Aristotle's conception of the "seed," which makes the efficient and the formal cause coincide. For Descartes considers both, the idea of God, and His attributes of perfection ingrained and innate in the human soul, even though as a potentiality.

In contrast to this ancient heathen conception, which has always been advocated, mainly to sidestep the principle of revelation, is the Bab's doctrine, that the sea of divine Being, as Creator, is, has ever been, and will ever be, separate and distinct from the sea which comprises the world of creation.(2) A creator, or artisan, cannot be conceived as in substance immanent in his creation. The latter is merely his handiwork, revealing his creative power. Nor can His creation ever be merged back into the sea of His divine Being. Hence, neither God, nor His idea, nor His attributes of perfection, can be considered as ingrained,

(1) Meditation III, by Descartes, tr. by J. Veitch.
(2) The Persian Bayan, by The Bab, 4:1.

and innate, in human reason. Between the two, there is not only numerical, but also substantial and formal, difference. Hence, the analogy of "seed" is confusing and inapplicable. It is on this ground that the Bab chooses the example of the mirror. For, between the sun and the mirror, there is not only numerical, but also substantial and formal, difference. And the Bab especially stresses that distinction when he says that the "image," that is, the sum total of forms, is not located in the mirror, but in the image, or the reality reflecting itself. (1) That image remains above, and beyond, the mirror which reflects it. In other words, not only God is an external object in respect to the human soul; but also His attributes of perfection, and the source from which they are derived. Therefore, man in his state of nature, has neither an idea of God, nor of His attributes of perfection. He can merely acquire them in the course of his spiritual and cultural development, which carries him far beyond that level. Thus, both the formal and the efficient cause of human evolution, are beyond, and external to, the human soul. This last—the human soul—is merely the material cause. It constitutes that formless clay, in which the creator gradually moulds His divine image, or attributes of perfection.

But though both: the Efficient and the Formal Cause, are separate from, and external to, the human soul; that does not necessarily imply that they do not coincide as appearance to reality. According to Plato, for example, they do coincide, even though they are deemed separate from physical being. We have observed the Bab say, that other than God is His creation; (2) and also that God created the Primal Purpose; and this, in turn, created all other objects. (3) Therefore, the attributes of perfection, or forms, which are realities "other than God," and that we refer to Him; spring from the Primal Purpose, and the spiritual and cultural end, it pursues. Furthermore, the Primal Purpose is, according to the Bab, identical with the divine nature revealed in the prophets as appearance to reality, or revelation

(1) The Persian Bayan, by The Bab, 4:1.
(2) Ibid. 3:6.
(3) Ibid.

137

to the revealed. In other words, the "Image" of God, which symbolizes the forms, or perfections we attribute to Him, is focused in the divine nature revealed in the prophets. And their human personality acts merely as a mirror which reflects that divine light. In that case, we can say that even between the divine, and the human, nature of the prophets, there is numerical, as well as formal, and substantial difference. For the one is in substance creator, and the other in substance created; the one is the reality worshipped, the other is, as the Bab says, the first to worship.

Now, if the "Image" of God is located in the divine nature revealed in the prophets, and that constitutes the focal center of all the forms and attributes we refer to Him; then we can justly consider it the Formal Cause of human evolution. We can at the same time distinguish between the divine nature revealed in the thought, words and deeds of the prophets, which are fully accessible and intelligible to man, on the one hand; and the divine essence and substance, which is utterly inaccessible and unintelligible. The first, then, may be considered as the knowable Formal Cause; and the latter the unknowable Efficient Cause of man's spiritual and cultural life. But can such a view hold its ground philosophically?

Philosophy cannot positively deny the existence of substantial objects in the world of nature. It can only assert that if they exist, they are inaccessible to human thought. Hence, philosophy centers its interest on the phenomenal world with its properties, functions and interactions; in other words, on their "appearance," not their substantial "reality." And this "appearance" constitutes the formal aspect of things, as distinguished from their unknowable substance and reality. In other words, this distinction arises from the peculiar nature of human thought, which itself is a relation, and applies to all aspects of understanding, religious as well as scientific. As Baha'u'llah says, human thought is limited to the field of attributes.

Now, the prophet, in whom the divine, and the human natures, contact; by the one acting as mirror, reflecting the light of the other; corresponds to the phenomenal aspect of things in the realm of nature. Through that mirror or prism, which constitutes the human personality of the prophets, the Primal Purpose reveals itself in its many forms, and attributes, of perfection, and thereby becomes the supreme object of human understanding. Those forms cannot be considered as identical and coincident with the divine substance, for they are its creation, and are related to a cultural purpose and end; but yet they are not independent and self-subsisting. They constitute the "appearance" of that "reality." The one is the Efficient, the other the revelation or Formal Cause. And this truth can be established historically as well; for the prophets were in fact the formal cause, and source, of the spiritual and cultural life, established by revealed religion down throughout history.

5. THE CULTURAL SIGNIFICANCE OF CONSIDERING THE PROPHETS AS THE FORMAL CAUSE OF HUMAN EVOLUTION: A result of this Aristotelian conception of God, and the identification of the Formal, with the Efficient Cause, is, that it does not distinguish between the field of nature, on the one hand, and that of culture, on the other. It does not leave room for a differentiation between physical creation, and cultural regeneration of humanity; between natural and the specifically spiritual evolution of mankind. And the basic distinction between the two, is that in the one, unlike in the other, the human faculty of reason, free will and love, obtain full scope to participate. To say of inanimate objects, even of plant and animal life, that they are in potency, and ever seeking a higher form; that as mere potentiality they feel the urge for actualization of their power; that they constantly long for a higher level of being, a fuller perfection of their innate endowments, and that the driving force is in the nature of love—such a belief, to say the least, is highly conjectural. For it assumes in inanimate objects, and physical nature, the purposefulness, and intelligent activity, which man pursues in his peculiar province of spiritual and cultural evolution. It is to attribute to nature the consciousness, and purpose, which is exclusive to man. For it is only in the field of culture, and spirituality, that we can say, man, guided by his intellect, and

by a conscious love for higher values and forms, seeks to acquire attributes of perfection. In other words, the conception of God as Formal Cause, clear, distinct and separate, applies more strictly to the field of culture and the spiritual life, rather than to mere physical and inanimate being.

Furthermore, it sounds stupid to speak of grades of existence in the sphere of physical nature. Objects of nature either are, or are not. There is no intermediate grade of being. A stone does not acquire fuller existence by falling to the ground, where its actualization resides. Even a youth cannot be said to have attained fuller existence by reaching manhood. Things in nature either are, or are not, no matter what is the stage of their evolution. But there are grades of being, when we consider the spiritual and cultural life. And that gradation depends upon the extent man has transcended his natural level of being, and the measure of perfections he has acquired. For a reborn or regenerated soul stands on a higher plane of existence. The perfections he has acquired raise him beyond his previous animal existence, into the sphere of culture and spirituality. It is in this respect, and because of such acquired perfections, that an individual is deemed reborn, or raised from the dead. Therefore, the formal conception of God, which is based upon the principle of grades of existence, relative to the extent human capacities have acquired perfections, that is have assumed characteristics that are essentially formal; such a conception is bound to be primarily applicable to the spiritual and cultural development, rather than to inanimate existence and physical being.

Descartes teaches that creation "is a type of efficient, not purposive agency. Purposive action in the service of final ends is, he contends, an essentially anthropomorphic type of activity. Though it is indeed the highest of which man is capable, it is not on that account any the more applicable to the Divine." (1) We thus see Descartes deny the Aristotelian principle that, physical nature is moved by a Formal, or even a Final Cause, or that objects in nature, possess an inner urge which leads them

(1) New Studies in the Philosophy of Descartes, by N. K. Smith, p. 165.

140

to the actualization of their potentialities. He saw that to assert the formal principle of motion in the field of physical nature, means to attribute consciousness to physical being; or rather, to subscribe teleology, which implies an inner conscious urge, to physical objects themselves. And that he regarded as highly conjectural, figurative and anthropomorphic. His main concern, therefore, was to prove, that in physical science, movement can be fully accounted for, by measuring the forces operating in the plane directly contiguous to the body itself; without supposing notions such as potentiality and actuality which are anthropomorphic, and bequeathed by Aristotle. In other words, heavy bodies fall, and light bodies rise, not due to different types of potentialities they possess, and different forms of actuality they seek; but because the forces operating directly on them, drive them in different directions. In other words, he indirectly proved that, in the field of physical nature, the operation of the Formal Cause cannot be maintained.

But if according to Descartes, the formal cause has no distinctive part to play in the field of physical nature, it has its role in the realm of culture, and the spiritual life. Man, though born on the level of physical nature, has all the capacities of acquiring perfections: intellectual, moral, social and aesthetic. And the forces which develop those capacities, and direct and stimulate their growth, is first a vision and understanding of the qualities of perfection, and then a stimulating and driving force in the nature of admiration and love. The function of a teacher is to provide such a formal cause to the intellectual development of the student; and the driving power the latter needs is an inner urge for knowledge. The moral development of man is the result of the love and admiration the individual feels, for one whom he deems exemplary, or the embodiment of the higher forms of conduct. Social reform starts with a vision of the ideal state of society, and a burning desire to realize it. The artist visualizes a certain form, which he considers beautiful, and then tries to depict it. In all these cases there is a formal cause, a reality that stands as embodiment of perfections, and then, a conscious and intelligent urge to attain them as end. This is not conjectural; it is factual, arising from a field of activity that is peculiarly human. Descartes could not deny the operation of such a formal cause in man's cultural life. He merely failed to locate its actual source. His belief in innate ideas, located that cause in man's own individual consciousness; while factually it was in the divine nature revealed in Jesus Christ.

6. THE DIFFERENT TYPES OF CAUSES GIVE DIFFERENT CONCEPTIONS OF GOD: Aristotle had distinguished four types of causes: the efficient, the final, the formal, and the material cause. Every one of these causes has since led to a different conception of God, and to a different type of proof for His existence. That applies even to the material cause; for pantheism, which deifies all being, or considers the Universe as God, tends to maintain that the basic stuff and substance, of which all things are composed, is essentially divine. We can prove the existence of such a God, by reducing all substantiality to law and order, and considering it as divine in nature. The best representatives of that school in the past, were the Stoics. Secondly, stress on the final cause, led the mystics to conceive that man's ultimate end is substantial identification with God. It is to be submerged into the universal sea of His being. To such mystics, the means of proving the existence of God, is to show the validity of that sudden experience, which they term ecstasy, and consider it as union with the Godhead. For that unity with the universal and eternal, as a final Cause, which man in certain states of consciousness—or, as some prefer to term, aberration—feels, is considered only as an earthly sample, of the unity the human soul will experience in after-life. Thirdly, the conception of God as efficient Cause of the universe, both natural and spiritual, physical and cultural, is sustained by the logical need for a first Mover that is unmoved; or a necessary Being which is the ground of all contingency. This school of thought was represented during the age of Descartes by the Deists. Finally, when the Formal Cause is deified, it leads to Theism, which regards God as the source and personification of all virtues; of truth, goodness, justice and beauty; that is, of the spiritual and the cultural life.

142

And it tries to support belief in such a God, by tracing to the origin of these supreme forms or values.

Thus, it is this formal conception, which considers God as the source of all perfections; and the proof that it establishes for His existence, is that it factually constitutes the foundation of the spiritual and cultural life. Hence it is this conception, and this proof, which stand as of primary importance in theology, and in the life of the individual, seeking spiritual rebirth, and cultural regeneration. The conception of God as Efficient Cause, or prime Mover; as such, has no cultural significance, and provokes no theological interest. And that proved to be true, as the result of the discussions pursued by the Deists. Though these staunchly advocated the existence of God as first Mover, they soon died out as an effective force, because they had no spiritual and cultural message to offer, as derived from that conception alone. The conception of God as an Efficient Cause, acquires significance and interest, only when He is considered, at the same time, the Formal Cause of the spiritual and the cultural life of mankind. Similarly mysticism, with its conception of God as Final Cause, has failed to exert any appreciable influence upon man's cultural life; mainly because it has failed to stress the Formal one as well, because it has provided no adequate ground for revelation, for the Primal Purpose as source of cultural values and attributes of perfection they imply. Likewise Pantheism, with its conception of God as the primary substance and element, of which the universe is composed, has exerted little influence on human evolution, because it has failed to attribute special significance to the Formal Cause as the source of all values and perfections. In short, the Formal Cause is the mainstay of the spiritual and cultural life of man; and the proof it advances for the existence of God, thus conceived, is that theology and moral philosophy seek it as their supreme quest. Hence, any conception of God which fails to find an adequate place for the Formal Cause in its system of thought; fails to bear adequate significance for human thought. And any proof for the existence of God, which does not establish categorically that basic conception, is devoid of any cultural significance. And it is upon this main theistic issue that all other

143

conceptions of God, and all other proofs for His existence, have floundered. They failed, because they were unable to locate the prime Mover of the spiritual and cultural life, and the supreme exemplar of characteristics, or forms, essentially divine.

7. THE BAB ON THE EFFICIENT, THE FINAL, AND THE MATERIAL CAUSES: We saw the Bab say, that the fundamental conception of all thought is the principle that, all other than God, is His creation. Further, that God created the Primal Purpose; and the Primal Purpose, in turn, created all other things. (1) In other words, God alone is the ultimate Efficient Cause of all things. The human soul, though a spiritual reality, can be creative, only in so far as it participates in God's creative work, and lets the Divine Purpose guide his activity. Hence, we cannot follow Plato's analogy and compare the human soul to the captain of a ship; that is, consider it an unmoved mover. It is at best, the helmsman who steers the ship on its course, as directed by a superior authority, which charts its destination.

Such being the case, the human soul, like the physical universe, constitutes the material cause: the clay, that the Efficient Cause moulds and remoulds, always adding to it a new form, and raising it to a higher state of being. It is sustained by being ever reborn; otherwise it will wither away. This divine substance thus constitutes an "ocean," which is absolutely distinct from the "sea" of His creation, that includes the human soul. With His Essence, the Bab says, in his preface to the Bayan, nothing can "resemble," nothing can "equal," nothing can "combine." He is "unique" in His empire and dominion.

Such being the absolute and substantial difference, between the Creator, on the one hand, and His creation, on the other; we cannot define the final cause, and end of human progress, as the submergence of the soul in the sea of divine Being, and hence, the final unity of their substance and nature, as mystics maintain. No reality, says the Bab, can trespass the limits set in its creation and recreation. (2) A spirit attached to a creature, he says, is

(1) The Persian Bayan, by The Bab, 3:6.
(2) The Persian Bayan, by The Bab, 3:6.

always a creature. (1) Humanity cannot be even sustained in its being, except through its constant rebirth, effected through the periodic appearance of prophets, to regenerate it, overcome the forces of destruction that dominate it, and give it peace and security. How can we, therefore, maintain that the human soul can be substantially united with God, and become one with Him in essence and nature? With its premise that between the universe as a macrocosm, and the human soul as a microcosm, the difference was not formal, but numerical, and merely in magnitude; Platonism could logically entertain that notion. But according to revealed religion, the difference is not only of magnitude, but also formal. And when the difference is formal as well, as revealed religion maintains, then the end of human evolution cannot be interpreted in terms of unity of substance; but only of acquired qualities, forms and attributes, which by their very nature remain contingent, and never attain necessity and the absolute. Descartes, who followed Plato in maintaining the principle of innate ideas, and hence, of formal similarity between God and human nature; compromised with that basic tenet of Christianity, and introduced in his thought that tendency, the full logical implications of which he could not claim to accept. For example, in his discussion on the possibility of error in human thought. (2) But if the Final Cause of human evolution cannot be interpreted in the mystic way, as the substantial unity of the human soul with God, how can we attribute meaning and significance to the statement, often repeated in the Sacred Scriptures, when referring to God as the "beginning and the end; the first and the last; the alpha and the omega"; which the Bab reiterates in his preface to the Persian Bayan?

It is true that individual physical objects in the universe are creations of God; hence that He constitutes the unmoved Mover of the physical universe; and the Efficient Cause of its being, and its source, or "beginning." But the significance of those expressions is more fully grasped when interpreted spiritually, and culturally, as well. We observed the Bab apply the term, "Paradise

(1) Ibid. 2:9.
(2) Meditation IV, by Descartes.

145

on earth," to the state of perfection an individual reality can attain while in this mortal life.(1) In such a case, the "Paradise on earth," of human society, would be the next prophetic dispensation, that is, the appearance of the new prophet, as the fulfilment of the promise of the past; when all the hopes and aspirations of the previous dispensation will be realized(2) when a new divine "Presence" in the world will occur. The "Paradise on earth" of Christianity, for example, would be in the return of Christ, as foretold. As these dispensations are cyclic, the attainment of "Paradise on earth" is eternally recurring, and periodic. In other words, man's historical evolution has been to emerge out of one "Paradise on earth," one self-revelation of God, one divine "Presence," and to proceed to the next, as his supreme attainment. And this constitutes the spiritual and cultural meaning of the term "we are from God and to Him do we return"; that "He is the first and the last the beginning and the end."(3)

In short, the Efficient Cause, that is, the Creator of the Universe, is unintelligible, and inaccessible to human knowledge or intuition. Similarly the material cause, taken in its absolute sense. For total formlessness, is an intellectual abstraction, and hence, non-existent. As creation is to subject an individual reality to a higher form, an absolutely formless reality would be uncreated; while, "all things other than God are created." Furthermore, being absolutely formless, pure matter cannot act as object of knowledge and understanding. Hence, the material cause—if matter is taken absolutely, is both non-existent and unintelligible. Only in its relative sense, as the material substance of which an individual is composed, can it be the object of knowledge; and in that case, knowable primarily to the creator of that individual reality. Such being the case, only the Formal and the Final Causes, constitute the objects of contemplation, and human understanding. And these are the revelation of the Primal Purpose, and the ultimate end of human evolution. And because they constitute the source

(1) The Persian Bayan, by The Bab, 3:13.
(2) Ibid. 2:17.
(3) Ibid. 4:7.

146

of all higher forms, and the end of human evolution, they establish the ground of the spiritual and cultural life of mankind.

8. DESCARTES CONSIDERS THE CONCEPTION OF GOD AN INNATE IDEA: To Plato, the idea of "the Good," or God, was like all other ideas, innate. Aristotle parted company from his master, in that he maintained, that knowledge of God, like all other forms of understanding is derived from sense-perception, from the observation of the product of God's creative activity, and hence, His operation as Prime Mover of all natural phenomena. Thomas Aquinas reverted from the Platonic conception, which Augustine had incorporated into Church belief, to the Aristotelian principle which denied that we have an innate conception of God, and asserted instead that our knowledge of Him, and of His attributes and existence, all are inferred from sense experience, and the causal connection we assume to prevail in the universe. And upon such basic empirical principles he tried to establish the validity of his proofs for the existence of God. These, however, were far from convincing to the Skeptics, Deists and atheists, who in the 16th. century were assailing the Church, and its basic tenets and doctrines. And the point they chose to attack was mainly the assertion of God's attributes of perfection, which we observed, is the source of man's spiritual and cultural life. Granted there is a God, acting as efficient Cause, and Creator of the universe, the Deists would say, how do we know that He is the supreme source of truth, goodness, justice and beauty? The Thomistic reasoning, that these formal aspects of the divine nature, were inferred from human experience, was not fully convincing. Hence, we see Descartes revert to the basic Platonic principle of innate ideas and maintain that, just as we can prove our own existence through the inner light of reason, so we can prove both the existence of God, and of His many attributes of perfection, through that inner apprehension.

"By the name God," Descartes says, "I understand a substance infinite (eternal, immutable), independent, all-knowing, all-powerful, and by which I myself and every other thing that exists, if any such there be, were created."(1) "It only remains to me," he says further, "to examine into the manner in which I have acquired this idea from God; for I have not received it through the senses . . . nor is it likewise a fiction of my mind, for it is not in my power to take from or to add anything to it; and consequently the only alternative is that it is innate in me."(2) In other words, this idea of God was moulded into the very structure of the mind of man, at the time of his creation or individuation. Hence, like all other ideas, it is innate. And the proof for its efficacy is the one applied, to establish his own existence, and the existence of all other inner ideas, namely, direct apprehension, clarity and distinctness. Summarizing his argument Descartes says: "It is absolutely necessary to conclude from this alone that I am, and possess the idea of a being absolutely perfect, that is, of God, that his existence is most clearly demonstrated. There remains only the inquiry as to the way in which I received this idea from God; for I have not drawn it from the senses, nor is it even presented to me unexpectedly, as is usual with the ideas of sensible objects, when these are presented or appear to be presented to the external organs of the senses; it is not even a pure production or fiction of my mind, for it is in my power to take from or add to it, and consequently there but remains the alternative that it is innate, in the same way as is the idea of myself."(2) Thus, the idea of God, like any other idea, is innate and potentially existent in the individual mind of man; and becomes actualized as operated upon it; by that infinite Being of Whose existence and substantiality, we are clearly and distinctly assured. As we shall observe, human mind contains no "potential" idea of God, innate in its structure. It merely possesses the "capacity" to receive it, when contemplating His revelation, as a distinct object of sense perception and understanding.

Furthermore, the analogy here does not fully apply. "I think," is an act; not a conception, idea or definition. Hence, "I think,

(1) Meditation III, by Descartes, tr. John Veitch.
(2) Ibid.

148

therefore, I am," proves only the awareness that accompanies a conscious purposeful activity; and the existence of myself as the subject of that I act; and of that awareness. The dictum does not establish the existence of any innate idea or definition, such as Descartes asserts. In other words, I obtain the certainty of my existence, as the result of that conscious act, while thinking. In the case of the existence of God, there is no corresponding activity on my part, of which I am conscious; to establish as a result the principle that He exists. Unless I should consider my own activity that of God, and thus identify myself with Him. And such a pantheistic attitude is far from Descartes' mind, as expressed in his definition of God, given above.

9. THE IDEA OF GOD IS ACQUIRED BY MAN: Is there no alternative to the principle that, the idea of God is innate in man; that it was moulded in the fabric of his thought at the time of his creation or individuation? Is there not any explanation that would better fit the process of human culture, which history records? Descartes' innatism was Platonic. Is there a religious one as well? To state that the idea of God, and of His perfections, are innate, is to disregard the phenomena of man's cultural evolution. For that idea has operated as the cornerstone and mainspring of cultural principles and values. From it the nature and destiny of man was derived, and spiritual and cultural values defined. And this basic idea of God, has been variously interpreted and understood, at different periods of human history, giving rise to different cultural systems of thought. There was, for example, the pagan and naturalistic definition of the nature of the deity, which identified it with the physical universe, with its two variants: the Platonic, which considered it as the universal Soul, transcendent to physical being; and the Aristotelian, which regarded it as the Form of all forms, and immanent in nature itself. There was also the pantheistic conception, which identified God even with physical elements. At the dawn of the Christian era there was a deification of the Emperor, as representative of the power and majesty of the Empire. Which of these ideas of God, we may ask, was innate

149

in man, was directly apprehended by him; and being clearly and distinctly defined, was true?

Jesus Christ said that no one knows the Father; which means that He is utterly undefinable, and hence, far from being a clear and distinct idea. And his mission was to combat the pagan conceptions, overcome them, and teach his own instead. Were it not for the mass conversion that followed, and the ascendancy of his idea of God; the pagan conceptions would have remained dominant, and the new spiritual and cultural era would have not dawned upon humanity. This historical fact proves that none of the conceptions of God, not even the abstract idea of God as a necessary Being, was innate in man; that humanity acquired the one which promised to be of supreme spiritual and cultural value, namely, the one offered by Jesus Christ.

Furthermore, man's cultural evolution is grounded mainly upon the gradual, and adequate, understanding of the basic conception of God. For, as we said, it is from that conception, that cultural values are derived. Therefore, the higher cultural values Christianity could offer, was due to the fact that it possessed a higher conception of God, and a more adequate means of establishing His will, and purpose for man, than contemporary pagan philosophies could offer. Had this conception been innate in man, as Descartes deemed it to be, there would have been no basic diversion between the Christian, and the pagan systems of thought, and cultural values. A certain basic similarity would have existed between them. In such a case there would be no ground for discarding the pagan, and embracing the Christian instead. And as a consequence there would have not been the regeneration effected through the latter.

In short, three principles can be deduced from the history of Christian culture: first, that the conception of an absolutely transcendent God, and of Jesus Christ as His sole intermediary and mouthpiece in that age, was not an idea ingrained and innate in the mind of contemporary man. Secondly, that it was a principle acquired and gradually implanted in the mind of those who embraced the Faith, and followed the teachings of the Gospel. Thirdly, that it was not a principle gradually reached

150

through experience and understanding; but imparted as part of a revelation of God, and in pursuance of a divine cultural purpose. In other words, the adequate idea of God, was given to man, not at the time of his physical birth, as Plato and Descartes believed; but as the initial step in man's spiritual and cultural training, and rebirth, which conversion necessarily implied.

10. DESCARTES' PROOF FOR THE EXISTENCE OF GOD: "It appears," he says, "that the existence can no more be separated from the essence of God than the idea of a mountain from that of a valley, or the equality of its three angles to two right angles, from the essence of a (rectilineal) triangle; so that it is not less impossible to conceive God, that is, a being supremely perfect, to whom existence is awanting, or who is devoid of a certain perfection." (1) Descartes started by defining God as a supreme and perfect Being. That perfection implied substantiality, and here, existence. But how can we define an unknowable reality; unless we identify it with the formal and intelligible, that is with a conception, or idea, in our mind. Only the knowable can be defined, and its forms determined. Only if God be considered supremely formal, can He be made subject to definition. Only in a rationalistic system of thought, which maintains the supremely intelligible, the supremely real; can God be defined. An unknowable creator cannot be defined. In a rationalistic system of thought, whether of the Platonic or Aristotelian type, which considers the intellectual and intelligible entities, as the supreme forms of reality, constituting its very substance, essence and nature, a transition from rational necessity of being, to an actual one, does not involve a gap, or necessitate a leap, which are unjustifiable. For both are deemed rational both immediate to the same consciousness. Ideal existence, in such a rationalistic system of thought, is identical with substantial existence. In other words, because the ideal is the supremely real, substantial and necessary; and the actual and physical, mere appearance or semblance of it; what possesses a rational

(1) Meditation V, by Descartes, tr. by J. Veitch.

151

being is fully objective and existent, even though it be only in thought.

But if we discard rationalism, and in the manner of revealed religion, consider God, and in fact the substance of all things, as beyond the realm of understanding, beyond the grasp of a mere "observer"; then rational existence would not entail, or be identical with, substantial existence. If thought be regarded as a mere accident of being, if it be one of the many forms of relatedness which prevail in nature, what is intelligible to man, might not actually exist, nor what is, be necessarily intelligible. Hence, in systems of thought other than rationalism, perfection cannot necessarily imply being. For example, the conception of a perfect triangle, in a rationalistic system of thought, is truly and substantially existent; while in an empirical system, it is not. It is in fact doubted whether a perfectly equilateral triangle is existent anywhere in nature; whether it is not a mere construction, existent only in thought.

The Skeptics, Deists and atheists, whom Descartes confronted, and whose views he tried to rebut, were not rationalists of the Platonic type, as he was. They were empiricists of the extreme order. And their point of view conformed, at least in this respect, more with that of revealed religion. For they also maintained that thought is an accident of being, and that the realm of subjective, rational existence, must be clearly distinguished from that of the positive, objective one. Descartes' view, therefore, that the idea of God as a perfect Being, entails the idea of absolute existence, can hold ground only in a rationalistic system of thought. It fails when the rationalistic premises are discarded; that is, when God is considered, not as the Universal Soul, and the Soul identified with Mind or Reason. It fails when the universe, including reason, is viewed "other than God," and therefore, as His creation.

11. ARE PROOFS FOR THE EXISTENCE OF GOD STRICTLY VALID? Proofs for the existence of God are based upon two assumptions, neither of which is acceptable by revealed religion, but are asserted only in pagan systems of thought.

First, the assumption that man is the measure of all things, of things that are, that they are; and of things that are not, that they are not. Secondly, that ultimate reality is essentially knowable.

Man, we have already observed, can assume before nature only the role of an observer; never of a creator. For nature is not man's handiwork, that he should grasp its substance and nature. His knowledge is limited to the appearance of things: to the relation that one reality bears towards another, to the functions and attributes they manifest. If such are the limitations of his understanding of nature; how can he claim that, with his own reasoning, he can establish the existence, nature and substance of that supreme Reality, of which he is a mere creature. Existence and non-existence, are attributes, or predicates, that define and set limits. How can the created, who is limited, define what is by its nature, unlimited; in fact, whose function in the universe is to set limits? Hence, to attempt to prove the existence of God, is to try and define Him, and set the limits of His nature. It is to assume the arrogant attitude, of acting as the measure of His existence and non-existence. And such a claim on the part of man, is utterly unjustified, if we follow the Bab, and say, that all other than God is His creation.

Naturalistic systems of thought, that identify God with Universal Soul, and consider the human soul as a microcosm, of the universe as the macrocosm, can upon the premise that, "like can know its like," maintain the legitimacy of proofs for the existence of God. For existence, and non-existence, are the least that such knowledge can provide. But when God is considered as creator of all other than Himself, and hence, utterly transcendent and inaccessible to human thought and being, no ground is left for such knowledge. For there would be neither formal nor numerical likeness between the two, to operate as basis of knowledge, even if the principle of "like knows its like," be admitted.

The second point to bear in mind, and which we seem to overlook, in demanding proofs for the existence of God, is that even Aristotle did not maintain that the efficient Cause of being is essentially knowable. And it was for that reason, and to make ultimate Reality knowable, that he tried to identify the efficient with the formal Cause. To undertake the proof of the existence of the efficient Cause, is to undertake the proof of the knowledge of the existence of a reality which is admittedly and essentially unknowable. And there is the fallacy of begging the question in advancing such a proof. For, if the efficient Cause or creator is unknowable to the created, His nature, substance and being are also unknowable. And it is fallacious to assume that intelligibility, and deduct from it existence, as Descartes does. What is knowable is the phenomenal operation of that reality not its noumeral being. Therefore, proof for the existence of God, turns out to be the proof for the existence of His revelation as formal Cause; that is of the efficient Cause after being identified with the formal Cause of man's spiritual and cultural life; of that reality which Plato identified with "the Good," and Aristotle with the Form of all forms; a Cause that is essentially knowable, and which, being formal, constitutes the supreme object of human knowledge and understanding. Aristotle considered the formal Cause the necessary, and in respect to it, he deemed all other beings as contingent. For the formal Cause was in act, what all other objects were in potency. In other words, what Aristotle in fact established was the existence of the supreme object of man's rational life. And in that process there was no logical gap to traverse, no occasion for a leap from the province of purely rational being, to that of objective existence, from what is deemed as rational necessity, to what is in fact. Aristotle's failure, was, like that of Plato before him, a failure to locate the sphere of operation of the formal cause, which was essentially spiritual and cultural; and also, a failure to designate the focal center of that Cause, which, to revealed religion, constitutes the self-revelation of God within the field of human understanding, namely, the divine nature revealed in the prophets, a failure characteristic of pagan thought as a whole.

12. REVELATION IS THE OUTSTANDING PROOF FOR GOD'S EXISTENCE: To an observer, appearance is the only

sign of the existence of reality. That is true in the sphere of natural phenomena; it is also true in the field of divine revelation. This is the reason why the Bab says that blessed are those who see nought, but the manifestation of God in all things. (1) We should, however, hasten to add that it is not God's substance and essence that we observe in all things, as pantheists claim; but the revelation of His Primal Purpose. For, according to the Bab, God creates the Primal Purpose, and the Primal Purpose, in turn, creates all other than Him.

But there are strata of being, upon all of which the Primal Purpose operates. There is the sphere of inanimate nature, that of plant and animal life, and also that of the spiritual and cultural development of man. In all, God's revelation is manifest to the discerning eye. The rays of His Primal Purpose radiate through all spheres of creation, but with different intensity and degrees of reflection. In all the different strata of being we observe the reign of His "law and order," which is the direct result of the operation of His Primal Purpose. (2) It is only the capacity of that object which determines the extent those rays of the Primal Purpose are received and reflected; reveal their divine illumination, and spread its light in turn upon the surrounding region.

Such being the case, the structure of every atom of dust, the growth of the tiniest weed, the nesting of every bird, proclaims the dominion of the Primal Purpose of God; but the supreme proof of His sovereignty and operation is the spiritual and cultural evolution of man. And in this sphere, the divine nature revealed in the prophets, operates as the channel, through which the Primal Purpose, pursues its highest creative activity. Should we examine the trend of human development "from the days of the first Adam, until the end for which there is no end," says the Bab, we shall observe that events bear witness of a great design, (3) with the perfection of man and his social order as its goal. And that design, followed by the Primal Purpose, is

(1) The Persian Bayan, by The Bab, 2:8.
(2) Ibid.
(3) Ibid.

155

proclaimed, and pursued, by the successive prophets that have appeared.(1) And, as the supreme revelation of the Primal Purpose, upon this plane of existence, is in the field of the spiritual and cultural life of man; it is from its operation there, that God's existence is best inferred. And as it is through the divine nature revealed in the prophets, that the Primal Purpose operates, it is through the attributes these reveal in their thought, words and deeds, that God's existence is verified. It is through their "appearance," that the existence of God's "reality" is proven.

When we look at the law and order which prevails in the universe, from the heart of an atom, through plant and animal life, to the spiritual and cultural development of man, the existence of God as a transcendent substance, is inferential; as inferential as the relation of a phenomenon is, to the reality it represents, in the sight of an "observer." But the operation of the Primal Purpose is manifest and distinct, especially when we consider it as revealed through the successive prophetic dispensations that history records, all serving the same spiritual and cultural purpose, all striving to lead man to individual and social perfection. And from adequate understanding of the reality and mission of these prophets, we can best attain certainty as to the nature of God, as prime Mover and creator of all things. If all things speak loud of the Primal Purpose of God, the spiritual and cultural evolution of mankind, throughout the ages, is the most commanding and convincing.

13. INTEGRATION IN NATURE IS SIGN OF A DOMINAT-ING CREATIVE PURPOSE: Creation, motion, generation are primary realities in a universe that is dynamic. Unchanging laws, and abstractions, are universal conceptions derived from such types of motion or activity. This is what Baha'u'llah meant when he stated that adjectives are derived from verbs. Attributes are modes of activity. Hence, the concept of creation is derived from the act of creating. We cannot attribute that supreme quality to God, if He were not eternally creating. Creation, therefore,

(1) The Persian Bayan, by The Bab, 2:8.

156

Baha'u'llah says, is an eternal process. It has had no beginning, and it will have no end.

In answer to Dr. August Forel, Abdu'l-Baha says: "Now, formation is of three kinds, and of three kinds only: accidental, necessary and voluntary (or purposeful). The coming together of the various constituent elements of beings cannot be accidental, for unto every effect there must be a cause. It cannot be compulsory (that is, through inner necessity), for then the formation must be an inherent property of the constituent parts, and the inherent property of a thing can in no wise be dissociated from it, such as light that is the revealer of things, heat that causes the expansion of elements and the (solar) rays which are the essential property of the sun. Thus under such circumstances the decomposition of any formation is impossible, for the inherent properties of a thing cannot be separated from it. The third formation remaineth and that is the voluntary (or purposeful) one, that is, an unseen force described as the Ancient Power, causeth these elements to come together, every formation giving rise to a distinct being."

Here, Abdu'l-Baha identifies the process of creation with that of integration, or generation, which we observe in nature and in the spiritual and cultural life of man. The process, he says, cannot be accidental, because in a universe of constant integration and disintegration, there is no place for accidents. These two forces have to be balanced; or rather, integration should be dominant, if the universe is to last or evolve, if the formless is to obtain form. Hence, there should be a purposeful cause dominating its operation. Furthermore, this cause cannot be considered as inherent, or immanent, in nature itself, as a constituent element of it; because in that case disintegration will cease, and the result will be a block universe. For, through the process of disintegration; we obtain formless matter, for further integration. The only alternative remaining, is that the cause of this integration is a power, or purpose, that transcends nature and dominates its motion. And we term that force the Primal Purpose of God.

Should we take this notion of creation, that is, as purposeful

157

generation, or integration; we find being formed into a hierarchy starting with physical objects, proceeding through plant and animal life, and ending in man; with his spiritual and cultural evolution, as the supreme form of generation and integration. In fact, we find all other created things, serving the interests of this last type of formation. It is, therefore, the existence of the Unmoved Mover, of the spiritual and cultural evolution of man, which constitutes the supreme quest of religion and theology, as well as philosophy. And this Unmoved Mover is what Plato sought, and termed "the God"; and Aristotle identified with the Form or all forms. It is the existence of this reality that he tried to establish as culmination of all his thought. To both, this Unmoved Mover, was the Formal Cause of the spiritual and cultural life of man. But being pagan, neither could locate it, either really or historically. But any proof for a theistic, as contrasted to a deistic, God; is bound to be a proof for the objective veracity of the Primal Purpose of God, as expressed through the divine nature revealed in the prophets.

14. THE EMPIRICAL APPROACH TO THE EXISTENCE OF GOD: We have observed that Descartes' proof for the existence of God, which he based upon the Platonic doctrine of innate ideas, failed because there are no such innate ideas in man. The idea of God, like any other idea, is acquired by man through the gradual process of cultural development, and growth of understanding. He acquires it as part of his conversion to the spiritual and cultural life; and makes it the ground of his intellectual approach and interpretation of things. Descartes' proof stands upon premises that the idealistic system of Plato assumes. It is only within that context that it possesses some significance. Should we discard that system of philosophy, and set aside its premises; we will have to deny the efficacy of that proof as well. And that is exactly what Thomas Aquinas was led to do, when he discarded the Platonic, and adopted the Aristotelian system of thought. The doctrine of innate ideas was discordant with his principle that knowledge is derived from sense-perception; and

therefore, he discarded it, and together with it, the proof of the existence of God based upon it.

But the empirical system of Aristotle also failed to inspire certainty, establish the theistic doctrine, and discern the source from which God's attributes of perfection are derived. A conception of God, based upon purely cosmological considerations, led logically to an unmoved Mover; but such a near notion, of an ultimate Efficient Cause of being, could not have spiritual and cultural value and significance. It presents mere bone, stripped of flesh, blood, life and beauty. It needs attributes of perfection, to satisfy spiritual and cultural needs of man, and become an object of contemplation and humble worship. And in that respect, the empirical cosmological proof for the existence of God, if taken alone, fails lamentably. Plato and Aristotle were conscious of that fact, and therefore, sought to identify God with "the Good," and with the "Form" of all forms; that is, with the source of the attributes of perfection, which constitute the highest object of contemplation and love. Neither the ontological, nor the cosmological, proof of the existence of God, could establish these attributes of perfection, without leaving a yawning gap between, logical necessity and rational requirement, on the one hand, and positive objective existence of the same, on the other; a gap which philosophy, to the present day, deems unjustified to leap over and traverse. Abdu'l-Baha refers to these perfections when he says in his letter to Dr. A. Forel, "As to the attributes and perfections such as will, knowledge, power and other ancient attributes that we ascribe to that Divine Reality, these are the signs that reflect the existence of beings in the visible plane and not the absolute perfections of the Divine Essence that cannot be comprehended."

Does this mean that there can be no proof for the existence of a God, as Efficient Cause of being, that would establish the theistic doctrine as well, and satisfy cultural and spiritual requirements? Neither of the two basic pagan systems of philosophy, in fact, no pagan system, which sidesteps the principle of revelation, as advocated, for example, by the Gospel and the Koran, can establish adequately the existence of God as "the

159

Good," and the Form of all forms. For it is only through revelation that God's being, as well as attributes of perfection, become objects of empirical understanding and contemplation. Thomas Aquinas was fully justified in reasoning from the motion he observed in nature, to the Prime Mover as a Cause; but such a prime Mover must at the same time be formal. What Thomas Aquinas, and Descartes, considered as divine attributes of perfection, they are what we have termed spiritual and cultural values. Just as much as physical and natural processes are objects of empirical understanding; so must truth, goodness, justice and beauty be. They are all objects of sense experience and contemplation; for they are all forms, types of behavior, classes of objects, appearances and phenomena. The problem is to discover the Prime Mover of cultural values as well; these forms of human behavior, and thought, which we universalize and conceptualize into values which we term attributes of perfection, contemplate, love and desire to acquire.

15. THE NEGATIVE ARGUMENT FOR THEISM: To establish the perfections, generally attributed to God as efficient Cause of all things, including the spiritual and cultural life, theists have been wont to use a negative form of argument. In answer to Dr. A. Forel, Abdu'l-Baha states it as follows: "For instance," he says, "as we consider created things we observe infinite perfections, and the created things being in the utmost regularity and perfection we infer that the Ancient Power on whom dependeth the existence of these beings, cannot be ignorant; thus we say He is All-Knowing. It is certain that it is not impotent, it must be All-Powerful; it is not poor; it must be All-Possessing; it is not non-existent, it must be Ever-Living. The purpose is to show, that these attributes and perfections, that we recount for that Universal Reality, are only in order to deny imperfections, rather than to assert the perfections that the human mind can conceive. Thus we say His attributes are unknowable."

In this form, the negative argument for theism, if applied to the efficient Cause of being, leads necessarily to anthropomorphism, which is unacceptable to modern thought. In fact, it has acted as a stumbling block to its approach to the theistic outlook. For it entails a rational construction of a God, that would conform to ideals which man entertains, and represents perfections he imagines in the light of his own shortcomings. It constitutes the creation of a God, that would assume the image of a perfect man; and imposes upon that unknowable reality, characteristics which are essentially human. But there is also a positive lesson to be derived from this negative argument. For it establishes the indispensable need for a formal Cause of man's spiritual and cultural evolution. It stresses the requirement of a rational system of thought, for a reality which possesses in full actuality, the perfections man can possibly conceive as goal, and which he has to visualize, before attempting to attain it. In other words, the negative argument for theism shows the need of man for a God that personifies supreme humanity, and embodies the perfections which are indispensable for man's spiritual and cultural evolution, upon this sphere of existence. And this God, is the Formal Cause, which both Plato and Aristotle earnestly sought, but only revealed religion could designate objectively and historically.

16. THE HUMAN NATURE OF THE PROPHETS ACTS AS THE MIRROR WHICH REFLECTS THE FORMAL CAUSE: We have already observed how Aristotle identified the Efficient with the Formal Cause of all motion; and conceived God as the "Form" of all forms, or the supreme "Good." He thus attempted to make God, the highest and purest object of human knowledge and understanding. He considered that ultimate reality to be the most knowable, on the ground that it is fully formal, that it constitutes pure idea, undefiled by unintelligible matter. Descartes follows this rationalistic conception, when he maintains that the idea of God, is innate in man; for that implies that He is knowable and intelligible. But he adds that, if man fails to know Him adequately, it is only because he is handicapped by his physical senses, that is, by the element of matter, which resides in his body, and distorts the activity of his soul.

161

To try and explain the reason for the limitations of human understanding; on the ground that the physical senses detain, and distort the operation of thought; makes the former a source of evil and a handicap; and thereby weakens the case of the Formal Cause, which is the supreme object of human understanding, both intelligible and sensible. For, the Formal Cause does not impart only ideas and forms. Jesus, for example, did not only impress his disciples with new forms of belief, and conduct. He did not only say "Blessed are the meek: for they shall inherit the earth," as a supreme principle of conduct; or "Be ye therefore perfect, even as your Father which is in heaven is perfect"; as an ideal state of individual being; or "But seek ye first the kingdom of God, and his righteousness; and all these things shall be added unto you," as a future state, of universal human brotherhood, where perfect peace and security will reign. Jesus did not only inculcate in the mind of his disciples, such universal moral and social forms of being, to recast their spiritual and cultural life, and remould their thought. He also exemplified them in his deeds, and manner of behavior. Besides acting as source of "Truth"; he also played the role of an "exemplar." He lived the life, as an individual substrate of the divine perfections, to become the supreme object of sense perception as well. His disciples heard his voice saying these things; saw him practice meekness, sit with the humble, treat the sick. They felt the warmth of his love, as well as his dominant personality. As an "exemplary," Jesus was the supreme object of human contemplation, and his deeds, of positive sense perception. In other words, the divine nature in him, revealed itself within the field of human individual sense perception. And that constituted a positive divine "Presence," concrete and objective, for all humanity to contemplate. As such, Jesus Christ constituted the Formal Cause of human perfection, individual and social. He revealed the forms, human life should take, to attain its destiny. If the Jews failed to recognize that divine "Presence," it was because of pride and prejudice, or distorted notions of the spiritual life, which dominated their thought. For these conceptions misinterpreted the deeds they perceived. The evil resided, not in

162

sense perception, but in the distorted notions that the Jews, during that period of their history, possessed.

The flaw in Aristotle's principle of teleology, which Descartes assailed, was that he maintained the immanence of forms, as potential in all things. If the difference between God, the human soul, and nature, was not qualitative and formal, but quantitative and numerical; then forms were immanent in all things, seeking actualization and expression, as a seed seeks to unravel its characteristics in the form of a tree. It is this conception of potentiality and immanence, that vitiated the dynamism of Aristotle, and rendered his teleology inacceptable to Descartes. But Descartes erred when he also denied its existence as a transcendent dynamic force, as a "revelation" of the Efficient Cause, imposing upon matter, characteristics it contained, and could impart: imposing its forms, to raise that concrete individual object to the level of its own being and likeness. And that transcendent nature of the Formal Cause, and its effect, is best expressed in the spiritual and cultural life of man. For it is manifestly expressed in the role of the prophets.

17. THE CLAIM OF JESUS AND MOHAMMED TO BE THE FORMAL CAUSE OF MAN'S SPIRITUAL AND CULTURAL LIFE: Jesus was referring to God, the Father, as the Efficient Cause of all being, and of the spiritual and cultural life of man, when he said: "There is none good but one, that is God."(1) Similarly the Koran is explicit in saying: "God! There is no God but He! His are the most excellent names."(2) Attributes of perfection all proceed from God as their ultimate source, but they are revealed through the divine nature of the prophets, such as Jesus and Mohammed. This nature which is the Primal Purpose, acts as the prism through which the simple light of God projects itself to manifest its many hues and beauty; that is, it projects itself, to reveal those attributes of perfection, in a manner human understanding can fully grasp and even sensually detect.

(1) Luke 18:19.
(2) Koran 20:8.

163

These two principles, namely, that all attributes of perfection proceed from God, the Father, as their ultimate source; and that the prophets stand to humanity as their supreme exemplars, establish the doctrine that God is the ultimate Efficient Cause, and the divine nature revealed in the prophets, the immediate Formal Cause of man's spiritual and cultural life. For the principle of exemplary, which is applicable to both Jesus and Mohammed, and which they both claimed to represent, involves the conception of formal cause. It is along this trend of thought that Jesus said: "All things are delivered to me of my Father: and no man knoweth who the Son is, but the Father; and who the Father is, but the Son and he to whom the Son will reveal him."(1) "I am the way," he said. "the truth and the life, no man cometh unto the Father, but by me."(2) The Father as Efficient Cause could not be the object of human understanding; and hence, act as direct source of man's spiritual and cultural life. Jesus and Mohammed, as revealations of the divine nature, within the realm of human understanding, could fulfill that task.

What were the parables of Jesus except supreme principles, forms and values, regarding the nature of the Kingdom of God to be established on earth, put in contexts that were matter of fact, and empirically verifiable. In other words, the thought, words and deeds of Jesus, were revelations of his Father's wisdom, goodness, justice and beauty; which in their absolute essence transcended human thought, and hence, could not become the means of man's spiritual and cultural development. Social justice demands positive understanding, on the part of man, of the divine will and purpose. It necessitates an intellectual grasp of the basic principles necessary for the establishment of the Kingdom, or City, of God upon the earth. And such an understanding needs positive exposition. An unknowable Efficient Cause, such as the Father was represented to be, cannot make man visualize beauty, and thus inspire him to construct an adequate aesthetic life, truly uplifting to his soul. But the personality, the loving ways, and the gracious deeds performed by Jesus accomplished that cultural

(1) Luke 10:22.
(2) John 14:6.

164

task. It recasted Roman aesthetic life, to serve spiritual ends. Jesus set a formal standard of beauty which became an object of visual contemplation, and a source of inspiration that commanded a worshipful attitude on the part of the Christians for centuries to come. All these basic elements of culture could be generated by the Father as the Efficient Cause, only through the process of revelation, of a Formal Cause, such as the mission of Jesus Christ. For only as such could they become the object of positive human understanding, and empirical experience.

18. THE KORAN AS THE FORMAL CAUSE OF MAN'S SPIRITUAL AND CULTURAL LIFE: Islam appeared soon after the great religious wars, Justinian waged against the Vandals and Goths; for their professed Arianism, which had spread over the major part of Western Europe and North Africa, had disrupted the unity of his Christian empire. The divinity of Christ was the main point of contention of the Church, with this heretical sect, which had appeared in Christianity. The controversy, and the armed conflict which resulted, had caused much bloodshed, and considerable devastation of previously flourishing cities and populated countryside. The purely intellectual controversy, had ended by establishing the identity of Christ with God the Father; and attributing to them the same substance and nature, though admitting their separate personality. But that solution remained unclear in many minds; and seemed mysterious in nature, and enigmatic. The object of the Koran was to avoid confusion on such a basic principle, and therefore, distinguished clearly between the human and the divine natures, resident in the prophet; both of which are essential to render him a mediator between God and mankind, and an exemplary of His attributes. The Koran, therefore, denied that Jesus was the Son of God in a physical sense—as the masses generally considered him to be— and stressed instead, that he was "the spirit of God"; which can neither be physically born, or give birth. Mohammed tried to avoid the appearance of such a controversy in Islam, by stressing the difference between his own human person, and the Koran, as the revelation of God to him, a mere messenger to mankind.

165

Of himself he says: "I am a man like you. Revelation comes to me." (1) Elsewhere he says: "It is He who sent, of the illiterate, an apostle from among their numbers, to read to them His verses, purify them, and teach them the Book and Wisdom." (2) Thus, to avoid the controversies that broke asunder the ranks, and killed the spirit, of Christianity; Mohammed admits his humanity, and lays his stress on the Koran as the divine revelation imparted to him. The Koran, which was in fact his literary production, he attributes to God as source of its revelation; and presents it as the Formal Cause of man's spiritual and cultural advancement.

"The Merciful," he says, "taught the Koran, created man, and imparted to him speech." (3) In other words, the "merciful" God, "taught" him the Koran, that he may thereby "create" mankind, and regenerate it spiritually and culturally. "We have revealed it," he says, "as a Koran in Arabic, that you might grow in reasoning." (4) Further he says: "These verses of the Book, revealed to you by your Lord, are truth." (5) "This Book we have revealed to you," God is made to say, "that you may bring man, out of darkness, into light." (6) "This Book (imparts) insight to man, and guidance and mercy to people of certainty." (7)

Mohammed does not, however, limit that revelation of divine Wisdom to his own message and dispensation. For "Wisdom" is revelation imparted to all the prophets down the ages. And bearing that message, and revelation, these constitute, each in his own age, the source of spiritual and cultural life. To put it in our own terminology: they all constitute the Formal Cause of man's cultural evolution.

These were not idle claims, made by Jesus and Mohammed. The Gospel and the Koran, each in turn, created a cultural revival of, what we have termed, perennial religion; by reanimating its spirit, reasserting its divine purpose, and regenerating its forms and values. These sacred Scriptures, which were revealed by

(1) Koran 41:6.
(2) Ibid.
(3) Ibid. 55:1.
(4) Ibid. 12:2
(5) Ibid. 13:1.
(6) Ibid. 14:1.
(7) Ibid. 45:20.

God, through these successive prophets, became in fact the source of the basic values man needed to reestablish his culture upon firm, healthy, and spiritual foundations. The wisdom they contained became the basic truths regarding the nature and destiny of man, that thinkers gradually adopted, as primary premises of their thought. Their ethical precepts became the foundation of the moral life of man for ages to come, and set the norms of his conduct. The conception of a universalistic society, where social, racial, national and class distinctions were to be set aside, became the "City of God," or "City of Peace" they visualized, and ardently tried to further throughout the world. The Koran was considered even in style, and rhythm, an object of beauty; and a source of inspiration for later poets, writers and stylists. In short, Plato and Aristotle sought a God that would be the supreme Good, and the Form of all forms. Jesus and Mohammed, with the Gospel and the Koran, fulfilled that function in man's cultural history. This constitutes an empirical fact that history can verify.

19. BAHA'U'LLAH ON THE PROPHETS AS THE FORMAL CAUSE OF MAN'S SPIRITUAL AND CULTURAL EVOLUTION: Baha'u'llah is still more explicit in affirming this principle; namely, that God as Efficient Cause of being, and the ultimate creator of man's spiritual and cultural life, is absolutely unknowable; that He cannot, therefore, be directly apprehended, either as object of human knowledge, or intuition; that He is unknowable even as regards His unity and being. Hence, that attributes we ascribe to Him, and consider divine, are one and all, qualities we find positively reflected in the life and teachings of the prophets; who are His revelations, and therefore, predicable to them alone. And such revelation of the divine attributes through them, renders them the "Good," and the "Form of all forms," philosophy has been diligently seeking, ever since Socrates directed his attention and interest, away from physical nature, to the moral, intellectual, social and aesthetic life of man.

"For man's apprehension of Thee," Baha'u'llah says, "is but the apprehension of Thine own creation; how can it reach up to

Thee? And all human praise and glorification of Thee pertain unto Thy servants; how can they be deemed worthy of the court of Thy oneness?" (1) "The glory of Thy might beareth me witness! Whoso claimeth to have known Thee hath, by virtue of such a claim, testified to his own ignorance; and whoso believeth himself to have attained Thee, all the atoms of the earth would attest his powerlessness and proclaim his failure." (2) In other words, knowledge, and hence, praise can strictly speaking, be directed only to what is intelligible, and not to the Efficient Cause, who is absolutely inaccessible to human understanding. An absolutely transcendent reality cannot be the object of intelligent praise on the part of man.

Referring to the prophets, Baha'u'llah says: "Al praise be to Thee, O Lord, my God! I know not how to sing Thy praise, how to describe Thy Glory, how to call upon Thy name. If I call upon Thee by Thy Name, the All-Possessing, I am compelled to recognize that He Who holdeth in His hand the immediate destinies of all created things (i.e. the prophet) is but a vassal dependent upon Thee, and is the creation of but a word proceeding from Thy mouth. And if I proclaim Thee by the name of Him Who is the All-Compelling, I readily discover that He is but a suppliant fallen upon the dust, awe-stricken by Thy dreadful might, Thy sovereignty and power. And if I attempt to describe Thee by glorifying the oneness of Thy Being, I soon realize that such a conception is but a notion which mine own fancy hath woven, and that Thou hast ever been immeasurably exalted above the vain imaginations which the hearts of men have devised." (3) Thus all the attributes of perfection predicated of God, are characteristics prophets reveal; and in virtue of that function, in the process of human creation and recreation, they can be considered the Formal Cause of man's spiritual and cultural development.

Baha'u'llah goes further and stresses, that through their creative work, and their operation as Formal Cause of human evolution,

(1) Prayers and Meditations of Baha'u'llah, tr. by Shoghi Effendi, p. 222.
(2) Ibid. p. 123.
(3) Ibid.

that is, in revealing God's purpose and attributes of perfection, these prophets bear witness that they are in substance and origin divine. In other words, it is through the revelation of the prophets that the theistic theses can be vindicated. In one of his prayers he says: "Praised be Thou, O Lord my God! I supplicate Thee by him Whom Thou hast called into being, Whose Revelation Thou hast ordained to be Thine own Revelation and His Concealment Thine own Concealment. Through His Firstness Thou hast confirmed Thine own Firstness, and through His Lastness Thou hast affirmed Thine own Lastness. Through the power of His might and the influence of His sovereignty the mighty have apprehended Thine omnipotence, and through His glory they who are endowed with authority have acknowledged Thy majesty and greatness. Through His supreme ascendancy Thy transcendent sovereignty and all-encompassing dominion have been recognized, and through His will Thine own will hath been revealed. Through the light of His countenance the splendors of Thine own face have shone forth, and through His Cause Thine own Cause hath been made manifest. Through the generative power of His utterance the whole earth hath been made the recipient of the wondrous signs and tokens of sovereignty, and the heavens have been filled with the revelations of Thine incomparable majesty, and the seas have been enriched with the sacred pearls of Thine omniscience and wisdom, and the trees adorned with the fruits of Thy knowledge. Through Him all things have sung Thy praise, and all the eyes have been turned in the direction of Thy mercy. Through Him the faces of all have been set towards the splendours of the light of Thy countenance, and the souls of all have been inclined unto the revelations of Thy divine greatness."

"How great is Thy power! How exalted Thy sovereignty! How lofty Thy might! How excellent Thy majesty! How supreme is Thy grandeur—a grandeur which He Who is Thy manifestation hath made known and wherewith Thou hast invested Him as a sign of Thy generosity and bountiful favour. . . ."(1)

(1) Prayers and Meditations of Baha'u'llah, tr. by Shoghi Effendi, p. 294.

The gist of this whole reasoning is, what we observe the Bab say, namely that God, the divine Essence, generated the Primal Purpose; and the Primal Purpose in turn created all other things, including the spiritual and cultural life of man. And this Primal Purpose is none other than the divine nature revealed in the prophets. This constitutes the Formal Cause of being, the existence of which Descartes denied. And naturally the far-reaching results of this divergence of view will become clear, when we shall deal with the spiritual and cultural life, and the extent to which it is free, rational and purposeful.

Chapter
V

THE REALITY AND DESTINY OF MAN

1. THE NATURE AND DESTINY OF THE SOUL ACCORD-
ING TO PLATO: In Timaeus, Plato says that when God, as
creator desires to create, "He looks to the unchangeable and
fashions the form and nature of His work after an unchangeable
pattern." Because His pattern is unchangeable, His creation is
"fair and perfect." Had He looked to a "created pattern," His
creation would not have been "fair and perfect."(1) For were
that pattern of the type that would change, it would have entailed
the imperfection of His creation, and failed to produce that
perfect, and fair, being that He desired to produce. Plato was a
rationalist, with unchanging Ideas, in the nature of mathematical
formulas, acting as the ideal type of being. He considered all
other objects, which are subject to constant and necessary change,
as devoid of that perfect type of existence. Being subject to
change, they lacked even that stability and permanence which
true knowledge and understanding require from their object.
Hence, they are not, strictly speaking, real; and constitute objects
of mere opinion. The physical body of man is in the nature of the
latter; his soul of the former. Hence, the soul, which Plato
identifies with mind or reason, is perfect and unchanging, seeking
in turn the unchanging ideas in its environment, as the true and
real objects of knowledge and understanding.

Because Plato conceived the soul to be perfect, and unchanging;
he was led to the belief that all ideas are innate, and knowledge
a mere recollection. As we have already observed, he regarded
these Ideas as inborn, moulded in the fabric of the soul at the

(1) Timaeus, by Plato, 28.

time of its creation. Thus, in his system, perfection, unchangingness and innatism, constitute essential attributes of the soul, and logically, these imply one another.

This perfect and unchanging soul, which contains all ideas innately, was, according to Plato, the dominating reality in man. It was represented as the master of all passions and desires, curbing the will, and controlling all the activities of the body, as an unmoved mover. Its role was likened to that of a captain, or pilot, guiding his ship through the sea of life. The pilot is not part of the boat, but its master, guiding its course and destiny. Should the ship be struck by the hands of adversity and destroyed, the captain would survive. Similarly, when the body of man perishes and disintegrates; and his physical powers are gone, the soul remains. In fact, it is delivered thereby from the world of constant change, and deception, and enters a realm where all things are abiding, perfect, and eternally unchanging.

Such a conception of the soul, leaves little scope for its development, and evolution, and constant regeneration. According to Plato's metaphysics, the human soul is a microcosm, representing the universal Soul, as the macrocosm. It is in fact, a segment or particle of the latter; differing from it, not in form, in attributes, and characteristics, but only in magnitude. It proceeds from the universal Soul, which is God, not in the form of generation, and as an individual, coming from non-existence into being, the product of a transcendent will, and creative purpose; but as the result of division or fission, as a segment of a line is cut from one which is infinite in extension. And being initially the product of mere division, there is no ground for the soul to acquire new forms to be regenerated, to rejoin the universal Soul. Its destiny, therefore, is in reversing the process of division, through which it was separated from the universal Soul; and following the process of addition, discarding thereby its individuality and identity; as a drop loses them, when merged in the ocean.

2. THE NATURE AND DESTINY OF THE SOUL ACCORDING TO ARISTOTLE: In his Anima, Aristotle distinguishes between two possible forms of motion: essential and accidental.

He also divides it into four species of motion, namely, in space, quality, that is, alteration, and then diminution or augmentation.(1) None of these essential species of motion, Aristotle argues, can be properly applied to the soul. The only form of motion, to which it can be subjected is the accidental, and that is due to an external cause. "Supposing the soul to be moved at all, one would say that sensible things would be the most likely to move it."(2) This principle can be considered as the basis of his empiricism, and the ground for justifying sense-perception. But sense-perception, according to him, cannot be considered as moving the essence of the soul. The motion it effects is, therefore, bound to be accidental, and of a temporary nature.

Thus, if Plato considered the soul as an unmoved mover, and likened it to a pilot, who directs the course of a ship, but is himself unmoved by it; Aristotle compares it to the sailor who, though he does not move himself, that is essentially, in respect of his quality, quantity or in space, yet he is carried along accidentally by the boat from one place to another. In other words, Aristotle, like Plato, cannot envisage any essential motion for the soul; of the type he terms "qualitative," and which is formal, in a manner as to modify its nature. And this attitude, as we shall observe, is due to the rationalistic trend of his system of thought, which he inherited from Plato.

Aristotle says that, "by the soul of the universe Timaeus clearly intends something of the same sort as what is known as Mind."(3) In other words, he admits that Plato considered Mind, as the supreme reality in the universe. It is along the same line that he himself proceeds, when he identifies the soul with the intellectual faculty of man. "The soul," he says, "is that whereby primarily we live, perceive, and have understanding: therefore it will be a species of notion or form, not matter or substratum."(4) There are, he says, three possible applications for the term "substance." It might be taken to apply to form, or to matter, or to the individual composed of matter and form. It is to form,

(1) Aristotle's De Anima, by R. D. Hicks, p. 21.
(2) Ibid. p. 23.
(3) Ibid. p. 25.
(4) Ibid. p. 57.

that Aristotle, as a rationalist, attributes priority in substantiality; and that on the ground that it constitutes the actuality of the body. The "soul is substance in the sense that it is the form of a natural body having in it the capacity of life. Such substance is actuality."(1) He then compares the soul to an axe and says, that just as "axiety" applies to the notion of an axe, so does the term "soul" apply to the notion of the living body of man as an individual being. "It would appear that in most cases soul neither acts nor is acted upon apart from the body. . . . Thought, if anything, would seem to be peculiar of the soul. Yet, if thought is a sort of imagination, or not independent of imagination, it will follow that even thought cannot be independent of the body."(2) Furthermore, all qualities we attribute to man, constitute notions, and hence, are identical with the soul. "So, too, the attributes of the soul appear to be all conjoined with body: such attributes, viz. as anger, mildness, fear, pity, courage; also joy love and hate; all of which are attended by some particular affection of the body. . . . If this be so, the attributes are evidently forms or notions realized in matter."(3)

In other words, Aristotle, like Plato, considered the soul as an intellectual, and intelligible, notion or idea; and as such, unchanging; but he differed from his master in considering it immanent in the body. And on the ground of this principle of immanence, he considered the soul as moving with the body; rather than merely directing its course as an unmoved mover, which is essentially separate, and transcendent. Being a type of intellectual notion, a sort of formula, according to which the body of man is composed and functions, it is necessarily unchanging. "It is quite impossible for the soul to have the attribute of motion at all,"(4) he says. It is as impossible, as it is for a formula to change, and still represent a certain composition. And that was the result of his rationalistic interpretation of the reality of man; a rationalism which desires to have all reality unchanging, and the object of knowledge and understanding.

(1) Ibid. p. 49.
(2) Ibid. p. 7.
(3) Ibid.
(4) Ibid.

But the rationalism of Aristotle had to provide a logical ground for his empiricism. Hence, he does not hold firmly to the immobility of the soul; he leaves ground for an exception, namely, that accidental type of motion which results from contact with external forces, such as the action of the environment upon the senses. In other words, he does not conceive the soul, as Plato did, that is, absolutely separate, dominating and controlling the body and the senses; but considered it to be affected by them, though accidentally. And this susceptibility to outside stimuli, gave rise to his conception of "capacity" in contrast to "potentiality."

3. THE SOUL AS A CAPACITY: Unlike Plato, Aristotle regards the soul, not as the source of all possible ideas and forms; but as a container in which notions can be gradually gathered and preserved. "It has no other nature than this, that it is a capacity. Thus, then, the part of the soul which we call intellect (and by intellect I mean that whereby the soul thinks and conceives) is nothing at all actually before it thinks. . . . Therefore, it has been well said that the soul is a place of forms or ideas."(1)

This further notion of the soul, as "capacity" to receive and retain forms, or ideas; was the ground on which Aristotle distinguished between the two meanings of potentiality. When Plato was trying to prove that, ideas are inborn in the mind of even an untutored slaveboy, he used the example of mathematical truths, and tried to show that they are not acquired, but innate, and merely recollected to become actualized, as the occasion for their use arose. In other words, that they were potentially, already existent in the mind of the boy, that is, were dormant; and had merely to be recollected to become actual. Aristotle considers this to be only one meaning for the term potential. But there is another, which he considered more applicable to his own system of thought, and satisfied better the needs of his empiricism, such as when, we say that such a matter has the "capacity," or characteristics necessary to assume such a form, or the mind

(1) Aristotle's De Anima, by R. D. Hicks, p. 131.

has the "capability" to receive, and contain, such a mathematical notion or idea. A piece of wax for example, does not possess all possible impressions; but it is said to have the "capacity," or ability, to receive and preserve a form, stamped on it.

4. BEING IMMANENT IN IT, THE SOUL PERISHES WITH THE BODY: Aristotle discarded the Platonic conception that the soul is separate and transcendent to the body: moving the latter, but unmoved by it, containing in itself as potentiality all forms and ideas. Instead, he advocated the empirical principle, that though essentially the soul is unmoved, accidentally it is, by different affections gathered through sense perception. It is hence, a "capacity" receiving and storing notions and ideas; acting as form of the body and inseparable from it. But in identifying the soul with the body as its form, and considering it not separate, but immanent in the latter; Aristotle subjected it to the same fate; unable to survive its death and disintegration. "But reasoning, love and hatred," he says, "are not attributes of the thinking faculty but of its individual possessor, in so far as he possesses it. Hence when this possessor perishes, there is neither memory nor love: for these never did belong to the thinking faculty, but to the composite whole which has perished, while the intellect is doubtless a thing more divine and is impassive." (1)

As a rationalist, however, Aristotle had to consider the soul, which he identified with mind, as part of universal Reason or God. Hence, he could not consider it as subject to motion and affection. But when individualized; and as such, was the form of a specific body, the soul would be subject, and be moved accidentally by them, and thereby act as mere "capacity." With the destruction of the body, which is the ground, and reason, for that individuality and separation, all affections, resulting from accidental motion, would cease; while the soul as a mere particle of the universal Soul or Reason would abide.

Thus, the memory of all things we have accumulated through knowledge and understanding: the faculty of love we have developed gradually in life, the many attributes of perfection that

(1) Aristotle's De Anima, by R. D. Hicks, p. 33.

we have painstakingly acquired, the sense of justice, goodness and beauty we have developed as the result of constant, diligent and repeated practice, and in pursuit of an aim and ideal—all these come to nought when we enter the grave, and our body disintegrates. In other words, according to Aristotle, there is no qualitative movement in the nature of man; which is abiding. There is no ground for a transmutation of the individual, his rebirth and regeneration. There is no destiny of which his life, with its strife and suffering, is a mere prelude and preparation.

When the human soul is considered as an unmoved mover, as Plato conceived it to be; or a reality that is moved only accidentally, and not essentially, and ceases to exist when separated and abstracted from the body, of which it constitutes a mere form, as Aristotle deemed it to be; in such cases what room, what ground of justification, is left for individual cultural and spiritual development, which is of an abiding nature? If no field for further progress is left, as with the former; or no possibility of essential motion, as in the system of the latter; how can there be a scope for spiritual and cultural growth? In the one case there is no lack of divine characteristics which remain to be acquired; in the other no possibility of qualitative change, in the very essence and nature of the individual. Furthermore, if, as with Aristotle, the soul is so intricately bound to the body of the individual, then what is its destiny, what constitutes the purpose of its being: the fruit of its arduous labor during a life-time? Is the spirit of man, the accomplishments and characteristics it acquires on earth all like the foliage of a tree which falls and disintegrates, merely to provide humus and enrich the soil, for future growth of plant life in general? Is there no sanctity in the individual man, to justify the survival of his soul as an abiding entity? In that case, what is the object of the spiritual and cultural life, why should man not remain on the plane of bare physical nature, give way to its lures, and partake of its pleasures?

5. THE DOCTRINE OF THE ACTIVE INTELLECT OF ARISTOTLE: Not only "love and hate," but also "reasoning,"

is considered by Aristotle as an attribute of the individual, in respect of which he acts as a "capacity." And this passivity, which "capacity" implies, necessitates an active intellect. For with every passivity there should be an active agent. Feeling this logical implication of his system of thought, Aristotle maintains that to this passive receptive individual intellect, there is an active one. "As in the whole nature," he says, "to something which serves as matter for each kind (and this is potentially all the members of the kind) there corresponds something else which is the cause or agent because it makes them all, the two being related to one another as art to its material, of necessity these differences must be found also in the soul. And to the one intellect, which answers to this description because it becomes all things, corresponds the other because it makes all things, like a sort of definite quality such as light. For in a manner light, too, converts colors which are potential into actual colors. And it is this intellect which is separable and impassive and unmixed, being in its essential nature an activity. For that which acts is always superior to that which is acted upon, the cause or principle to the matter." (1) Thus, Aristotle considers this active intellect, which we may identify with his universal Reason, and which is in the nature of Plato's "Good," the source of illumination to man's individual understanding. Just as light brings out the color of things, so does the illumination, shed by that active intellect, actualize the potentialities hidden in the human soul, and reveal the significance of facts, experience detects in nature. But neither Plato, nor Aristotle, states that this active Reason logically implies a transcendent God, or reality, of which it is a mere function, as Socrates did in his apology. In other words, neither identifies the active Reason with the Primal Purpose as source of illumination.

6. "POTENTIALITY," "ACTUALITY," AND "CAPACITY," IN THE LIGHT OF REVEALED RELIGION: We shall observe in the sequel, when dealing with the Bab, and Baha'u'llah's point of view, regarding the reality and destiny of man, that what both

(1) Aristotle's De Anima, by R. D. Hicks, p. 135.

systems of thought—the Platonic and the Aristotelian—lacked, to render them objectively significant, and hence, of cultural value; adequate understanding of the principle of revelation, and the location of its center of illumination, namely, the prophet of God in their age. We shall observe that the two conceptions of "potentiality" and "capacity," differentiated by Aristotle in De Anima, are not contradictory, as they may seem superficially; but rather, that they are fully complementary, and in fact, interdependent; to provide the ground for the spiritual and cultural evolution of man. Furthermore, we shall observe that Plato's principle of unmoved mover, and of innate ideas, of potential wisdom which needs merely the occasion, to be recollected and made actual; acquires spiritual and cultural value, when applied, not to the individual human soul, but to the divine nature revealed in the prophets. Similarly, the conception of Aristotle, that the human soul is a mere "capacity," that its intellectual capability is in the nature of a lack, with the possibility of acquiring, and becoming actual, applies in reality to man. We can, therefore, fully distinguish between "potentiality" proper, which applies to the prophets; and "capacity," which is characteristic to man; the one imparting, and the other partaking of, wisdom and understanding. Neither alone can explain the historical development of man's spiritual and cultural evolution.

7. THE MEANING OF CREATION; AND PERIODIC RECREATION OF MAN: Should we discard the untenable conception, that God created the world in six days, as applying to physical being; and maintain with Baha'u'llah, that this universe of ours is both ancient and everlasting; that it had never a beginning, nor will it ever have an end; then the principle of how it was originally formed, will cease to bear any significance, or objective validity. It would be a hypothetical notion, not only devoid of meaning, but vicious, in the sense that it brings in question the eternity of God's creative power, and the ancientness and everlastingness of His dominion. But in such a case, how will the first chapter of Genesis fare? Will it have to be discarded as foundless tradition of dubious origin?

179

If there is one God, Who acts as the ultimate source of truth, and the prophets are, one and all, His mouthpieces, sent to guide mankind, at different critical stages of its gradual development, then, to understand any point left obscure in the scriptures of one, we should seek enlightenment in the explanation offered by the subsequent ones. This is the basic principle of interpretation to which the Koran refers when it says: "O people of the Book! My apostle has come to clarify much that you consider obscure in the Scriptures."(1) Zoroaster was a prophet of God who succeeded the Hebrew ones. Therefore, we have a right to refer to him for the elucidation of the statement in Genesis.

The first verse of Genesis reads: In the beginning God created heaven and earth, in other words, physical nature. No one can harbor any doubt concerning this truth, if "beginning" is taken logically and not temporally. For physical nature should precede the appearance of man and his spiritual and cultural development. It constitutes an essential preliminary to such a growth. Nowhere is it asserted that this physical environment was produced within six days. The second verse states that a "void" prevailed upon the earth, that it was without "form," that "darkness was upon the face of the deep." There is no reason why this "void," "formlessness" and "darkness" should be interpreted physically and not spiritually and culturally, if in this latter sense it gives sense and becomes historically verifiable. Especially if the first verse states definitely that heaven and earth were already existing. "And God said, let there be light: and there was light," refers to spiritual and cultural "enlightenment"; for that is a familiar figure of speech used in all subsequent Scriptures. In other words, the six days should, in preference, be taken to refer to the spiritual and cultural evolution of man, to the period needed by humanity to attain maturity, as the result of successive and cyclic divine manifestations. And this is in substance what Zoroastrian eschatology maintains when it asserts, that human history is divided into six cycles of one thousand years each, every one of which is inaugurated by the advent of a savior, sent by Ahura Mazda to deliver humanity,

(1) The Koran, 5:15.

and at least temporally, overcome the prevailing forces of evil that dominate; until, in the fulness of time, that is the end of the cycle, universal peace and brotherhood is established, and the forces of evil are finally routed and destroyed.

Such an interpretation of the first chapter of Genesis would far better conform with the principle of the eternity of God's creative power and dominion. For these Zoroastrian cycles are not deemed to have had a beginning, or to end. Such an interpretation conforms with human thought and logic; with modern scientific discoveries; with the trend of religious and cultural development during the last few thousand years, history records; and even with the subsequent stories of the Old Testament. For these narrate how Hebrew culture sprung at one of the critical moments of human history; when paganism was at its height, and the spiritual atmosphere man breathed, in the nature of a "void." They tell how, guided by the spirit of God, the Hebrews developed gradually a culture and a spiritual life, which attained its climax at the time of David; how they became a torch spreading divine illumination, and the principles of true spiritual culture, in a society steeped in "darkness," and devoid of "forms," or adequate values.

Creation is not mere imparting of being. It implies as well, rendering actual and objective, an idea, or a sketch, or form in an individual; which might be a person, an institution, a civilization or a culture. Spiritually and culturally, a child starts life formless. And his development along that line is termed rebirth, regeneration and a new creation. Hebrew religion, Zoroastrianism, Christianity and Islam, all appeared when a spiritual and cultural "void," and "formlessness," prevailed in the world, and "darkness" spread its shadows upon mankind. The prophets of these successive religions, shed a new light of guidance upon humanity, which separated and distinguished between the "night" that prevailed, and the "day" that was to dawn. These were individual acts of creation, verifiable by historical records. They were the kind of integration into higher states of being, which we saw Abdu'l-Baha meant by creation, in his letter to Dr. Forel.

The prophets of Israel spoke of the coming of the new Jerusalem; of the City of God; of a state of universal peace and brotherhood; when goodness and justice will flow, like a river of living waters, down from Zion, to quench parched humanity. Similarly, Zoroaster spoke of the ultimate victory of the spirit of goodness; and complete destruction of the forces of evil; before the dawn of that Messianic age. Likewise, Jesus spoke of the coming of the Lord, and the establishment of the Kingdom of God on earth, as it is in heaven; and the early Christians awaited that, and termed it "the great event." Among many other references to that coming age, when "the City of Peace" will be established, the Koran dedicates a whole Sura, or chapter, to that "great event." All these were expressions of a universalistic social idea, form, and sketch of being, for humanity at large; which, through the trend of history, has been gradually taking shape, and realized objectively. They refer to a social status gradually to be created. They refer to the integration of the nations, races, classes and creeds into a world community, where spiritual values will dominate. This creative process was to be spiritual and cultural; not physical and material only. In fact, compared to such a creative process, and its consummation in the establishment of the "City of God," physical and natural being is mere "void," "formlessness" and "darkness."

Pagan culture, we have observed, was essentially naturalistic. The physical universe, and the forces which it deified, were natural. Even mind and reason, were considered essentially natural faculties, though identified with God, as a particle of His substance and being. Such a naturalistic culture could not consider the field of nature a "void"; for reality in all its stages was regarded within its sphere. It is otherwise with the prophets of God who consider the spiritual and cultural life, as a stage beyond the field of nature. Hence, measured by spiritual standards, which these advocate, nature is "formlessness" and "void." Under such circumstances creation was to proceed beyond it, to a higher state of being. Because pagan philosophers, especially the physicists, considered the cultural life, part of the physical and the natural, "void" and "formlessness" were bound to be physical and natural. Hence, they were concerned to explain, how there came to be nature as it is, positive, dominated by physical law and order, and revealing beauty. To the prophets, these physical aspects of being were mere groundwork, "dust" and "clay," for their paramount interest was the higher state of existence which was spiritual and cultural. Hence, it was this spiritual and cultural type of "void," that they tried to overcome, and that process was deemed creation.

8. THE CONTRAST BETWEEN THOMAS AQUINAS' CONCEPTION OF CREATION AND THAT OF AUGUSTINE: We have already observed how this principle of creation, which is foundational in a system of thought, and which constitutes the parting of ways between revealed religion, on the one hand, and pagan thought, on the other; how it had preoccupied Arab thinkers in the Middle Ages; how it had become the main point of contention, between orthodox elements, and students of Aristotelian thought. Thomas Aquinas repeatedly refers in terms of admiration to Avicenna, one of the most outstanding figures among them. He refers to him as "the master," as he designates Aristotle as "the philosopher." From these he received, among others, the Greek conception of creation as emanation, or division and fission; as well as the basic tenets of rationalism. Furthermore, following the example of Mohammedan Aristotelians, he tried to reconcile these pagan conceptions with tenets of Christianity, as the Mohammedan Aristotelians, tried to do with the Koran. The significance of this attempt of Thomas Aquinas is that subsequent European thought was partly a logical development of it; and partly a hostile reaction. Descartes was confronted with that controversy, and it is in that light that his thought can be adequately appraised and understood.

Thomas Aquinas defined God as supreme Being; and creation as imparting of being, without adding that this becoming and motion should be into a higher form and stage of existence: what Augustine, as we shall presently observe, termed "improvement." In other words, he upheld the doctrine of emanation, or Platonic division, advocated by Neoplatonism, and incorporated into religious thought by Avicenna. In his Summa Theologica, Thomas Aquinas defines his conception of creation, and contrasts it with that of Augustine by starting to set aside the interpretation the latter gives to this foundational conception in all systems of thought. He says: "For Augustine says (Contra Avd. Leg. et Proph. i): 'To make concerns what did not exist at all; but to create is to make something by bringing forth some thing from what was already. . . .'" Creation, we have observed, is of the individual. And the individual, with the forms it is made to assume, constitutes a new reality. For then it acquires a new nature, a new definition, new characteristics, new functions, and new types of action and reaction to its environment. It is qualitatively different from what it was; for its dominating forms are different. Hence, we are fully justified to say that the individual, with these forms, did not exist previously. In other words, "improvement" and "coming from non-existence into being," are not contradictory notions. The principle of creation, as advocated by revealed religion combines the two, in one dynamic process.

Thomas Aquinas then proceeds to say, that "Augustine uses the word creation in an equivocal sense, according as to be created signifies improvement in things, as when we say that a bishop is created. We do not, however, speak of creation in that way here, but as it is described above." Thomas Aquinas thus departs from Augustine, who considered creation as "improvement," that is, as imparting of a new and higher form; and instead defines it as mere becoming a separate entity. And this, we know, is the ancient pagan, and Platonic, conception of creation; as division, and segmentation, of the universal Soul, into individual human souls.

"I answer," Thomas Aquinas proceeds to say, "that as said above (Q. XLIV A. 2) we must consider not only the emanation of a particular being from a particular agent, but also the emanation of all being from the universal cause, which is God; and this emanation we designate by the name of creation." (1) Explaining the point of view of Aquinas on the subject, E. Gilson

(1) Treatise on the creation, Ques. XLV, Art. 1.

says: "We speak of creation whenever something which was not, begins to be . . . creation which is the emanation of all being, consists in the act whereby all things pass from non-being or nothingness to being . . . 'from' signifies in no way material cause; it means simply sequence." (1)

Augustine's conception of creation implied more than a mere "sequence"; it designated a new "form," and a material cause; for a bishop is created from a lower grade of ecclesiastic, which can be relatively regarded as "matter" acquiring a new "form," and thereby raised to a higher state of being.

9. THE NEOPLATONIC POINT OF VIEW: We said that pagan thought was primarily interested in physical nature, and its generation from a primordial physical "void" or chaos. Being essentially naturalistic in their outlook, and interest, pagan philosophers considered even the spiritual and cultural life of man, as aspects of nature and its phenomena. Mysticism was such a pagan system of thought; for it was essentially pantheistic, and identified God with nature; and hence, the spiritual life with a phase of nature. The highest concern of mysticism was so to interpret the gradual devolution of the human soul from God, that is, from the universal Soul, as to justify logically its process of return to Him, leaving no individual and personal survival to mar its fulness.

Neoplatonism, which sprung into being, in the third century after Christ, found in this mystic system of thought, a seemingly spiritual movement that might stay the progress of Christianity, by presenting an alternative to it in the field of the spiritual life. Its main object was to divert the mind of the people from the person of Jesus Christ, and from his claim to be the sole channel of divine revelation in that age. To combat this principle, Neoplatonism had to show that such a belief is needless; for the divine nature is not peculiar to Jesus, but is characteristic of the human soul as such; though the individual is not conscious of it. The old Platonic conception of emanation, that is, of proceeding from God through the process of division, afforded a premise

(1) Thomas Aquinas, by E. Gilson, p. 132.

185

that would lead logically to such a conclusion. For it would establish initially a formal and substantial similarity, and unity, between the universal, and the individual human soul. Plotinus stressed that ultimate reality is spiritual, but like Plato and Aristotle, he identified spirit with reason, or principle of intellection. God was, therefore, universal Reason, or source from which all individual reasons emerged and flowed. The first outpouring of this formal reality, constitutes the "intelligences"; the second is the individual human soul. As the intelligences, and the soul of man, were in essence principles of intellection, that is mind or reason, there could be no formal difference between them. The one was on a large scale, what the other was in miniature form.

10. A HISTORICAL EXAMPLE OF SUCH CREATION IN THE SOCIAL LIFE OF MANKIND: Pure matter, and pure form, are both intellectual abstractions. Unformed matter does not exist; and pure form is an abstraction, which is generated and exists in the mind of the creator, as an idea, or sketch, waiting to be actualized. This matter may be at various stages of formation; but in every stage it is formless, when compared to the new, and higher one, it is to assume. For example, mankind, as matter, might pass through different stages of development; but in every stage it can be considered "formless," if compared to the new form God, as its ultimate creator, desires to impose upon it, and thereby regenerate it, and usher it into a higher stage of being. For example, Roman intellectual conception, regarding the reality and destiny of man, which constituted the source of all cultural values, moral, social and aesthetic, was basically naturalistic, and tended towards materialism and the domination of power. That culture was mere matter, clay, or dust of the earth, which was presented to Jesus to give new form, and thereby regenerate. Through his sermon on the mount, parables, sayings, and the exemplary life he led, he presented mankind a new conception of the reality and destiny of man. To counteract Roman physical power, he advocated meekness, forgiveness, self sacrifice; and stressed, that through individual rebirth, human

186

salvation can be attained; in other words, Roman culture could be recasted, and reformed. His were totally new forms, and in clear contrast with the Roman. He imposed them upon prevailing culture, using it as clay. He, and his followers after him, succeeded in that task, and regenerated, or "improved" it, making it more wholesome for the spiritual life of man, and for his rebirth.

11. THE MYSTIC CONCEPTION OF THE DESTINY OF MAN: When mind, or principle of intellection, is said to emerge, or pour out of the substance of God, and constitute a separate entity, and distinct reality, acquiring an individuality of its own; the formal aspect of that substance cannot be considered as changed. If the formal aspect of a reality, is regarded as the seat of its substance and essence, as rationalism does, then its definition, that is formal aspect, remains the same. In such a case, individuation would be a passing aspect, and a seeming appearance. The substance itself would remain formally the same. This is what the principle of emanation, or creation through division, tried to maintain, namely, to give logical necessity, and entailment, to the mystic system of thought, and its conception of the destiny of man, as reversion to the sea of divine being.

Emanation is a principle of devolution, devised to justify a certain specific conception of human destiny. It is a method of proceeding from God, that would logically imply, and explain, a return to, and final substantial union with Him. But if viewed closely, the doctrine of emanation is a principle of disintegration, not of integration. It is a contrast to the conception of creation, as "improvement," and imparting an ever higher form; and not a definition of it. It is a sort of disintegration of the deity; while God is an ever creative agent, working for formation and integration. The principle of emanation applies only to the reality revealed in the prophets if considered as self-revelation. For that revealed, divine reality is formally identical with the divine Essence. In that case there is no individuation, to imply disintegration. It is an outpouring of Grace, which is universal. Mysticism, and its pantheistic tendencies, which identified God with nature, could logically consider the soul as an emanation of

God. But Christianity, with its basic doctrine, that God transcends nature, as a creative agent, cannot countenance such a basic belief, without vitiating its whole system of thought. The principle of creation, as "improvement," does what nature, left to itself, will completely undo. For humanity, if left alone, will forget its spiritual destiny, dissipate its energy along conflicting lines, lose its cultural forms and values, and relapse into the "void." It is the creative and sustaining power of God, which counteracts that natural trend, regenerates humanity, and integrates it into an ever higher stage of being.

12. EMANATION APPLIES ONLY TO THE DIVINE NATURE REVEALED IN THE PROPHETS: The principle of emanation, as we have observed, rests upon one fundamental condition, namely, the identity of form, and substance, between God and the reality that has issued from Him; an identity that we find exemplified by the sun and its rays, or the tree and its shoots. If that be the case, then its application will be, not to the human soul, but to the Logos, the Holy Spirit, or as The Bab terms it, the Primal Purpose, which animates the prophets. For though there is no formal and substantial unity between man and God; there is between the Spirit of Christ, and the Father; between the Primal Purpose, and the divine Essence. And it is because of that substantial, and formal unity, that creative ideas are considered innate in the Spirit of Christ; and that it possesses the divine attributes in their full actuality. The two are qualitatively the same. Intellect, or reason, is only one of the many attributes of perfection that reality reveals, within the sphere of human understanding. It is only one of the many colors manifested, when the light of God shines through the prism of the personality of Jesus, or any of the other prophets.

And when this outpouring of the divine reality, is restricted to the divine nature revealed in the prophets; the phenomenon does not assume the type of a natural disintegration, an almost mechanical devolution of the supreme Being. It becomes a purposeful activity on the part of God; an act of Grace, done to impart spiritual and cultural life; a project of the Primary

Purpose, that animates all prophets alike. For unless the sea of the divine Being surges, and reveals itself; its infinite attributes of perfection will not become positive objects of empirical understanding, imparting to man the truth regarding his nature and destiny.

13. THOMAS AQUINAS' CONCEPTION OF THE NATURE OF THE HUMAN SOUL:

Expressing the point of view of Thomas Aquinas, E. Gilson says: "At the apex of the world of forms we find the separate Intelligences; at the lowest stage we encounter sensible forms, entirely enclosed in matter, between the two is situated the soul, neither pure Intelligence, nor a simply material form. . . . By its very definition, the soul is entirely form and not susceptible to any admixture of matter. . . ." (1) Neoplatonism had considered the Intelligences as the first out-pouring of the divine substance and being, and the human soul as a further emanation of these Intelligences. Thomas Aquinas objects to this belief, and considers the latter as a direct emanation of God. It is true that the human soul is the direct creation of God, as the efficient Cause of all being; but its creation is not in the nature of devolution and division, but rather of "improvement" of the soul as matter. Furthermore, its spiritual and cultural life, its regeneration into an ever higher state of being, is the result of the direct operation of the creative power of the prophets, as its formal Cause. Moreover, the human soul is not a formal reality, as Thomas Aquinas conceived it to be. Form or idea, as Aristotle defined it, implies full actuality; which leaves no scope for change, and inner motion and development. It is a definition that is unchanging. Change pertains to an admixture of matter and form, and therefore, to an individual reality. For only an individual can constantly assume a higher reality and thereby, improve. The soul is such an individual reality, and possesses both form and matter; but this matter should not be confused with physical body and being. The soul is a spiritual substance, with infinite capacity, seeking an ever higher form of actuality. It is this receptivity resident in the soul,

(1) Thomas Aquinas, by E. Gilson, p. 204.

which distinguishes it from the divine nature revealed in the prophets, which is dynamic. This receptivity makes the human soul dependent upon the prophets for its development. Being pure capacity, the human soul is constantly created and recreated, by acquiring new forms. And proceeds to fulfil its destiny, with every new form it assumes; that is by contacting the Spirit of Christ, which animates all the prophets, appreciating its perfections, practicing them, and making them acquired characteristics of its own. Should we follow the view of Thomas Aquinas, and consider the soul as pure form, we would have to follow its logic, and end with the idea held by Aristotle, namely that, being form, it is not subject to change, except accidentally; except as a non-moving sailor, carried by a moving boat. Religion, and the spiritual and cultural life of man, rests upon two pillars, namely the essential actuality of the spirit of Christ, revealed in all the prophets; and then the capacity and receptivity of the human soul. The former is the formal Cause and hence perfect, and unchanging; the latter is pure capacity, and therefore, non-formal. And it retains that capacity for improvement, even in the worlds to come. Such being the case, the potentialities of the human body, fade into insignificance, when compared to the infinite capacity of the human soul as a separate spiritual entity.

14. THOMAS AQUINAS' CONCEPTION AS TO THE NATURE OF THE MOTION THE SOUL POSSESSES: In the first article of his Treatise on man, in the Summa Theologica, Thomas Aquinas defines the soul as "the first principle of life"; and adds that "life is shown principally by two actions, knowledge and movement." Hence the soul is "an act of the body," in these two respects. It is because the soul is an act, he says, that it makes the body move; for the body is pure potentiality and seeks realization through an act. Furthermore, he refers to Aristotle's Physics and maintains, that there is a mover which is moved neither per se, nor accidentally. Such a mover can produce only an invariable movement. But there is another kind of mover that "though not moved per se, is moved accidentally"; and for this reason the movement that it generates

is variable. There is also a mover which is moved per se. Under that category falls the body of man. In other words, Thomas Aquinas adopts the definition of the soul advanced by Aristotle; namely, that it is a mover that is moved only accidentally; not per se, and as an essential element of its nature. Thus, being the "first principle of life," and the form of the body, that is, a type of formula, according to which the human body is formed and functions; the soul is essentially an unmoved mover. If it moves at all, it is the type of motion Aristotle defined, when comparing it to that of a sailor who though unmoved, moves with the boat which carries him.

15. THOMAS AQUINAS MAINTAINS THAT THE SOUL MOVES AS FORM DOES, NAMELY, BY AWAKENING DESIRE: Thus, being form, the soul cannot act on the body, as an efficient cause would. It operates solely as other forms do, that is, as a formal cause acts; namely, by attracting what stands to it as potentiality, to the perfections or actualities it possesses. Every higher principle of life, Thomas Aquinas says, includes within itself the lower principles as well. The principle of intellection, for example, includes within itself and as part of its reality, the principle of sensation, (1) and thus down the scale to the principle of growth peculiar to plant life. It is the feeling of privation of the lower reality, which stands as potential to the higher experiences, and the desire for full actualization it awakens, which makes it move and seek the higher. And the higher generates that motion by attracting it to itself. (2) "The reason is because nothing acts except so far as it is in act; hence a thing acts by that whereby it is in act." "The intellect does not move the body except through desire." (3) It is through such an attraction and stimulation of desire that the soul, as act, operates upon the body, and makes it move from potentiality to actuality. According to The Bab, potentiality exists only in the Primal Purpose, not in the created—not in the material cause, but in

(1) Philosophy of St. Thomas, by E. Gilson, p. 214.
(2) Ibid. 207.
(3) Sum. Theo., Q. LXXVI, a. 1.

the formal. Illumination transcends sensation. It is not potential in sensation. Sensation can accept illumination, or remain in the dark. Hence, the desire is not due to the existence of a potential, but to the consciousness of a lack.

16. THOMAS AQUINAS CONSIDERS THE SOUL IMMANENT IN MAN: The soul is not considered by Thomas Aquinas as an entity separate from the body, as viewed by Plato. He follows Aristotle in this respect as well, and regards it as organically united with the body, and together constituting a complete man. "Man contains two incomplete beings in himself: matter which is body and form which is the soul. The matter, being pure potency requires in order to be really a body and not simply matter, the actuality imparted to it by its union with form. But neither is the soul a complete being; and this must unhesitatingly be asserted. Not only the soul as vegetative or sensitive, but also of the rational soul itself."(1) Thomas Aquinas tries to establish this point, namely, that the soul is only part of the complete man, on two premises: first, the definition of an individual man; secondly, on the fact that the soul does not seem to operate in the field of sense perception except with the help of the body. But, according to the Bab, both the physical body, and the soul of man, are mere matter, and possess only the capacity to acquire the form. The form is in the transcendent reality. As the Bab puts it, the image is in the reality beyond, not in the mirror itself.

17. THOMAS AQUINAS' VIEW ON THE BASIS OF INDIVIDUATION: In Neoplatonic thought, individuation was considered to be the result of the separation of the human soul, from the universal Soul, or substance of the divine Reality; and its admixture with physical matter, or body. Therefore, it was the element of matter that caused this individuation. Eliminate it, or transcend it, Neoplatonism would say, and you revert back to the universal Reality; out of which you originally emerged. Thomas Aquinas also considered individuation as due to the

(1) The Philosophy of St. Thomas, by E. Gilson, p. 216.

admixture of form with matter. For the two: matter and form, together constitute an individual. Form alone, being a universal, could not operate as ground of individuation. A definition has to comprise the whole of an individual: its form as well as its matter. Hence, the definition of man should include, not only his soul as the form, but also the body as its matter.

Under the principle of emanation, or division of the universal Soul into individual human ones, the difference is bound to be numerical and not formal. Such a conception of generation, and emergence out of ultimate reality, cannot consider individuation to be the result of formal difference; for it is premised and assumed that they are formally alike. It is, therefore, bound to be the result of its admixture with the body. But if the principle of creation is maintained, and generation is considered to be the result of acquiring ever higher forms; formal difference between individual souls, is bound to occur, and be maintained. For there can always be degree of acquiring that form; and the nature of the form so acquired. In such a case the ground of individuation is located within the soul; irrespective of physical differences that might accompany it. This conception of individuation becomes still more valid if we consider the human soul, not immanent, but separate from the body. The individuality of different captains is located, not in the boat they happen to guide, but in the qualities they reveal, and measure of ability they manifest, in guiding their boat and reaching their respective destiny.

We define human personality without taking into consideration man's physical body. We center our attention and definition upon man as a spiritual reality, possessing specific characteristics, both individual and social. Cannot individuality be similarly defined, and the two made to coincide? It is because of the premises he adopts, and takes for granted, that Thomas Aquinas feels obliged to include the human body in his definition of man. Change those premises, and the definition will no more require the body as basis of individuation. Furthermore, is physical existence, or body, a necessary element in every form of individuation? Even a purely formal reality, such as a chemical formula, possesses a distinct individuality, though it is fully conceptual and formal. That individual reality distinguishes it from all other formulas, and imparts to it characteristics all its own. The physical composition of the elements is not required to generate that individuality. When the body is not considered the ground of individuality, then there is firm reason to maintain, that such distinctiveness which it implies, will wax greater when the body is set aside at death, and man continues to develop spiritually, and acquire ever higher forms, in the worlds to come. Thus, the principle of individuation can be purely formal, as between two equations or definitions.

18. THOMAS AQUINAS' "AGENT INTELLECT": The metaphysics, logic, and the conception of the human soul as formal, developed by Aristotle, led him to the adoption of the doctrine of an "active intellect," to which the passive intellect of man, that is, the ordinary intellect which receives impressions through the senses, is mere matter and potentiality. The same conception we find advanced by Thomas Aquinas, under the term "agent intellect." Before presenting his own point of view, however, he states that of Aristotle as follows: "The philosopher says that it is necessary for these differences, namely, the possible and agent intellect to be in the soul. I answer that, the agent intellect, of which the philosopher speaks, is something in the soul. In order to make this evident, we must observe that above the intellectual soul of man we must suppose a superior intellect, from which the soul acquires the power of understanding. For what is such by participation, and what is subject to motion, and what is imperfect always requires the pre-existence of something essentially such, immovable and perfect. Now the human soul is called intellectual by reason of a participation in intellectual power, a sign of which is that it is not wholly intellectual but only in part. . . . Again it has an imperfect understanding, both because it does not understand everything, and because, in those things which it does understand, it passes from potency to act. Therefore there must be some higher intellect, by which the soul is helped to understand." (1)

(1) Sum. Theo., Treatise on Man, Q. LXXIX, a. 4.

Thomas Aquinas starts his comment on the words of "the philosopher," or Aristotle, by saying: "The agent intellect . . . is something in the soul." In other words, he endorses the point of view of Aristotle, in contrast to that of Plato, namely, that it is a separate reality. He, however, ends his exposition of his own point of view, by referring to the doctrine of Christianity, namely, that "the agent intellect, according to the teaching of the Faith, is God Himself, Who is the soul's creator."

If such be the case, and the "agent intellect" is God: the "Father," as conceived in Christianity; we confront the objection of Plato stated in Timaeus, namely, how can we obtain any access to it, to make it the object of human understanding? Especially if He is conceived, as it is done in Christianity, namely, that He is "unknowable." The "agent intellect" must needs be accessible to man. And that can be secured only through His self-revelation. Furthermore, to act as the "agent intellect," that supreme reality has to be formal in nature; and contain the forms humanity is bidden to acquire in the process of its evolution. It has also to be the seat of potentiality: of a before and after, as the Bab says, in its process of revelation. And that reality, we have observed, is the Primal Purpose, or divine nature revealed in the prophets; the spirit of Christ which animates them all.

There are, thus, two possible alternatives as to the seat of this "agent intellect": the first is the Aristotelian view, namely, the human soul; the second is the divine nature revealed in the prophets, or what the Bab termed the Primal Purpose. Therefore, Thomas Aquinas ought to have said that the agent intellect is, "not God Himself," namely, the Father, Who is the efficient Cause, and hence, unknowable; but rather, the Primal Purpose, or Jesus Christ who acted as the formal Cause of man's spiritual and cultural life. To Thomas Aquinas, the two conceptions, namely, that the agent intellect is "in the soul," and the other, that it is God Himself, were not contradictory. For he conceived the human soul, as an emanation of the divine substance, and formally the same, though individualized. In other words, the agent intellect could be both at the same time, without any contradiction in his thought. Proceeding from God as emanation; or, as Plato maintained, division; stresses formal likeness between God and the human soul. This doctrine corroborates the thesis of Neoplatonism, advanced to combat early Christianity, and its belief in revelation vouchsafed through Jesus Christ. For that sets aside the necessity of Jesus Christ, of the prophets who appeared before him, and of his return in the fulness of time as channels of revelation. The thesis of Neoplatonism was that revelation was not peculiar to the prophets, but is a phenomenon characteristic of all human souls, and that is to what the thought of Thomas seems to lead.

In logic, the function of the active, or agent intellect, as viewed by Aristotle and Thomas Aquinas, is to provide human thought the major premises it needs, for deducting true conclusions. In empirical thought, the function of the active intellect, is to interpret the data presented through the senses, and give them truth, unity, and significance. Now, can these two functions be adequately fulfilled by the active intellect; if it is conceived as proceeding from the human soul itself? When dealing with the epistemological issue we observed, that true knowledge is the prerogative of the creator, not of the created. He who creates a certain object, according to a definite design, and a specific sketch, knows with certainty the purpose entertained, and the nature of the thing produced. Hence, it is the creator who knows the nature of the reality and destiny of man; not man himself who is created, and can act only as an observer who contemplates reality, assumes certain truths, and formulates certain hypotheses, always subject to modification. Independent human thought, on ultimate issues; such as the nature of the reality and destiny of man, is bound to be uncertain. And with that basic uncertainty lurking in the human soul and intellect, how can it function as the source of major premises of thought, and principle of interpretation of all facts presented through the senses? And it is from the conception of the reality and destiny of man, that all spiritual and cultural values are deducted.

19. BACKGROUND OF DESCARTES' CONCEPTION OF THE NATURE AND DESTINY OF MAN: Such was the background of contemporary thought, on the subject of the nature and destiny of man, which to a great extent influenced the philosophy of Descartes. Plato, Aristotle and Thomas Aquinas, all agreed that the soul of man is an unmoved mover. Being primarily intelligible, and a principle of intellection, and hence, formal, and rational in substance and nature, it could not be regarded as possessing a movement per se. If it had any motion, it was conceived accidental to its nature and essence; just as a notion, or form, or idea, or definition cannot be considered as possessing motion in the very substance of its being. Motion is the result of a "capacity" acquiring ever newer and higher forms; not of a reality that is already in act, as the soul was deemed to be, drawing other things to itself, as a formal cause does.

If there was a basic difference between Plato, on the one hand, and Aristotle, on the other; it was whether the human soul was like a captain detached from the boat, and merely steering it to its destiny; or it was a form of the body, and hence organically one with it; that is, whether it was separate, or immanent, in the human body: a difference which permeated the two rival schools of thought and distinguished their views on outstanding issues.

The doctrine of creation in six days, which the masses accepted on faith, was so repugnant to the philosophic mind, that the doctrine of emanation, as advocated by Thomas Aquinas, seemed the only rational explanation to which reason could subscribe. And this conception ascribed to the human soul, a source of being and a form of proceeding from God, which was plausible, and raised its dignity, by considering it essentially divine in nature. The very principle, that the idea of God is innate in the human soul, a principle to which, we have observed, Descartes subscribed, is the logical outcome of the metaphysical notion of emanation. For it is the doctrine of emanation which entails the principle, that the idea of God is innate in the human soul, or that both alike are principles of intellection. The doctrine of creation, as advocated by revealed religion, and interpreted by

197

Augustine as "improvement," on the other hand, could in no wise establish such a substantial likeness, and justify the existence of such innate ideas in the human soul. For in this case, the innate ideas enter the human soul, only as a result, and to the extent, that it acquires them, by coming in contact with the formal cause of its spiritual and cultural life. We can thus attribute to Descartes an implied acceptance of the doctrine of emanation which Thomas Aquinas had accepted and bequeathed to Christian thought. For his conception of the soul seems to bear those features, and thus resemble to a great extent the notion incorporated in the latter.

20. DESCARTES' CONCEPTION OF THE NATURE OF THE SOUL: Such being the case, the human soul could not be considered a physical entity, such as materialists deemed it to be. "Now, it is plain," Descartes says, "I am not the assemblage of members called the human body; I am not a thin and penetrating air diffused through all these members, or wind, or flame, or vapor, or breath, or any of all the things I can imagine; for I supposed that all these were not, and, without changing the supposition, I find that I still feel assured of my existence." (1) The human soul, being an emanation of God, as the supreme principle of intellection, was itself according to Descartes, in the nature of reason and a thinking substance. He says: "But what, then, am I? A thinking thing, it has been said. But what is a thinking thing? It is a thing that doubts, understand (conceives), affirms, denies, wills, refuses, that imagines also, and perceives." (2)

This truth, that the soul is a thinking substance, is deemed by Descartes to have been attained empirically, that is through his own inner experience; for it constituted the ground of his "cogito." We may be able to doubt every aspect of our being, even the existence of our body; but that very doubt implies the certainty that we are thinking. The soul, being so identified with the principle of intellection, it becomes also the principle of being

(1) A Discourse on Method, by Descartes. Meditation II, tr. by J. Veitch.
(2) Ibid.

and its criterion. For Descartes considers thought such an absolute criterion of being, that he maintains, not only that the act of thinking is sufficient ground for certainty as to the existence of the soul; but also that to cease thinking is proof for its non-existence. "I am," Descartes says, ". . . I exist: this is certain; but how often? As often as I think; for perhaps it would even happen, if I should wholly cease to think, that I should at the same time altogether cease to be."(1)

21. DESCARTES CONSIDERS THE SOUL AS OBJECT OF DIRECT INTUITION: Descartes did not agree with Aristotle and Thomas Aquinas that the soul is an "assemblage of members called the body"; but he endorsed their principle that it is a thinking substance. Now, though he accepts the rationalistic notion, that the soul is an object of understanding, he parts company with that school of thought, by saying that it is directly apprehended or intuited. He maintains that it is a reality that can be clearly, distinctly, and intuitively apprehended. This constitutes the subject of the latter part of his second Meditations.

There, Descartes compares the mind to a piece of wax that, under the influence of heat, may lose its shape, smell and hardness, and become liquid; that is, lose all its sensible characteristics, both primary and secondary; and yet retain its substantial being. This substantial being, he says, is not perceived through the senses, nor does it constitute the object of imagination. "It is the mind alone which perceives it." "The perception of it," he says, "is neither an act of sight, of touch, nor of imagination, and never was either of these, though it might formerly seem so, but is simply an intuition (inspectio) of the mind, which may be imperfect and confused, as it formerly was, or very clear and distinct, as it is at present, according as the attention is more or less directed to the elements which it contains, and of which it is composed." "What then! I who seem to possess so distinct an apprehension of the piece of wax—do not know myself, both with greater truth and certitude, and also much more distinctly and clearly?" "Bodies themselves are not properly perceived by

(1) A Discourse on Method, by Descartes, Meditation II, tr. by J. Veitch.

the sense nor by the faculty of imagination, but by the intellect alone; and since they are not perceived because they are seen and touched, but only because they are understood (or rightly comprehended by thought), I readily discover that there is nothing more easily or clearly apprehended than my own mind." Thus, Descartes attempts to establish the principle of rationalism, namely, that the ultimate reality in man, that is, his soul, is clearly and distinctly apprehended. The soul is not only a thinking thing, but also the most clear and distinct object of thought.

22. DESCARTES CONSIDERS THE SOUL A SEPARATE ENTITY: But though Descartes follows Thomas Aquinas in considering the soul as the principle of intellection; yet he parts company with the latter as to the extent it is bound to the body; that is, as form to matter, with no separate existence of its own. He defines the body as what is subject to spatial considerations, such as length, breadth and depth, none of which applies to the soul. Descartes says, that the very fact that these two, that is, the soul on the one hand, and the body on the other, can be so distinctly and clearly defined and distinguished, is sufficient ground and reason for considering them separate in their reality and existence. "It is sufficient," he says, "that I am able clearly and distinctly to conceive one thing apart from another, in order to be certain that the one is different from the other, seeing they may at least be made to exist separately."(1) "It is certain that I (that is my mind, by which I am when I am) am entirely and truly distinct from my body, and may exist without it."(2) Direct human apprehension, we have observed, constituted to Descartes the criterion of being and truth. That was the basis for the validity of his "cogito." Inasmuch as the separate existence of the soul from the body is so apprehended, he considered them to be also separate in fact, though he deemed them to interact, through what he considered to be the penal gland, which constitutes their point of contact.

(1) A Discourse on Method, by Descartes, Meditation VI, tr. by J. Veitch.
(2) Ibid.

23. THE FUNCTIONS OF THE SOUL ACCORDING TO DESCARTES: In his second Meditation Descartes mentions three attributes or functions for the soul: the first is expressed in the power of nutrition and motion. This is completely dependent upon a concurrence of the body. The second is sense-perception. This also cannot function without the respective organs of sense. The third is thinking. This attribute pertains, according to Descartes, to the soul alone as a thinking thing. He includes under thinking the power to doubt, understand or conceive, affirm or deny, will or refuse, imagine or perceive. The power of imagination and of memory, seems to pertain to the second class, and be penal in pattern. Thus, whereas Thomas Aquinas made the soul and the body fully and intricately bound together as form to matter, Descartes considers them as possessing clear and distinct reality, nature, and being of their own, and separate in their functions and attributes. But yet, he does not go to the extent that Plato did when he considered them to be as a captain to his ship, separate one from the other. "I am not," he says, "only lodged in my body as a pilot in a vessel, but that I am besides so intimately conjoined, and as it were intermixed with it, that my mind and body compose a certain unit." (1) Answering a query he explains this point further. He says: "I thought I took sufficient care to prevent anyone thence inferring that man was merely a spirit using the body." (2)

What Descartes states regarding the function of the mind, both in sense-perception and imagination, shows that to him it constitutes an unmoved mover, along the line Thomas Aquinas conceived. For according to Descartes, it is the mind which, as passive and active—passive in perceiving, active in willing— moves the body in pursuing its purpose. Thus he does not seem to depart from the ancient philosophic principle, that the soul is per se unmoved; and that its motion is accidental to its nature. He seems to uphold the view, maintained by Plato, that divine perfections, or ideas, were moulded by God in the human soul, when it was originally created, not as a capacity to acquire forms,

(1) A Discourse on Method, by Descartes, Meditation VI, tr. by J. Veitch.
(2) New Studies in the Philosophy of Descartes, by N. K. Smith, p. 142.

but as a potentiality containing the actual, and revealing it, as the occasion arose. "On considering the nature of God," he says, "it seems impossible that he should have planted in his creature any faculty not perfect in its kind, that is, wanting in some perfection due to it."(1) Hence, according to Descartes, error is not due to any infirmity or inadequate development, of the soul, in having the proper idea, but to insubordination of the will: its venture beyond the limits of understanding, or faulty judgment when making a free choice. Hence, basic conceptions of culture, regarding the nature of God, and the reality and destiny of man, as well as the values that are based on them, were all implanted in the very substance of the human soul; and the soul given full capacity to apprehend them. "Accordingly," says Descartes, "it is true that when I think only of God (when I look upon myself as coming from God), and turn wholly to Him, I discover (in myself) no cause of error or falsity."(2) In short, the human soul is unmoved per se, because it proceeds from God as an emanation of His divine substance, as a microcosm "divided" from the macrocosm; and not as an entity possessing capacities and capabilities which it can develop, through them acquire new forms, and be thereby perfected.

24. DESCARTES' VIEW ON THE ACTIVE INTELLECT: We have observed, how both Aristotle and Thomas Aquinas, felt the need for an active, or agent, intellect, which, being in act, would impress itself upon the passive intellect, and thereby impart to it actuality; but they both located it in the soul itself. Descartes, however, could not subscribe to this immanence. In this respect he was more Platonic in tendency, for he tries to maintain an element of transcendence. To him active intellect was not a mere form, nor passive intellect mere matter, which, when combined, would constitute a complete whole. In his conception of the active intellect, he seems to combine elements of both systems: the Platonic and the Aristotelian.

Descartes believed on the one hand, with Plato in innate ideas,

(1) A Discourse on Method, by Descartes, Meditation IV, tr. by J. Veitch.
(2) Ibid.

hence, he considered the active intellect, as that faculty of man, in which those ideas are stored, and which as such transcends both the faculty of perception which is purely receptive, and as such passive; and also the faculty of imagination, which is dependent on physical factors, and therefore, is not pure intellection. In his Meditation VI, Descartes considers this as, the "active faculty capable of forming and producing" ideas; in other words, he defines the active intellect as the store-house in which the ideas are found innately. And to keep clear of the Aristotelian principle that this active intellect is mere form, immanent in the body, Descartes proceeds to state that "this active faculty cannot be in me (in as far as I am but a thinking thing), seeing that it does not presuppose thought, and also that those ideas are frequently produced in my mind without my contributing to it in any way, and frequently contrary to my will." In other words, Descartes tries to avoid the immanental principle, that the active intellect is part and parcel of human thought, and thus deny that element of transcendence which was specifically Platonic, and in the nature of illumination. He admits that element of separate existence, by proceeding to state that, "this faculty must therefore exist in some substance different from me, in which all the objective reality of the ideas that are produced by this faculty is contained formally and eminently," that is, a mind in which the ideas are innate. But is that substance, in which the ideas exist innately, human or divine?

We have elsewhere observed, that to Plato a pressing problem was that, if the creator be considered the measure of all things, and the source of all creative ideas, then the insurmountable difficulty would be, to find the means of obtaining access to His thought, and learning His will and purpose. Similarly, in Meditation VI, Descartes states: "But as God is no deceiver, it is manifest that He does not of Himself and immediately communicate those ideas to me, nor even by the intervention of any creature in which their objective reality is not formally, but only eminently contained." There is no such communication, because there is no clear and distinct apprehension of it by man. Hence, the only alternative Descartes finds left, is that "those ideas arise from corporal objects." And this is the empirical Aristotelian tendency, upon which Descartes establishes the reality of the objective world as source of those ideas. But this conclusion is not contradictory to his principle, that the active intellect, resides in the purely rational element of the soul, for that he considered to be part of the universal soul which he identified with God.

25. THE DISTINCTION BETWEEN POTENTIALITY AND ACTUALITY: Potentiality implies the immanence of a certain reality; while capacity assumes its transcendence, but possible acquisition. When the individual human soul is considered to be a part, or particle of universal substance, or God; when the difference between the two is regarded as only numerical, and a question of magnitude; and not qualitative, formal and substantial; in such a case, we can speak of "potentiality." On the other hand, when the human soul is considered mere clay, in the hand of the divine artist, moulded and remoulded to assume a constantly new form, and thereby acquire ever higher aesthetic value, we cannot strictly speaking refer to it as "potentiality"; but only of "capacity" and "capability." For, similarity of form and quality, would then be a condition acquired and a perfection achieved. In such a case, the forms which bring about similarity, are not inherent and innate in the created; but rather impressed upon, or moulded into, the substance of the object, to make it qualitatively like the original sketch; or conform with the purpose entertained by the creator. In other words, "potentiality" can strictly apply only to a reality that has emanated from God; while "capacity" and "capability" qualify one that is created, and destined to "improve."

26. DESCARTES CONSIDERS GOD IMMANENT IN NATURE: Now, if nature fulfils the function of acting as repository of general ideas, which operate upon man's perceptive faculties; then its function verges on the divine, and can be identified with God. And this is what Descartes maintains in sympathy with Aristotle. He says, "For by nature, considered in general, I now understand nothing more than God himself, or the order and

disposition established by God in created things; and by nature in particular I understand the assemblage of all that God has given me." (1) He thus endorses the principle of the immanence of God in the universe, and in the human soul, as part and particle of it; with the potentiality of revealing all ideas. And this is a basic ancient pagan conception, in contrast to that of revealed religion. Such a conclusion is in full logical conformity with both: the principle of emanation of the divine substance, as propounded by Thomas Aquinas, and also with the notion of illumination which Plato had maintained. The human soul would then be divine though possessing the ideas only "potentially," to be actualized when recollected. The result is a reconciliation and compromise between illumination, as coming from God in the Platonic sense, and illumination as a "natural light," imparted by nature as the repository of all ideas. But, here again, the principle of the emanation of nature from God, served only the original purpose for which it was devised by Neoplatonism, namely, to help set aside the necessity of revelation, as vouchsafed to Jesus Christ, and to the other prophets of God.

27. THE DIFFICULTIES OF THE CARTESIAN OUTLOOK IN THE FIELD OF CULTURE AND THE SPIRITUAL LIFE: The difficulty of the Cartesian principle starts, when we try to go beyond the field of physical nature, to that of the spiritual and cultural life of man. A piece of stone, suspended in the air, has the potentiality of falling; but can we say the same of the cultural life? Are the divine attributes of perfection, whether intellectual, moral, social and aesthetic, found "potentially" in nature? Is man "potentially" cultured, and with a spirtual outlook; or has he merely the "capacity" to acquire them? Can there be creation, further integration and regeneration, or "improvement" of man's spiritual and cultural life, that is, can the human soul acquire spiritual forms, by reverting to nature, as the emanation of God's being and substance? We have already had the occasion to show that, if left to itself, nature tends to disintegration; that integration, whether physical or cultural and spiritual, is due to a

(1) Meditations VI, by Descartes, tr. by J. Veitch.

transcendent creative purpose. Man, as a natural being, has merely the capacity for spiritual and cultural evolution. The forms and values, he needs for that process, are found in the mind of the Creator, and His purpose for man. It is to that source that humanity should look for guidance, not to physical nature.

The basic predicament of Descartes in this connection was that "as God is no deceiver, it is manifest that he does not of himself and immediately communicate those ideas to me." Plato confronted a similar difficulty when he said that supposing we admit that God is in fact the measure of all values, how can we obtain access to his thought to know them? Plato, however, was a pagan philosopher. But Descartes was a professing Christian; and that is exactly the function the Christian revelation claims to have fulfilled. For that revelation constituted an immediate communication of those ideas to mankind. Just as the phenomena of nature divulge to man the forms that are the laws and principles, the Creator moulded into them; so do the words and deeds of the prophets, reveal to him the spiritual and cultural ideas, and values, the Primary Purpose has established for the regeneration of the human soul.

28. THE ACTIVE INTELLECT MUST BE OTHER THAN, AND ABOVE, HUMAN INTELLECT: If we consider the source of ideas and forms, as immanent in human thought, that is, maintain that man possesses them potentially, even if that be as a separate inner faculty; or if we regard it as immanent in nature, as an emanation of God and not merely as a separate entity; we are confronted with the difficulty of explaining the process of integration which creation implies. For ideas and forms cannot act as principles of integration when their source is in nature, or in human reason itself. For once there, even potentially, and below the level of consciousness, they are operative; and when operative, human thought would be actually already formed and integrated. Similarly, if those forms are innate and already existent, even potentially and subconsciously; disintegration of the spiritual and cultural life cannot occur. And we know as

historical fact that such disintegrations of human society have happened.

But if we consider the active intellect, that reality which imparts the spiritual and cultural ideas and forms, not a function of the human soul, considered as an emanation of God; then the result would be that the latter becomes thoroughly passive and receptive in its relation to the reality that contains them in fact and imparts them. As "capacity" it would always have to look to the source of those ideas and forms, to grow, evolve, and be regenerated. It would become dependent upon that "grace" which is proferred by the prophets of God.

The spiritual and cultural life, we said, rests upon two pillars, both logically and factually interdependent and complementary: the one is the actuality of the divine attributes in the prophets of God, as the formal Cause of human regeneration; the second is the receptivity of the human soul as a substance ever ready to acquire those forms. This basic spiritual principle, therefore, demands: first, that this formal Cause of the spiritual and cultural development of man, should be identified, not with the absolutely transcendent God, Who is far beyond human reach and understanding; but rather with His periodic revelations, in the reality of His successive prophets. Secondly, that the human soul should be considered a reality that in substance, nature and essence, is not such as to be "unmoved" per se, such as a form or principle of intellection is regarded to be; but rather a reality that can be, like a piece of clay, moulded and reformed; and thereby "improved," and raised from one stage of being to a higher. And this, we have observed, can in no wise be secured under the systems advanced by Plato, Aristotle, Thomas Aquinas or Descartes.

29. REASON IS A MERE FUNCTION OF THE HUMAN SOUL: The principle of intellection, or reason, is not as rational philosophers, among them Descartes, deemed it to be; that is identical with the soul; but rather, it is a mere function of the human soul upon this plane of its existence. As The Bab says, "the

outward body is the seat of the inner." (1) Descartes could from the act of his thinking deduct that he exists; because the human soul is an ever active reality, and thought is a form of its activity. That activity, according to Baha'u'llah, is sign of its being. For, in the world of creation, what is not moved, and hence, does not move, cannot have being. Furthermore, from the assertion "I think therefore I am," Descartes had no right to proceed to the notion that man exists so long as he thinks; or objective world processes being so long as it is thought. Man may act unconsciously and automatically and yet be. Thought is a sign of being, but not the criterion of being for they are functions he can perform. Nor is Descartes justified to conclude from his "cogito," that he is a thinking thing, that his soul is a principle of intellection, that it is mind. Man, as we have observed him maintain, has a will or principle of volition, as well as intellect or principle of understanding. It is wrong to confuse the two, as he does, for they have different natures: the one is passive, the other is active. And these are contrary notions with different definitions. Hence, they must be considered two functions of a higher reality, namely, the soul. They proceed together in states of conscious activity; but they may also act separately. For the one may be dormant, while the other acts. In states of conscious activity, we act in the light of our understanding, or think to realize a certain purpose through our activity. We can neither separate them absolutely and have conscious activity; nor confuse them as a single function and maintain their specific nature, definition and role. Neither can we say that the relation between the two is automatic, that the one is a mere reflex to the other; for activity may be against the dictates of considered deliberation, and hence, of thought. For, we might know what is wrong and injurious, and yet do it. The more adequate conception is that these are twin functions of a higher reality, which we term soul, while upon this earthly plane of its existence; that intellection and activity, or understanding and volition, are some of its many functions and capacities; that the soul is not a thinking thing, but an unknowable substance which, on its present level of

(1) The Persian Bayan, by The Bab, 5:12.

208

existence, thinks and acts intelligently, that is, perceives facts, imagines others, conceives universal laws, and from present deductions of past experiences, guides its future behavior. In short, the human soul is essentially unknowable, and hence cannot be defined as a thinking thing. All we can assert, pertains to its functions and characteristics upon this sphere of its existence. All else is pure conjecture. And these functions and characteristics might be transcended, as it grows and enters into higher realms of being.

Furthermore, as we have already observed, when discussing the principle of knowledge advanced by Descartes, understanding of the substance and reality of a thing, is the exclusive prerogative of its creator, not of its observer. We are in no sense the creators of our soul to know its nature and definition. We just observe its functions and characteristics, the capacities and capabilities it reveals upon this plane of its existence; not its substance and reality. Therefore, we can say it can think, will, and act; but we cannot jump from this to the conclusion that it is a thinking thing, a principle of intellection, a mere form, mind, or reason. The soul cannot be identified with any of its functions. These are some of its attributes and present capacities. What constitutes the real substance or stuff of the soul, the material of which it is made; that is the prerogative of the creator to disclose. And we have no better way to refer to it than spirit, which implies that it is not physical.

30. HUMAN "CAPACITY" TO ACQUIRE SPIRITUAL AND CULTURAL FORMS ENTAILS FREEDOM OF CHOICE: When the human soul, is considered an emanation of God, or a spark released from His substance and is "potentially" divine; it has merely to disengage itself from the physical and material forces, that separate and retard it from attaining its destiny. And when that task is completed, and the elements which caused its individualization are overcome, then the divine nature residing in it, becomes "actual" as a matter of course. In this process, which is almost mechanical, there is little freedom left to choose; first as to forms to be acquired, and then as to the extent they

should be practiced and made habitual, and ingrained in the soul.

It is otherwise when the soul is considered to possess the "capacity" to acquire the supreme forms, or divine attributes of perfection. The element of freedom then comes into prominence. For then man has to choose his own way, designate his goal, and guide his purpose. He has to choose the forms he desires to acquire, and the extent to which he wants them to become part of his nature. And when he has practiced them, and made them an integral part of his nature, he develops a certain individuality and personality of his own, derived from the combination of these forms, and extent of their growth. His case then is not that of a drop of water, that has originally emerged from the sea, and will ultimately flow back into it; or a substance reverting to its origin or a "potentiality" made actual. He is an individual being, acquiring ever more distinctive personality. And this individuality is the direct result of that freedom of choice, as to what form to acquire, and freedom as to the measure he should master them: a freedom which is his because his soul has merely the "capacity" to evolve, and acquire the divine attributes of perfection.

31. HUMAN "CAPACITY" TO ACQUIRE SPIRITUAL AND CULTURAL FORMS REQUIRES A RATIONAL PROCESS:

The rationalism of Plato, Aristotle, Thomas Aquinas, and Descartes, was based upon the hypothetical assertion, that the universal Soul is the universal Reason, and the individual human soul is a principle of intellection. But the process whereby human potentialities are made actual, was not of necessity rational and intelligent. In fact, mysticism, which fully embraced that basic principle of human "potentiality," and upon it based the course of the spiritual evolution of the soul, denied that the process of "return" is rational at all. It went even to the extent of holding that the rational life is an encumbrance, a positive handicap in that course. The "return" was considered the result of an inner urge: of the "potential" seeking the actual. Descartes himself tends in that direction, when he considers the process an "apprehension," rather than understanding of the truths involved, and the forms to be actualized. There was no necessity to understand the forms, when they were already ingrained in the soul, and man had merely to remove the obstructions, to let them appear and reveal themselves.

On the other hand, when man has merely the "capacity" of acquiring those forms, and divine attributes of perfection; even if it is not presumed that his soul is a principle of intellection, but merely is endowed with reason as one of his many faculties; then the process of his evolution is essentially and necessarily rational. For he can acquire them, by first understanding their nature, intellectually contemplate them, deliberate personally upon them, make his free choice between specific alternatives presented, and then create the necessary environment wherein he can realize his end. All these steps need intellectual understanding and guidance; though they are stimulated later by will, desire, and love for the beauty of the forms which are to be acquired. Such rational process does not operate when the soul is considered "potentially" divine.

32. HUMAN "CAPACITY" TO ACQUIRE SPIRITUAL AND CULTURAL FORMS ENTAILS A CREATIVE PURPOSE AND PROCESS:

The divine nature revealed in the prophets, what the Bab termed the Primal Purpose, the Word or Logos, which is an emanation of God, does have a burning desire, urge, will and purpose to repair to the sea of divine Being, when its mission upon this earth is fulfilled. It is like a surging wave receding into the ocean. But that process is not creative, in the sense that it is "improved" by it. It is a "potentiality" being actualized. There is no substantial and formal change involved in that process; for in the divine nature all supreme forms, all attributes of perfection, are already ingrained and inherent. There is no occasion for freedom of choice, rational deliberation, or for a creative process of "improvement" requiring a will and purpose to operate. It is a like reverting to its like. It transcends all these characteristics of the earthly, human process of evolution.

It is otherwise with the human soul, when it is not conceived as an emanation of God, an outflow of His substance and nature; but a spiritual entity created by Him with the "capacity" of

acquiring an ever higher form. Having that "capacity" and
capability to evolve, and thereby proceed to an ever higher state
of being; the process is creative. When the individual human
soul, submits his will to the supreme divine purpose, and seeks
to employ his "capacities" for acquiring divine attributes of
perfection, he freely and intelligently submits himself to a process
which is both purposeful and creative, a creativeness that the
process would not entail, if that soul were considered, as the
mystics consider it, an emanation of God, already possessing
potentially all the forms.

Thus, when this principle peculiar to the divine nature revealed
in the prophets, is extended to apply to the human soul, it loses
its spiritual and cultural creativeness. No logical ground is thereby
left for "improvement"; and it becomes a mere awakening to
what is deemed to be already a fact. When applied to the divine
nature revealed in the prophets, the principle of emanation
becomes the basis of divine grace, and guidance, for man's
cultural evolution and regeneration. When applied to mystics,
who claim it for the human soul generally, it becomes a doctrine
of stagnation, of losing that paramount creativeness which man
should possess, and which ought to urge him to "improve" his
spiritual and cultural life and environment.

33. THE BAB'S BASIC CONCEPTION THAT THE HUMAN SOUL FALLS WITHIN THE REALM OF THE CREATED:

We
have observed the Bab state, that the fundamental doctrine of all
thought, is the dictum of God, saying: "I am God; there is no
God but Me; all other than Me is My creation. O My creation,
worship thee me." (1) This doctrine, which The Bab considers to
be the major premise of all thought, establishes the basic nature
of the human soul, as a created entity; for it is "other" than God,
and hence, pertains to the realm of the created. To elucidate the
meaning of the term "creation," and bring out the distinction
between it, on the one hand, and that attached to it by the
mystics, on the other; the Bab says: "The sea of God's Being

---

(1) The Persian Bayan, by The Bab, 3:6.

does not enter the sea of the created"; (2) in other words, the term "creation" cannot be interpreted, when applied to the human soul, as an emanation, or outflow, or outgrowth of the divine substance and being. It is rather in the nature of "making" and "improving" and giving form. Furthermore, we observe The Bab say, that the type of likeness with God, the human soul is deemed to acquire, is of qualities and attributes; never of substance and essence; (3) for no reality can go beyond the limits destined for it; "a spirit attached to a created thing always remains created." (4) The Divine Essence is exalted, and beyond whatever can be termed "object"; (5) while the human soul is such an "object," or created entity. It is rather like a mirror reflecting the rays of the sun. (6) With no flight of imagination can we say, that the substance, and essence, and reality of the sun enters, and becomes enclosed, in the mirror. In it we can observe only the reflection of the sun: its shape, light, colors and other qualities. This principle of the Bab is in clear contrast to the doctrine of emanation, or outflow, of the divine substance, maintained by Neoplatonism; and the notion that the human soul is a microcosm: a particle "divided" from the universal Soul, as held by Plato.

To maintain the paramount station of Christ as an intermediary, and reconcile it with the principle of successive emanations conceived by Plotinus; some schools of thought have identified the spirit of Christ, or the divine nature revealed in Jesus, with the "intelligences" of Neoplatonism. They have considered it as the first direct "outflow" from God; and the human soul as a secondary one, emanating, not directly from the divine Essence, but from the spirit of Christ, as the intermediary. In contrast to this conception of the human soul, as a direct emanation or outflow of the spirit of Christ, we have the statement of the Bab that "we all were created by the intermediary of God," (7) and

(2) Ibid. 4:1.
(3) Ibid. 2:9.
(4) Ibid. 3:6.
(5) Ibid. 2:10.
(6) Ibid. 4:1.
(7) Ibid. 3:6.

likening that relationship to that existing between the sun and a mirror. He says that the "Point," or the divine nature revealed in the prophets, is like the sun, and the other "letters," meaning the soul of individual men, are like mirrors facing it, and receiving its light. (1) We have observed The Bab assert repeatedly, that in the relation between the sun and a mirror there can be no case of substantial and essential likeness, which the doctrine of emanation or outflow, takes for granted. In other words, the human soul is neither an emanation of God, nor an emanation of the divine nature revealed in the prophets; but rather, just as the human aspect of the prophets, is a mirror, in which the divine nature of God is reflected; so the human soul is a secondary mirror, in which the light shed by the prophets is made manifest. The one imparts the supreme forms which it possesses in full actuality; the other receives, and gradually acquires them, in its process of development. The one represents the creator, the other constitutes the created.

34. BAHA'U'LLAH ON THE NATURE OF THE SOUL: "Thou hast asked me," Baha'u'llah says, "concerning the nature of the soul. Know, verily, that the soul is a sign of God, a heavenly gem whose reality the most learned of men hath failed to grasp, and whose mystery no mind, however acute, can ever hope to unravel." (2) The Bab also refers to the human soul as a "sign." He explains the reason saying, that the term is used to stress the fact that it is not perceptible, but refers to a reality that is beyond. Acording to the Bab, the outward body is merely the seat of the inward body. Hence, any judgment passed upon the former, applies to the latter. Otherwise, pleasure and pain are experiences of the soul through the instrumentality of the body. As the soul is the mover of the human body, it can define it and state its limits and functions. But itself, being the mover, cannot be defined by the senses which are moved by it. The senses, which are instruments the soul employs, are subject to categories

(1) Ibid. 3:11, 7.
(2) Gleanings from the Writings of Baha'u'llah, tr. by Shoghi Effendi, LXXXII.

214

of time and space, of which it is itself free. And if empirical understanding is limited to sense-perception, it cannot possibly attain a knowledge of the soul which, because of its very nature, transcends it.

Plato tried to establish the intelligibility of the soul, by premising that it is a particle of the universal Soul, or Reason, and hence, identical in nature with human intellect which is an intelligible and knowable reality. Aristotle regarded the soul as formal, and therefore, essentially knowable. Descartes followed Plato and considered the soul as reason, but in touch with the body through a certain gland in the brain. Baha'u'llah's conception is an implied refutation of all these hypotheses; for it asserts that the nature of the soul far transcends human understanding. We cannot say it is reason, because intellect is a mere function of the soul. It is not form, because it is a created thing, and the product of creation is individual, and not universal and formal. It is not immanent in the body, because it will otherwise succumb to spatial considerations, and thus lead to a materialistic conception. And it cannot communicate with the body through a gland, for that implies location, and hence spatial considerations. "The human soul," Baha'u'llah says, "is exalted above all egress or regress. It is still, and yet it soareth; it moveth, and yet it is still. It is, in itself, a testimony that beareth witness to the existence of a world that is contingent, as well as to the reality of a world that hath neither beginning nor end." (1)

Human knowledge is limited to the functions, characteristics, attributes and relations that a reality reveals; in other words, to its appearances; never to its substantial reality and nature. That, we have observed, is the prerogative of the creator, who alone knows it, and can divulge it to others with authority. The substantial reality and nature of the human soul, therefore, according to revealed religion, is an unknowable reality, a mystery that the human intellect cannot fathom. Even if we could imagine to apprehend its nature, our vocabulary would fail to express it. Therefore, when Plato, Aristotle, Thomas Aquinas, or

(1) Gleanings from the Writings of Baha'u'llah, tr. by Shoghi Effendi, LXXXII.

Descartes, identified the human soul with mind, reason, or principle of intelligibility, they were confusing its substantial reality, with one of its functions; though we may admit, it is an outstanding one. And to confuse a reality with one of its functions is unjustifiable.

35. THE HUMAN SOUL POSSESSES THE CAPACITY OF ACQUIRING DIVINE ATTRIBUTES: "Upon the inmost reality of each and every created thing," Baha'u'llah says, "He hath shed the light of one of His names, and made it a recipient of the glory of one of His attributes. Upon the reality of man, however, He hath focused the radiance of all of His names and attributes, and made it a mirror of His own Self. Alone of all created things man hath been singled out for so great a favor, so enduring a bounty." (1) In every individual, the Bab says, (2) perhaps in every object, he adds, God has enclosed two signs of His creative power. With the one man knows God, or rather the divine nature revealed in the prophets, glorifies His unity, beholds Him alone as creator of all things, and other than Him, as created. This element of human nature is the seat of what we have termed the spiritual and cultural life, the ground of human personality. It guides and moves the body as an instrument of its activity; and in turn, it is itself moved by God, in acquiring perfections, and attaining its destiny.

"Consider the rational faculty with which God hath endowed man," says Baha'u'llah. "Examine thine own self, and behold how thy motion and stillness, thy will and purpose, thy sight and hearing, thy sense of smell and power of speech, and whatever else is related to, or transcendeth, thy physical senses or spiritual perceptions, all proceed from, and owe their existence to, this same faculty. So closely are they related unto it, that if in less than the twinkling of an eye its relationship to the human body be severed, each and every one of these senses will cease immediately to exercise its function, and will be deprived of the

(1) Gleanings from the Writings of Baha'u'llah, tr. by Shoghi Effendi, XXVII.
(2) The Persian Bayan, by The Bab, 4:1.

power to manifest the evidences of its activity. It is indubitably clear and evident that each of these afore-mentioned instruments has depended, and will ever continue to depend, for its proper functioning on this rational (spiritual) faculty, which should be regarded as a sign of the revelation of Him Who is the sovereign Lord of all. Through its manifestation all these Names and Attributes have been revealed, and by the suspension of its action they are all destroyed and perish.

"It would be wholly untrue to maintain that this faculty is the same as the power of vision, inasmuch as the power of vision is derived from it and acteth in dependence upon it. It would, likewise, be idle to contend that this faculty can be identified with the sense of hearing, as the sense of hearing receiveth from the rational faculty the requisite energy for performing its functions.

"The same relationship bindeth this faculty with whatsoever hath been the recipient of these names and attributes whitin the human temple. These diverse names and revealed attributes have been generated through the agency of this Sign of God. Immeasurably exalted is this Sign, in its essence and reality, above all such names and attributes. Nay, all else beside it will, when compared with its glory, fade into utter nothingness and become a thing forgotten."(1)

In this passage Baha'u'llah maintains that, just as the senses are instruments of mind, and can function only when the latter is positively operating through them, in other words, when mind moves them, and directs them; so is the mind, in turn, an instrument of the soul, or what he terms "sign"; and functions only when this latter is operating through it. He thus repudiates both principles held by rationalism, namely, first that the human soul is a knowable and intelligible reality; second, that it constitutes the principle of knowledge, and is identical with reason. The human soul, according to Baha'u'llah, is both unknowable, and transcends reason. The latter is a mere function

---

(1) Gleanings from the Writings of Baha'u'llah, tr. by Shoghi Effendi, LXXXIII.

of that higher reality, a mere instrument of its purposeful activity.

Plato and Descartes considered the human soul as the source of innate ideas, which God had implanted in its substance at the very time of its creation. This principle had led them to the belief that it was an unmoved mover, acting like a captain in a boat. Aristotle and Thomas Aquinas had, from different premises, also come to the same rationalistic conclusion. Having considered the human soul as the form of the body, these had to conclude that it was like any form, unmoved per se; that its motion was, like that of a sailor in his ship; carried accidentally by the progress of the boat. Thus, starting from different premises, all these rationalists had come to the conclusion that the human soul is an unmoved mover. And this was in keeping with their principle that the human soul is a microcosm divided from the universe as the macrocosm, sharing with it all Ideas and Forms.

In utter contrast to this basic rationalistic conception, Baha'u'llah compares the human soul, to a child in a nursery, trying diligently to learn the syntax. For the mind of the child is moved and "improved" in the process of its education. He maintains that the human soul is both moved and mover; that motion is not an accident of its being, but characteristic of its very essence and nature as a created thing: a reality which is born on the plane of nature, and then repeatedly regenerated, by acquiring ever higher forms, and being raised to ever higher states of spiritual and cultural development. In one of his prayers, Baha'u'llah refers to the human soul as the (Nafs el harakiyyeh), meaning a reality whose very nature, essence and substance is to move. Far from being an unmoved mover, an unchanging form, as Aristotle conceived it to be; it has the capacity of being moulded and remoulded by the hands of its creator. In fact, compared to its field of motion and development, that of the physical body falls to insignificance. For, as the divine perfections are infinite, the capacity of the human soul for acquiring them is also infinite. And such a "capacity" implies infinite possibility of inner and substantial motion and formal change. It was on such ground that Paul said: ". . . though our outward man

218

perish, yet the inward man is renewed day by day." (1) "When I was a child, I spoke as a child, I understood as a child, I thought as a child; but when I became a man, I put away childish things." (2) This childhood and maturity applies to the spiritual and cultural life as well; here on earth as well as in the worlds to come, when "the outward man perish."

36. THE METAPHYSICAL GROUNDS OF THE DISTINC-TION BETWEEN "POTENTIALITY" AND "CAPACITY," ACCORDING TO THE BAB AND BAHA'U'LLAH: We have tried to bring out the metaphysical distinction underlying the two conceptions: the one "potentiality," the other "capacity"; the first springing from the doctrine of emanation, the other from the principle of creation as "improvement" and "making"; the one stressing formal similarity between God and His emanation, the other asserting the initial formlessness of the latter. We also restricted the sphere of the first to the relation prevailing between God, on the one hand, and the divine nature revealed in the prophets, on the other; and attributed the second to the field of creation, in which, all things are "other" than God, belong. Let us now consider how the Bab and Baha'u'llah confront that issue.

We have repeatedly referred to the stress the Bab, on various occasions, lays on the fundamental principle, that the image we seem to observe in the mirror, is not in fact in it; but rather in the reality of which, the image seen in the mirror, is a mere reflection. For example, the divine attributes of perfection we observe manifest in the words and deeds of Jesus Christ, were not in the man Jesus, that is, in the human aspect of his nature; but rather in the Spirit of Christ which animated him; in the divine nature revealed through him to mankind. This is the ground of the statement of Paul: "But we all, with open face beholding as in a glass the glory of the Lord, are changed unto the same image from glory to glory, even as by the Spirit of the Lord." (3) In other words, the "glory of the Lord" was not

(1) 2 Cor. 4:16.
(2) 1 Cor. 13:11.
(3) 2 Cor. 3:10.

immanent in the human nature of the man Jesus, which was part of the world of creation, and acting as a mere mirror, though pure and undefiled; but rather in the Spirit of Christ, in the divine nature in him, which was an emanation of God, and therefore, His true image. For between these two there is formal unity and similarity.

In this connection Baha'u'llah says: "These sanctified Mirrors, these Day Springs of ancient glory, are, one and all, the Exponents on earth of Him Who is the central Orb of the universe, its Essence and ultimate Purpose. From Him proceed their knowledge and power; from Him is derived their sovereignty. The beauty of their countenance is but a reflection of His image, and their revelation a sign of His deathless glory. They are the Treasuries of Divine knowledge, and the Repositories of celestial wisdom. Through them is transmitted a grace that is infinite, and by them is revealed the Light that can never fade. . . . These Tabernacles of Holiness, these Primal Mirrors which reflect the light of unfading glory, are but expressions of Him Who is the Invisible of the Invisibles. By the revelation of these Gems of divine virtue all the names and attributes of God, such as knowledge and power, sovereignty and dominion, mercy and wisdom, glory, bounty, and grace, are made manifest."(1)

This unity and similarity of Forms, or of divine attributes of perfection, between the divine Essence, on the one hand, and the divine nature revealed in the prophets, on the other; is due to the fact, that the latter is an emanation of the former, a shoot from that ancient Tree, an outflow of that Ocean. It is otherwise, however, when the relation is that of creation, as is the case of the human soul. For the soul has merely the "capacity" to receive that light and reflect it. It is a mirror which has to be cleansed from dust and dross, to transmit the rays of Light it receives from a source far beyond itself, or the image of a reality which is separate and transcendent to its own being. There are no innate or ingrained forms in the nature of the human soul. For, as the Bab says, the sea of the divine nature, does not enter the sea

(1) Gleanings from the Writings of Baha'u'llah, tr. by Shoghi Effendi, XIX.

of created being. (1) Hence, we cannot maintain that in the mirror there is a reality which is "hidden." (2) Thus, whereas in the divine nature revealed in the prophets, there is a "hidden" potential reality, that is, infinite Forms and attributes of perfection, actualized and expressed as the occasion arises; in the human soul there are no such "hidden" forms or ideas. It has to acquire them. It merely possesses the faculty and capacity to receive those forms and practice them. And to fulfill that task, it has to turn to the prophets, to the reality which possesses those forms in full actuality.

To illustrate his point of view, Baha'u'llah chooses the example of a candle, and the light it emanates when kindled; and the dust which has to be removed from a mirror, to give the possibility of reflecting the image projected upon its surface. This represents a correct view of the distinction we have tried to make between "potentiality" and "actuality." For, "neither the candle nor the lamp can be lighted through their own unaided efforts, nor can it ever be possible for the mirror to free itself from the dross. It is clear and evident that until a fire is kindled the lamp will never be ignited, and unless the dross is blotted out from the face of the mirror it can never represent the image of the sun its light and glory." (3) To put it otherwise, a hand transcendent to the candle and the mirror has to intervene to bring out the change.

As the Bab says, we do not observe in the consciousness of the individual other than God. It is an error on the part of man, to think that his soul contains attributes other than what God has shed upon it. (4) But in the mirror itself, only the mirror exists. The reflection we observe, is the result of the projection made by the object beyond. Otherwise, the Bab says, the image we observe in the mirror, has priority over it, and that is unattainable. In every object, he further says, there is a sign from God, which possesses the possibility of proclaiming Him. That "sign" can be traced

(1) The Persian Bayan, by The Bab, 4:1.
(2) Ibid. 4:1.
(3) Gleanings from the Writings of Baha'u'llah, tr. by Shoghi Effendi, XXVII.
(4) The Persian Bayan, by The Bab, 4:1.

back to the Primal Purpose, which is in substance divine. And it is termed "sign" because it refers to a higher reality. In that sense all things are created by God and worship Him. For worship is to reflect the perfections shed upon that object, and to the extent it can acquire them.

These statements of Baha'u'llah and The Bab, present the conception of contingent things, with merely the "capacity" of receiving and acquiring perfections. God, the Creator, sheds illumination upon all things. His Grace is universal. But these can receive and acquire form and light, only to the extent of their capacity. The human soul, has been given the freedom, to turn to that source, and be thereby illuminated and regenerated; or turn its face away and remain in the dark. In its primitive state, the soul is naked and formless; it merely possesses the freedom to choose between following the Primal Purpose and its supreme values; or setting them aside and accept its consequences. But in following the Primal Purpose of its creator, lies its salvation and bliss.

The End of Book I